Called to the Prairie

Life in McKenzie County, North Dakota

1915 - 1916

From the Journals of the Rev. Richard C. Jahn

Edited by

Richard P. Jahn, Jr., Jan Dodge and Dennis E. Johnson

Catlinberg Publishing

ISBN: 978-0-578-14337-8

Publisher: Catlinberg Publishing
408 Ferncliff Drive
Signal Mountain, TN 37377

Cover and interior design: Sandra Tincher

Printed in United States of America

IN MEMORY OF

RICHARD C. JAHN

*For voluntering to go on this mission
and not shrinking back;
For writing your journals for all of us to enjoy.*

AND

EMIL BELLIN

*For taking Richard in when he was lonely,
For furnishing your cabin and animals,
For being a faithful partner in this ministry and
For being content with what you had.*

For you have need of endurance, so that when you have done the will of God you may receive what is promised.

For yet a little while,
and the coming one will come and will not delay,
my righteous one shall live by faith,
and if he shrinks back,
my soul has no pleasure in him.

But we are not of those who shrink back and are destroyed,
but of those who have faith and preserve their souls.

Hebrews 10: 36-39 (ESV)

CONTENTS

McKenzie County Map

Mountrail County

MCKENZIE COUNTY

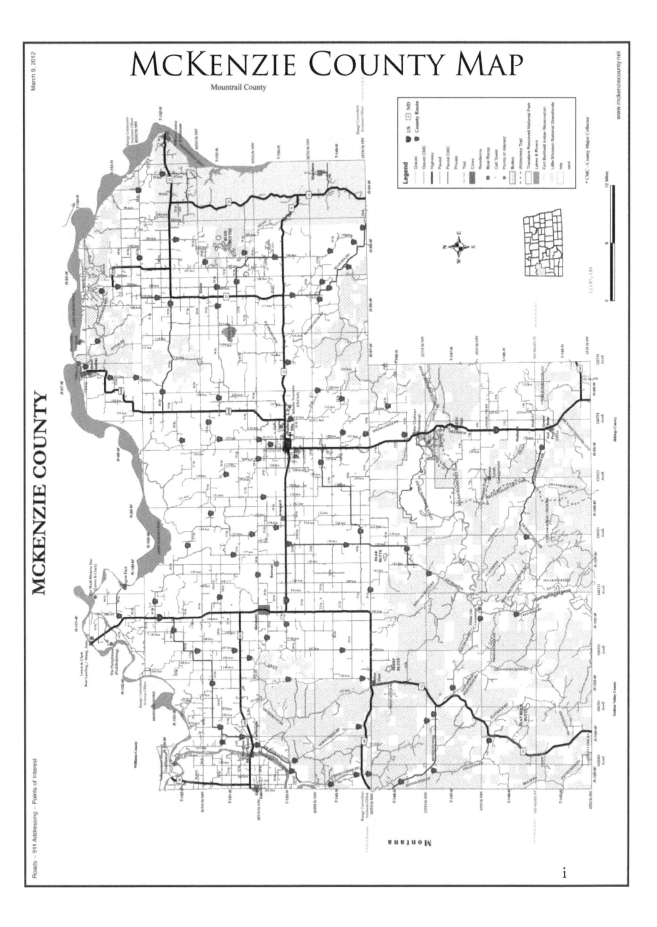

Legend

- US
- ND
- County Route
- Gravel
- Gravel CMC
- Highway
- Paved
- Paved CMC
- Private
- Trail
- Cities
- Residence
- Boat Ramp
- Cell Tower
- Points of Interest
- Buttes
- Wilderness Trail
- Lakes & Rivers
- Theodore Roosevelt National Park
- Fort Berthold Indian Reservation
- Little Missouri National Grasslands
- Gap
- sect

* CMC - County Major Collector

0   6   12 Miles

Montana

EASTERN McKENZIE COUNTY
WITH MODERN HIGHWAY 23

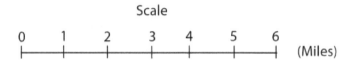

Scale

0   1   2   3   4   5   6

(Miles)

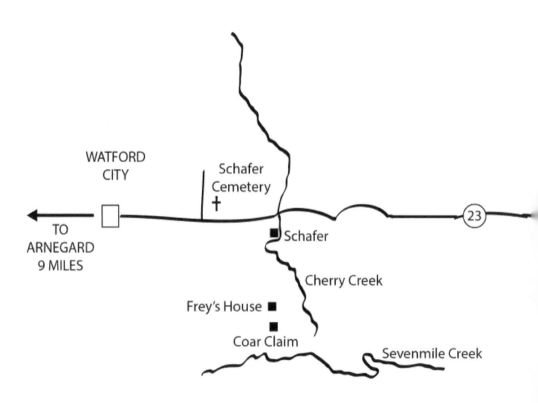

WATFORD
CITY

Schafer
Cemetery
✝

← TO
ARNEGARD
9 MILES

■ Schafer

Cherry Creek

Frey's House ■

■
Coar Claim

Sevenmile Creek

23

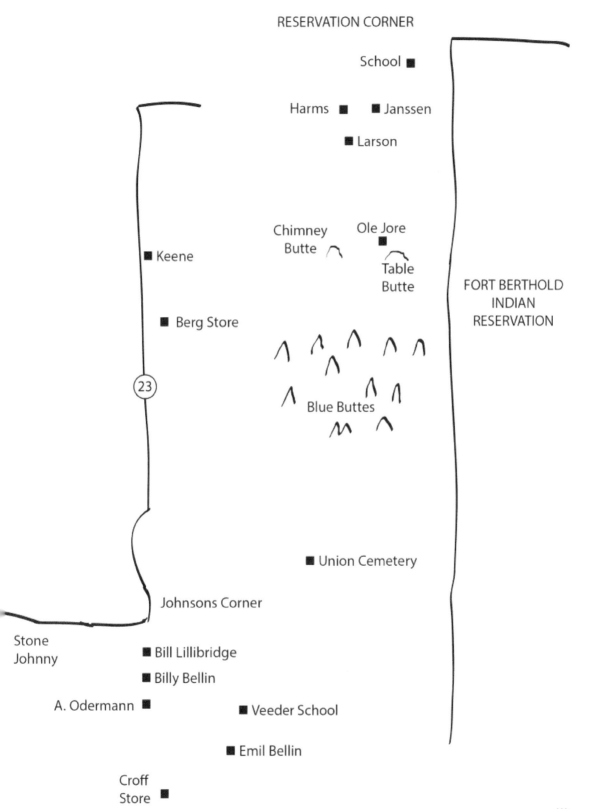

Charlson

RESERVATION CORNER

School

Harms   Janssen

Larson

Chimney   Ole Jore
Butte

Table
Butte

FORT BERTHOLD
INDIAN
RESERVATION

Keene

Berg Store

(23)

Blue Buttes

Union Cemetery

Johnsons Corner

Stone
Johnny

Bill Lillibridge

Billy Bellin

A. Odermann

Veeder School

Emil Bellin

Croff
Store

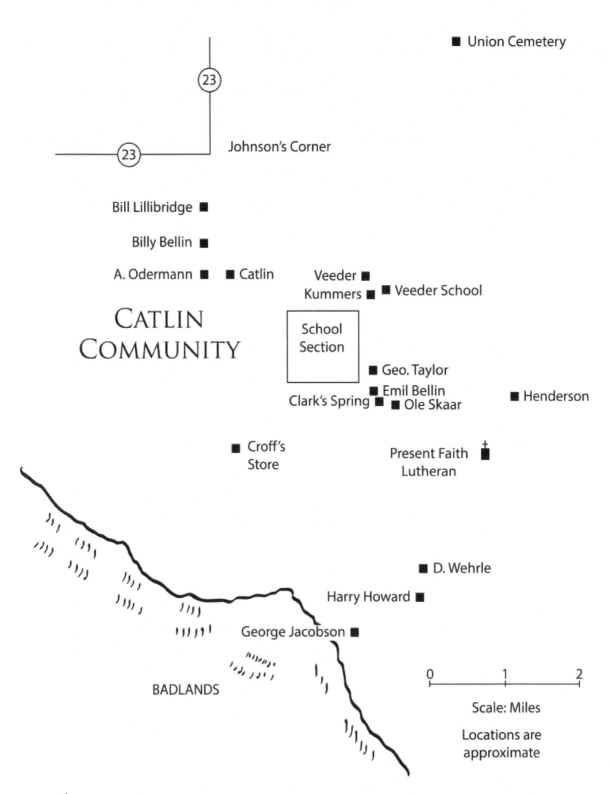

Union Cemetery

(23)

(23) Johnson's Corner

Bill Lillibridge ■

Billy Bellin ■

A. Odermann ■   ■ Catlin

CATLIN
COMMUNITY

Veeder ■
Kummers ■   ■ Veeder School

School
Section

■ Geo. Taylor
■ Emil Bellin
Clark's Spring ■ ■ Ole Skaar   ■ Henderson

■ Croff's
   Store

Present Faith ✝
Lutheran

■ D. Wehrle

Harry Howard ■

George Jacobson ■

BADLANDS

0   1   2

Scale: Miles

Locations are
approximate

ACKNOWLEDGEMENTS

The editors thank these loyal typists: Madison Jahn, Hayden Jahn, Kay Hartung, Elaine Kelly and Carol Walker.   Special thanks go to Silas Baird and David St. John, who corrected many technical issues in the manuscript and transcribed footnotes in Chattanooga. Sandra Horsman and David Jahn ably assisted with the index and photographs for the final draft. Jessie Veeder Scofield read the manuscript and made helpful edits. We also thank Nancy Henderson for her professional guidance and invaluable assistance with editing. And finally, we wish to thank Sandra Tincher for the hours she devoted to meticulously transform manuscript to finished form. The book we hold today is her design.

A special thanks goes to John and Cleo Kirkland for guiding the editors to Union Cemetery, Table Butte, Reservation Corner and Ole Jore's homestead. Also, we appreciate Gene Veeder for guiding us to the location of the Howard's house after it was moved to the Wherle farm. The editors are also grateful to Leroy Lillibridge for providing a rare photo of Croff's Store and farm. Don Jore submitted several photographs of the Jore family. We also are grateful to Arno (Bud) Bellin, Emil's son, who was very touched by this account and seeing photographs of his father again. He gave us the information for Emil's biography. Midland Atlas Company, from Watford City, published plats of the homesteads as they were located in the county in 1916, and this was incredibly useful.

Rick Jahn
Dennis E. Johnson
Jan Dodge
Co - Editors

EDITOR'S INTRODUCTION

This is an account of a yearlong visit by my grandfather, Richard C. Jahn, to McKenzie County, North Dakota in 1915 and 1916. Before this venture he was a young Lutheran ministerial student at Concordia Seminary in St. Louis, Missouri. A small congregation in Schafer, North Dakota had sent a written request for a minister, and this plea made its way to the seminary. The previous minister had relocated to Minnesota. This request, considered a Divine call by Lutherans, was announced to the students on October 7, 1915. Richard volunteered to go. The call specified that the minister would serve five or more small congregations in the area, some even in Montana. He was told that this would be a one-year stint where he would ride a circuit in and around McKenzie County, preaching in German and English. He would return to the seminary the next year.

Richard was no stranger to farm life in the Midwest. He was born in January 1895, near Amherst, Nebraska. Richard worked on some Nebraska farms as a teenager; however, his high school days were spent at St. Paul's College, a Lutheran boarding school in Concordia, Missouri. Thereafter, he entered Concordia Seminary in St. Louis. When this call came, he was no doubt comfortable and accustomed to the intellectual life of a seminary student in a big city.

When Richard died in 1977, he left a large accumulation of personal papers and books from his life as a Lutheran minister. We in his family knew he had gone to North Dakota as a student, but apart from a few of his recollections, the trip was unknown to us. For instance, we had no idea where in the state he had served. He had told me that he had lived in a shack, far from contact with others, 80 miles from the nearest railroad. I thought he lived alone. He never mentioned his cabin-mate, Emil Bellin.

In 2002, I discovered Richard's 1916 journal packed in a shoebox in my house. This box contained his not-too-interesting student journals from high school and seminary days. Or, so I had assumed. I had reviewed the shoebox items years before, but for some reason I looked through them again and opened this account of North Dakota in a faded red journal. With it was another journal that contained what is now Part Three of this book. I read them and realized he had lived in the thick of daily life with homesteaders and ranch hands. A few years later, after much searching, I came across Richard's 1915 journal. Together they give the reader a detailed look into a year of rural American life a century ago, when a seminary student lived and served among these gritty North Dakota farmers.

It was surreal. I felt that I was peering into a lost world, set in remote western North Dakota, a world that modern life had never known or surely forgotten. Here was a cast of characters—people and animals—immersed in their own daily adventures, and I felt I was the only witness to their story. His was no easy mission. I was stunned to read that to fulfill his duties, Richard was constantly on the move, in the open, often in appalling or dangerous situations. So were the homesteaders; they all just accepted it as a fact of life. Watford City had been a town for less than two years. There were virtually no decent roads or bridges. People (as well as animals) must have suffered constantly in the weather as they crossed icy coulees, snowdrifts and swollen creeks on horseback or sleds, often in sub-zero conditions. Yet none of them felt any need to lock their doors. One wonders if Americans today could display such fiber and trusting relationships.

Richard mentioned in the journals that he was taking photographs with his box camera, and I went on a serious hunt to try and find some. I was worried because I had never recalled seeing any such pictures. However, they were there; his North Dakota photographs were scattered among many others in family collections. Most were tucked away in closets in Chattanooga, Tennessee, Richard's last residence. It was a treasure hunt. Each one was a prize, and they made the story come visually alive. Richard wrote captions on many of them, and this proved to be a great help to the editors. Some of the photos could be precisely dated from the diary entries. It was exciting to match them with the journal. In addition, he bought pictures of local scenes at the small stores he visited. He seemed to be inclined to buy anything relevant to his world in McKenzie County, especially rodeo photos of cowboys whom he met.

Further searches through Richard's papers led to the discovery of a number of original letters from friends and family that he mentions receiving in Catlin and Schafer in 1916, as well as the original call itself. Thus, the story in this book has been compiled from source material that has fortuitously, or I should say, providentially, survived. One reason this book has been delayed is due to new material being unearthed. However, it is fitting that it has been published in time for Watford City's centennial in June, 2014.

I asked family members and some of my employees to help type the handwritten journals, which were penned in Richard's tiny script. This was a painstaking process. Then, with a manuscript and photos in hand, I wondered if anyone in McKenzie County would be as interested in them as I was. I knew no one there. Had the folks Richard written about really been there? Would anybody remember them or even care? To my great encouragement, the local residents prized their heritage and were more than receptive. I was fortunate to make contact with Jan Dodge, now recently retired from the McKenzie County Tourism Bureau, and I sent her a manuscript. Coincidentally, she and her husband Cameron owned Emil Bellin's farm. Jan assured me that the diary characters were real—many were revered ancestors of present-day residents—and she soon put me in touch with Dennis Johnson, an attorney and local historian from Watford City. They were enthusiastic about Richard's account and encouraged its publication. We became co-editors. They have added much local history and anecdotes in the footnotes here.

I made two visits to McKenzie County and travelled its eastern half, Richard's circuit area. It is truly a beautiful and romantic land, with striking buttes and other natural features. It lies close to Teddy Roosevelt's 1880s ranch and national park on the Little Missouri River. I met Emil Bellin's son Arno (Bud) in Watford City and interviewed him in 2006 before he died. He and I spent hours together at Emil's cabin site, where he had grown up. His biography of Emil is an appendix to this work. The editors also studied homestead records in order to locate the claims of the diary characters. Many of them, including Emil, are now resting peacefully in Schafer Cemetery, just east of Watford City. In addition, much more local history can be found today at the Heritage Center and the Pioneer Museum, both in Watford City.

This journal is published in three main parts. Richard's 1915 journal is the first. In the actual journal seven days were contained on each page, so he was constrained by space limits. He wisely obtained a larger journal for 1916, and the level of detail greatly increased. It makes up Part Two, the main portion of this account. Part Three was found undated, but he probably wrote it sometime soon after he returned from McKenzie County. He elaborates on the events of 1915 in significant detail. It appears to be an unfinished recollection, but still it adds useful information to the story. Maybe he realized that his 1915 journal entries left out much detail. Maybe he intended to add more to it to include 1916 events. We will never know. I do know that he never indicated to his grandchildren that he kept a journal or had photographs from his year in North Dakota. The editors decided to leave the entries just as he wrote and spelled them. Nothing has been taken out, and our comments are contained in the footnotes.

This account contains many interesting and touching events. Richard was 20 when he first arrived at the Watford City train station, and his observations sometimes reflect his youth. This was his first experience with grown-up ministerial responsibilities, and he still had two years to finish at the seminary. Later, in a 1924 journal, he reflected back on his performance in the North Dakota mission field in 1915 and 1916. He wrote: "Now that I have had some experience in the ministry, I find that I sadly neglected my mission field, owing not to a lack of zeal, but to almost unbelievable ignorance in the proper methods and means of carrying on such work. I did not even know enough to make house calls at the homes of the people. There was no fellow pastor within hundreds of miles to advise me either, so that I am, in a measure, excusable."

I don't quite agree with this self-assessment. Besides the weekly announcements in the local newspapers, the journal shows in many places where he personally invited people to church services. He preached a number of times to the tough punchers at the big ranches on the Little Missouri River. Overall, it was evident that the locals knew there was a minister in residence in Catlin, and they sought him out for his services on many occasions.

Richard understates it, but North Dakota surely tested him fully in body and spirit. At the same time, he portrayed life and relationships among a number of families during the early settlement period of McKenzie County. His account is a picture of difficult travel, temperamental animals, bitter cold, helpful neighbors, and faith in God, but optimism for the future. Although their farmsteads have all but vanished, the people described in this journal admirably struggled, endured, and left their legacy for us to admire.

Richard P Jahn Jr.
Co-Editor, Chattanooga, Tennessee

A WORD
FROM THE CO-EDITORS

The amazing journal of Pastor Richard Jahn is undoubtedly the greatest historical find for McKenzie County in its 100-year history. As a young, single man, Richard was in the midst of studies at the seminary when he decided to head to the wilds of western North Dakota. Along with hymnals and Bibles, he took with him a journal, pens and ink, a camera and a sense of adventure! For a year he recorded with faithful devotion and a sense of importance almost daily accounts of the sometimes happy, sometimes boring and sometimes grueling days of the early homesteaders. The journal brings us stories and events never heard before, such as what is perhaps the only documented killing of a man by a wolf in North Dakota. Richard's observations of the early homesteaders, their joys, triumphs and tragedies, along with his excursions to bring religion to the cowboys in the cattle camps of the badlands, all paint a vivid picture of what it really was like to be in a time when intrepid cowboys and homesteaders with saddles and plows forged the beginnings of McKenzie County. Their stories are in these pages along with wonderful photographs of their amazing frontier life. Pour a cup of coffee and light the kerosene lamp. Prepare for a journey back in time with the most excellent guide, the Reverend Richard C. Jahn.

Dennis Edward Johnson
Assistant Local Editor

The journals of Pastor Jahn are truly an incredible find for our community and McKenzie County, and we are indebted to his family for bringing them forward. They are a wonderful look back into the life and times of individuals and families that helps us relive those incredulous years of pioneer life. You will feel that you are walking in the footsteps of many as you experience the trials, disappointments and joys of everyday life. As we celebrate the past 100 years of our community, we realize the dedication of these individuals to their families and their community. Through this book, we realize that dedication is what made the difference between success and failure in this remote area of North Dakota.

Jan Dodge
Assistant Local Editor

T.B
R.C **SUN** **28** The sun came out bright this morn., but a keen wind was blowing, which increased to a storm by noon. I preached to 22 souls in Joe's kitchen and ate a "capital" dinner there. Although a heavy snow was falling and the wind cut icily, I pushed on to Res. Cor, where 14 people awaited me. Spent the night at Bob Jennsens, because Mrs. Draeger was sick. Mr. J. is very talkative and somewhat of a braggart. Very "terror" big.

MON **29** Got up at 8. Pan-cakes for breakfast; wrote my report to Rev. Hegendorf in fore-noon & talked a great deal. After dinner I prepared my confirmation lesson, had Minna Norms, W. Draegert & one Jannsen boy. Got through fine. Talked a good deal in eve. and went to bed at 11.00. A fine, sunny day. Had a miserable cot to sleep in, but managed some-how. Left Johnsons at 9-00. Stopped at

TUES **30** Berg to mail my letters and get some groceries. It was very cold with a heavy wind, which luckily was not directly in my face. Drove to Cabin, where I had 9 letters. Emil was not home, and there was no coal oil in the house; the lantern burnt out at 8.00 so I went to bed. Had no supper, because I expected Emil & Howard back.

WED **1** **DECEMBER.** Got up at 7.00. Tended to the horses and then sat down and wrote a complete sermon for next Sunday on I Joh. 14. Had bread and cheese of it in afternoon. Buched part for dinner. Howard & Emil came home at 6. 00. Emil's black mare (Belle) had taken sick & he left her at Lilly-Bridges. We loaded up 30 bu. of wheat for Mr. Howard to take to W.—

THURS **2** We got up at 3.30. Howard left by 4.30 — Emil & I were so tired that we went back to bed & slept till 9.30 — Then we made dinner and drove over to Howards. Emil fixed up the door & table for her, while I had a very interesting conversation. We got back home before dark and had a late supper. I had intended to study, but was too sleepy.

FRI **3** Got up very late. Helped Emil to haul hay & did not leave for Schafer till 2.00 P. m. It was a nice day and not very cold, but it was pretty dark when I got to Schafer. Bought some groceries and got a huge armful of packages etc from the P. O. Ma & Dora sent me butter & etc. It was very dark before I got my team put up at home. Did not do much studying, but went to bed early.

SAT **4** Got up at 9.00 Breakfast: grapenuts, crackers. Hitched up and drove to Watford, where I got a hair-cut, and bought some necessities. Met Howard on the Road. Emil's mare is doing fine, but his other horses are getting sick. Filled my "straw-bag" and made a mattress. Buched my sermon and looked up hymns etc. in eve. Am very short of coal and hay. Went to bed at 10.30

PART I: 1915

Figure 1: *RCJ, at right, with seminary buddies back in St Louis.*

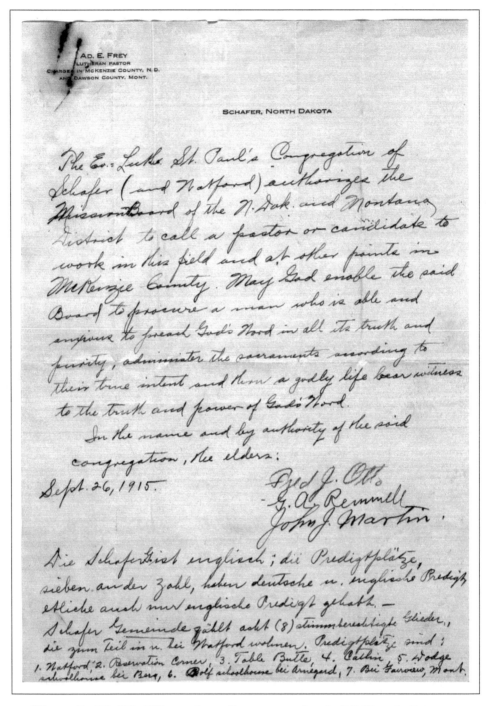

Figure 2: *The "Call" letter from the congregation in McKenzie County, North Dakota. Richard C. Jahn kept it with him for his entire life.*

CHAPTER 1

THE CALL TO MCKENZIE COUNTY

Thursday October 7

This is a rather momentous day. Fuerbringer[1] gave out a call[2] to McKenzie Co., N.D. and I applied for it. I have not intended to Vicar before but this place appealed to me. The roommates were mighty sore about my decision but my mind is firmly made up. Wrote to Mr. Deke asking for advice. Made the greater part of english sermon on Luke 14, 25-35 before devotion. It was mighty cold in night.

Friday October 8

Had steam again this morning. Finished my sermon during free lesson. Spent my afternoon by reading and talking. Made Fuerbringer's test on 1 John, because I figured that would help me next year, after devotion, while the other boys were playing pinochle. It was so cold that I slept between blankets. Got a letter from Ma.

Saturday October 9

Got up for devotion and breakfast. Attended auction and bought several books. After dinner I read the Oct. Cosmopolitan and then Bill Medo and I went to Fibbi's. I discussed my Vicar-post with him, and Bill applied for the Orange place. Went to Reineke's and had enough drinks to make ourselves dizzy. (Just in p.m.) Played pinochle and read in parisienne.

---

[1] Ludwig E. Fuerbringer (1864-1947). A longtime, distinguished professor at the Seminary (1893-1947), he became president in 1931. The students apparently nicknamed him "Fibbi."

[2] This was a formal request from the Schafer congregation asking that a minister be sent to them.

Sunday October 10

Bummed church in morning. Shaved and then read papers till dinner. After dinner Bill and I hiked to the "Grand Dutchess" (hippodrome) and saw ten reels of good pictures for 5¢ (Chaplin in "Shanghid"). Stayed in after supper and talked about various subjects with Bill. Ban and Bill went to bed while I stayed up a while yet.

Monday October 11

Witte came back this morning. Kuecher and Koldy preached in p.m. Got a hair cut at Linds. Got a letter from Jack this morning. I still have a bad cold. Typewrote an outline on a German sermon in evening. Witte and Schelp came up in the room and talked all evening. Went to bed at 11:00.

Tuesday October 12

Talked with Mrs. Brooks after dinner and promised to come down tomorrow night. Made the motion for Bill Medo as asst. librarian and he got it. Typewrote a sermon outline on Luke 4 in p.m. and another in same chapter in eve. Got a letter from Helen[3] today, which worries me considerably. Went to bed at 10:30.

Wednesday October 13

Dr. Pieper was sore this morning. -Got a letter from Deke, in which he advised me to vicar.[4] Accepted the call immediately through Fibbi. Typewrote a sermon outline[5], took a bath, shaved, and went to Holmann's for supper. Enjoyed the evening immensely. Took a walk to Grand Ave. with Emmy.

---

[3] This letter was from Helene Burmeister, RCJ's first cousin living in Lyons, Nebraska. He came close to marrying her, but they broke up in late 1917. She faithfully corresponded with him throughout his year in North Dakota.

[4] This was from Mr. A.H. Deke, who operated the Daylight Store, a general store in Concordia, Missouri. RCJ attended high school in Concordia and must have met him there. RCJ's family could not support him, and Deke proved to be a valuable benefactor throughout his seminary years. Mr. Deke's letter of support was obviously a critical factor in RCJ's decision to go. He formally accepted the call that same day.

General
Merchandise
Phone 90

Member of the Retailers Commercial Union and stockholder in The Retailer is King Co., the official organ of the Retailers Commercial Union. Your advertising patronage is respectfully solicited for our publication.
Address The Retailer is King Co., Farmington, Iowa.

CONCORDIA, MISSOURI, Oct. 12/15. 191

Mr. Richard Jann

St. Louis, Mo.

My. dear Richard:-

I was surprised to hear that you was ready to take charge of the ministry, and I am more then glad to know that Prof Fuerbringer has such confidence in you. It will be entirely satisfactor to me, if you are willing and think that you can and are able to fill the place and that you health will permit it.

You state that your salery will be 25.00 per month, Who pays your salery? and do you have to pay your traveling expense out of that? It seems to me that you aught to have your traveling expencis paid,Will you have to have a horse and buggy, or are the diferent Congregations on Rail Road? I suppose that whenever you preach at the diferent places that they will take up collections for your expencis.

I hope to hear from you real often when you get to work, and be faithful and trust in the almighty and nothing can down you. God bless you my Dear Richard, I am,

Your assistant.

A.H. Deke.

Figure 3: *Letter from A.H. Deke, Richard's supporter, encouraging him to go to North Dakota.*

5

Thursday October 14

Fibbi returned our exams on 1 John this morning and gave me my written call to ND. Alexander came up in p.m. and we beat Bill and Ban 12-3 in pinochle. Hans Bente gave us a test in Symbolics today. Typewrote two engl. sermon outlines. Went down to H. Reinecke's with Bill after devotions. Had one whiskey, one Slow G. Fizz, one Scotch Hi. Slept fine!

Friday October 15

Got up for devotions first time in week. Made up my mind not to go to class anymore.[6] Bill celebrated his birthday and my early departure by a joint blow-out. We invited Alex up and had one case of Griesedieck,[7] twelve sandwiches, hot chili, wine, pickles, ect.[8] After cleaning up on this we went to H. Reinecke's where Alexander set'em up. I drank six straight whiskeys and got pretty dizzy.

Saturday October 16

Bill Medo and Dietze were sick today, Dietze's stomach upsetting at frequent intervals and later Bill joining him. They both slept on couches and kotzed profusely. Attended the auction today where I bought some nice books.[9] Took a good hot bath which made me feel better. Went to bed after reading a while.

---

[5] RCJ knew he would need many sermons for North Dakota, thus the outlines. He would be preaching in German and English.

[6] At this point, RCJ was in the enviable position of not having to go to class or study for tests. He awaited his railway ticket, which would not come for several more weeks.

[7] A local beer, popular in St. Louis.

[8] These Lutheran men, true to their German heritage, showed no reluctance to imbibe alcoholic beverages. RCJ would make up for this in North Dakota, a dry state.

[9] An auction was held periodically at the seminary. Old theological works from deceased pastors were offered for sale to students. RCJ's collection of these books included some dating back to 1526.

Figure 4: *The farewell party of October 15, 1915. RCJ is seated second from right. Sandwiches and a few beverages are on the table.*

Sunday October 17

Bill Medo and I bummed again this morning. After dinner slept for a while until Deitze came up and borrowed my "auxiliarium." He intends to teach school this week and to preach next Sunday. In the evening Bill Medo and Sam Beckler and I went to Bethlehem Church and heard Prof. Arent preach. Dandy sermon. Ate two ice-creams before coming home.

Figure 5: *Ludwig Fuerbringer, nicknamed "Fibbi." Courtesy of the Concordia Historical Institute.*

Monday October 18

Got a letter from Ma and Dora. They are all wrought up about my intention to vicar. Bummed all lectures except Fibbi's. Bill Medo and I went over to the Publ. House where I bought several books. Hiked to the public library after that and to Rice Stix, where I bought some underwear and socks (winter goods).

Tuesday October 19

There is not much to be said about Tues and Wed. Fibbi announced a test on the Isagogics of 1 John and Revelation and introduction of the Old Testament. This is to come off Thursday (next week). Pips is pretty sore in class right now, because some kids made so much racket the other night.

Wednesday October 20

I have been patiently waiting for my railway pass to North Dakota to come. It seems as if there is a hitch somewhere, because it certainly is overdue. One thing that gets my goat is the stale question, "Yin,[10] when are you going to leave?" And I have to go on explaining the same thing over and over. Have been bumming all lessons.

---

[10] This was RCJ's nickname. It stayed with him for life.

Figure 6: *The Jahn family in 1915. From left: Erich (seated),
Richard (standing), Dora (standing), Mutti ("Ma" seated),
Paul (standing) and Jack (seated).*

Thursday October 21

Went to Fibbi's lesson, bummed the rest. Hans cursed because of my absence. Wrote an introductory sermon on Romans 1,16. Alexander came up just after I had typed a letter to Ma, and he and I played pinochle against Bill and Ban. Lost 2-3. Began to typewrite my sermon when Pips came up in the evening. We played some more pinochle.

Figure 7: *Franz August Pieper, seminary professor, nicknamed "Pips." Courtesy of the Concordia Historical Institute.*

Friday October 22

Bummed lessons again. Prof. Bente got sore and called me over to his house, but treated me nicely. Deitze came up to read his sermon to "Dutch" and he and Bill and I went down to Reineke's. Had three rounds of beer and one on the bar tender. Then we went over to the Chippewa lunchroom where we ate until we couldn't move. Deitze went right home. I went to bed soon.

Saturday October 23

I had packed my books that I could not take along in two boxes, one of which I got from Alexander. Took a long bath and packed most of my underwear in my trunk. "Goosie" Hinners was up with Monk and played cards.

Sunday October 24

While Bill Medo went to the "Redeemer" in the morning. I bummed church all day. Bill and I went out for an ice-cream and some fruit in the afternoon. After supper I wrote the greater part of a German sermon. Then Bill came up again and we talked about all sorts of subjects. Off and on I wrote a few words on my sermon. Went to bed at 10:30.

Monday October 25

Was rather disappointed this morning because my railway pass for N. Dakota had not come. Went to Fibbi's lesson, bummed the rest. Finished and type-wrote my German sermon. Ban and Hux Mueller preached today. "Goosie" Hinners was up in the room again and played pinochle. Bucked Fibbi's test in the evening and decided to take it tomorrow.

Tuesday October 26

Went to Bente's and Fibbi's lectures today. "Bricks" Wiedemann came back, and so Weber lost his room. Since Deitze is no resident member, we took Weber over in our room. I wrote the exam on 1-2-3 John, Apocalypse, apocryphal literature of NT and general Isagogics of O.T. at Fibbi's house this afternoon. I think I got through alright. Reinecke gave us a blow out, but I did not go down.

Wednesday October 27

Got a card from Ruth this morning and answered it during Hans' lesson. Mailed it before dinner and read around until dinner. Before supper Menzel came to me and took me up to his room. Reverend Nachtsheim was there and told me I could get my passes from Reverend Kretzmar tomorrow morning. Decided to leave for Chicago tomorrow night.

Thursday October 28

Slept till after breakfast. Went down to Rev. Kretzmar's for my passes and there bought a clergyman's ticket for Chicago at the Wabash office. Packed and roped my trunk and sent it to the station. After supper I played a fare-well game of pinochle with the bunch and then Ban and I left for the station. Took leave of the old scout there, perhaps for life and left on the 9:17 Wabash. Slept fine all night.

Friday October 29

Landed in Chicago at 7.00 a.m. After a good breakfast I boarded a "12th-5th Ave." car and looked at the city. Wrote a card to Ban from the Grand Central Station. Felt pretty lonely, because I was entirely unacquainted. Had a few Buds on Harrison Street. After a shave and massage I went in the Grand Central smoking room where I stayed till 6.30. Then I boarded the "Soo" Pullman for St. Paul Min. Went to bed at 9.00 and had a great sleep.

Saturday October 30

Arrived in St. Paul at 8.00. Walked up Siblsy Street till 4th Street and then 10 blocks to a clean restaurant. Found St. Paul to be a very dull place. Bought a street guide and finally found to St. Anthony and Sybelart, where the bank is located. Looked at it from the outside then beat it back and hung around the station. Left for Jordan at 5:00 and got there at 8:00. Talked with Rev. Frey and stayed over night at Morlocks. Nice people; slept fine.

Sunday October 31

Slept till 8:00. Ate breakfast at Morlocks and staid there till shortly before church time, where I returned to Rev. Frey's. Ate dinner there and then we discussed the Schafer parochy.[11] Bought a carriage heater and some gloves from him. Also borrowed $10. Walked around in Jordan, which is a beautiful town. After supper I packed and left on the 6:55 for St. Paul. Left St. Paul on the 10:45 Great Northern.

---

[11] RCJ's notes from this conversation survive. See Appendix IV. Frey gave him a quick thumbnail sketch of the main people at each preaching post. For example, he told RCJ who could play the piano, where he should spend the night, and who was a good cook. The leaders and outstanding parishioners were pointed out, and so were the indifferent ones.

Monday November 1

Ate a box of cracker-jack instead of breakfast or dinner. Spent the entire morning on the train and got very tired of sitting around. Had to change trains at Williston, N.D. and also spent the night there. Slept at Willis Hotel, which I found to be a nice clean place, and ate at Hogan's Café; good service, high prices. Tried to buck my sermon.[12]

Tuesday November 2

Was awakened at 5:00; dressed leisurely and took a breakfast of cereal and hot milk. Went down to the station and left for Fairview.[13] Met another traveler there, and since we had 2 hrs. time, we went out on a spree. Caught the accommodation and combination Freight and Passenger train for Watford. After a trip that seemed to last for ages, I finally got there. To my joy "Daddy" Roettger[14] was at the station and drove me over to Schafer. My trunk also arrived. I was introduced to Hofman's and Alex's and then we drove up to my shanty and began our batching.

---

[12] This was the term RCJ used to describe the memorization of his sermons. Apparently the students were taught that they should not read their sermons or use notes.

[13] Although Watford City was 50 miles south of Williston, the train from Williston proceeded west to Fairview, Montana, and south to Snowden. From there it reentered North Dakota and headed east to Watford City.

[14] This was Elmer A. Roettger. Adolphus Frey had left the area in September, and Roettger served as interim minister to the congregations until RCJ arrived. The trip from the train station at Watford to Schafer was about seven miles. The pair went two more miles south to Frey's recently-sold homestead. The house was still intact and on the site at this time, but it had been sold separately. Mr. Hoffmann had bought the kitchen and the Ladies Aid Society had bought the rest of the home. Later (see July 9, 1916), the ladies sold their part to lawyer C.C. Converse.

Figure 8: *This is a photo of Rev. Frey and two others at an unidentified location in McKenzie County. Rev. Frey probably gave it to RCJ while he was in Jordan, Minnesota. The photo states: "Klansler, Clacker, Frey – Rex, Lightfoot, Whitefoot." These horses must have belonged to Emil Bellin.*

CHAPTER 2

LONELINESS AT SCHAFER

Wednesday November 3

We arose at about 8 o'clock this morning. Fed the horses, ate breakfast and then started on the trail for Table Butte and Reservation Corner. 'Dad' wanted to show me the road before he left. We got to the Table at about three o'clock and there I met Mr. Jore, Mr. Buck,[15] their wives, Mrs. Eltin, Mrs. Harry Buck. Then we drove to the Res. Cor. Where I met Mr.Jannsen. Got to Draegerts about 7:00 in eve. Covered 45-50 mi.[16]

Thursday November 4

Got up at 8:00 and left at 10:00. We drove wrong several times and stopped at Jore's at 2:00; ate dinner there and fooled around so long that we did not start till 4:00; we intended to go to E. Bellin, a distance that I judged at 25 mi. It gets dark slow in the prairies, and we were lost several times. When we got to Catlin it was quite dark and we lost the road; drove around aimlessly till we saw a light, where they directed us. Even then we felt bad, but finally came to the deserted house. Broke in and helped ourselves. Mr. Bellin came home later on and prepared us an elaborate supper. Then we played casino till 1:00 am.[17]

---

[15] Mr. Frisby Buck homesteaded near Table Butte. Berg was a community a few miles south of Table Butte. It had a small store and post office.

[16] This was a long trip from Schafer, but it was RCJ's first look at his most distant preaching stations. The central home at Table Butte was Ole Jore's house, which still stands. RCJ had great respect for Ole. Conditions permitting, RCJ would preach at Jore's on Sunday morning, then have lunch and ride about seven miles to the Reservation Corner schoolhouse for mid-afternoon services.

[17] This was RCJ's first meeting with Emil Bellin. Much is written about Emil later in the diary.

Friday November 5

Got up late, changed our team, and hiked home the 20 mi. to our shack. Here 'Dad' got ready in a hurry and then we hiked for Watford. The train was very late, but I stayed there till it arrived and took Dad away to Cardena, while I remained home alone. Ate a lonesome supper and bucked my sermon for a while, but did not get finished with it.

Saturday November 6

Got up at 7:00, fed the team and then lit a fire and made breakfast. Then I got ready and left at 9:45. Got my mail in Schafer and then hiked 40 mi. to Table Butte. Did not have any trouble with the roads, although it had rained all morning. Got to Ole Jore's at 3:45. Read my Alma Mater[18] and studied my sermon. Talked a lot with him before going to bed. Slept behind a calico partition.

Figure 9: *Julia Jore and family. These folks all resided near Table Butte. Clarence Jore is in center, kneeling and Marit is behind him. Photo courtesy of Don Jore.*

[18]This was a literary magazine published by students at the Concordia Seminary. RCJ had been on its staff.

Sunday November 7

When I woke up this morning the ground was covered with snow and it was still falling. It got so bad that no-body came for services so my trip was in vain. The snow continued to fall all day and changed into a severe storm in p.m. so Mr. Jore could not let me go, but told me that it was impossible to get thru. I spent the p.m. by writing to Bill Medo and Dora. Read a Treatise on Phillippians in the evening. Went to bed early. It was very cold at night.

Monday November 8

This morning the storm had stopped. About 8 in. of snow had fallen, and in places the drifts were 2 ft deep. Luckily the snow was sticky, else a blizzard would have been inevitable. Mr. Buck went to Berg in a cutter and broke trail for me. Once in a while I found other trails to Schafer. Drove wrong once. Stopped for some groceries at Stephen's and it was so dark that I got lost. Finally found back to Schafer, where I spent the night.[19]

Tuesday November 9

A fierce So. East wind was blowing all night and this morning. Had a hard time to get home. Put up the team and then built a good fire. Had oatmeal crackers and peanut butter for dinner. Mr. Hofman came over for a load of straw in p.m. and stopped in for a chat. Hot wienies for supper. Wrote a letter to Rev. Frey and to Dad Roettger in eve. Went to bed at nine o'clock. It was mighty chilly, so I had hardly enough covers.

Wednesday November 10

This was a very stale day for me. I slept late, but even then it seemed as if the day would never end. I am growing so opprest once in a while that I wish I had never come. Even while I am reading the sense of loneliness never leaves me. So, I determined to attempt to board with Bellin till they move my house to town.[20]

---

[19]There were hotels in Schafer, and after this arduous day of travel RCJ stayed in one rather than go the extra two miles to Frey's house. Frey's house had been built in an isolated place.

[20]Far from his friends and at 20 years old, RCJ was overwhelmed with loneliness. This explains how he ended up living at Emil Bellin's cabin.

Figure 10: *Emil Bellin's log cabin, as RCJ would have seen it when he first arrived in McKenzie County.*

Thursday November 11

After a late breakfast I hitched up and drove to town in order to get some groceries. It was very cold and I froze my left cheek. Mailed my letters and came back early. I made my bed wrong by not having enough covers underneath me, and so I froze all night. Hardly slept a wink; felt very lonely; in fact, am feeling lonlier all the time. After doing my usual chores I collected my dirty linen and drove over to Mrs. Alex. I also wanted some coal, but she had none to spare. I felt very lonely, and since she was talkative I stayed until nearly 8 o'clock. After I got home I made room in the barn and carried in all the hay I could, so the cows would not eat it. Slept in kitchen, where it was warmer.

Saturday November 13

Got up at 8:30. Had a hard time to get a fire started, so I had a late breakfast. It is comparatively warmer today, the wind having gone down. Put the horses in the hay corral and cleaned the barn. Had dinner at 2:00. Went through my sermon several times. Felt very lonesome and strengthened my resolve to stay at Catlin if possible.

Figure 11: *Frey's house near Schafer, where RCJ was supposed to stay. It was built on the edge of a steep bluff. The top of the barn is visible on the left.*

Figure 12: *Frey's house viewed from the well, which was far below it.*

Figure 13: *The well at Frey's house. Next to it is an abandoned claim shack that apparently belonged to a Mr. Core (or Coar). RCJ would later have to store his belongings here after Frey's house was moved away.*

Sunday November 14

Got up bright and early and after dressing carefully I drove to Schafer to conduct services. My audience consisted of five women. In the big hall they made a very poor showing. At Watford the services had not been advertised through some misunderstanding, so there was no meeting. Wrote to Hux and Jack in eve. Salmon for supper.

Monday November 15

Drove to town this morning for my mail and some groceries. It looked very much like blizzard weather but it passed off again. Packed up the things I expected to take to Catlin tomorrow. Wrote a letter to Art Behn and Helen. It got late and since I had not packed everything, I decided to wait till tomorrow Wed. with my Catlin trip.

Figure 14: *View of Catlin, about 1914. The store and post office is at left. The land and store belonged to W.B. Croff. Photo courtesy of Leroy Lillibridge.*

Tuesday November 16

Got up late and cleaned the kitchen good and proper. Carried all the articles I intended to keep into house proper. Fixed a hamburger steak for dinner. Read most of the afternoon. I really did not feel like leaving the house at all. Were it not for the fact that I have no cook-stove and can't prepare a meal on my heater, I believe I would have stayed right there. My hope is that my house will be moved to Schafer soon.

Wednesday November 17

Got up early, but had so much to do, that I did not get away till 11:00. Bellin and Howard were hauling freight for Stephens; met them in Schafer before I left. It was warm and sunny, so that some thawing went on. Found the road all-right and got to Bellin's place at about 3:00. Emil and Howard[21] came at about 7:00. I was just washing dishes. After supper we talked till 1:15 AM. I slept on cot.

Thursday November 18

Got up at 5:30. Fed the horses and shoed Whitie. Young Veeder and Mr. Green came over and stayed for dinner. At about 2:00 Emil and I took Mr. Howard home. A fierce storm was raging and the drifting snow nearly blinded us. There was a Ladies Aid meeting at Howards. (met Mrs, Pollack and Olsen) When we drove home it was quieter. At 8:00 PM the thermometer registered 30° below zero, but the cold did not bother me.

Friday November 19

Mr. Howard knocked against our window at 5:00AM and got us out of bed; We had been up til 12:30. Emil and I loaded up the wheat and left for Watford. We hauled some flax-straw on old cow-barn and got a jag of hay. Had a heavy snow-fall in fore-noon. In the afternoon Emil went over to Morris' to help them thresh. They had quite a time to get the rig set up, so they did not

---

[21]This is the first mention of Harry Howard. His wife was Delia Howard, formerly Delia Green. Their homestead was in Delia's name. It was located about three miles from Emil's cabin. Delia had three girls by a previous marriage to Edward Henry Green, not the Ed Green mentioned often in the journal. RCJ would enjoy a close and supportive relationship with the Howards.

put any grain through. Emil got some groceries at Catlin.[22] We played casino in eve.

Saturday November 20

Got up at 5:00. After Emil left for threshing I cleaned his barn and went thru my sermon. Then I bridled up "Babe" and rode over to Morris' and watched the machine. They had a straw- burning engine. When I came home Mr. Howard had just come back. He had quite a trip; had to abandon his sleigh and use a wagon, because it thawed near Schafer. He made supper.

Sunday November 21

Got up at 5:00. Emil helped Morris in AM. Mr. Howard took his place in PM. We got Mrs. Howard and then drove over to Veeder's school-house for services.[23] There were 19 people present. I preached in English and German (collected: 81 cents). Took Mrs. Howard home and then came back to shack. It was mighty cold (32-)

Monday November 22

Emil went threshing for last time today. I washed dishes in AM and drove over to Howard's shortly after dinner. I instructed Mrs. Howard in Baptism (1st pt.) and found her to be a very interesting and interested pupil. I stayed and talked till 6:00 then drove home. After doing the chores Emil came home and ate supper with me. We played casino. I won most games.

---

[22] This was the name given to the community where Bellin's cabin was located. The only commercial building in the area was a store and post office operated by W. B. Croff. The area was later referred to as Croff. It was a good three-mile ride from the cabin to the store, but Emil and RCJ made it often. The present home of Mr. and Mrs. Leroy Lillibridge is built next to the store site. Catlin was about 13 miles from Schafer.

[23] This was a schoolhouse in Catlin named for Leon Veeder. It was close to Bellin's cabin. Over the years the building would be moved around, depending on the proximity of school-aged children.

Emil Bellin on "Babe"
Catlin, N-Dak.

Figure 15: *Emil Bellin. He was 25 when RCJ met him. RCJ was 20.*

Tuesday November 23

(Prof. Graebuer's birthday) We got up so late that we had breakfast at 9:00- hauled in a load of hay and cleaned out the barn. Ate dinner at 4:00. Harry Howard came over just then. Emil and I scooped 140 bu. of wheat on the two wagons, while Harry shod a horse. Had a late supper and went to bed early. Slept fine.

Wednesday November 24

Mr. Howard pulled us out at 3:30AM. After hurriedly getting ready Howard and Emil left with their loads of wheat for Watford. I was just washing dishes when Mr. Dolan came walking in. He was drunk but sobered up by dinner. I took him to Odermann's and drove to Catlin for my mail. In evening Lloyd Buell's threshing crew came over. I gave them supper and bedding.

Thursday November 25

Got up early and cooked breakfast for the threshing crew. Had potatoes, fried bacon, green peas, fried onions for dinner. Emil and Harry came home at 7:00 PM. We put up the horses and drove over to Howard's for an oyster stew. Played whist for a while (1-1). Had a very agreeable evening and came home at 11- played Tipperary 3 times.

Friday November 26

Mr. Green came over early in the morning, and we hitched up and drove into the "breaks" or the bad lands of the Little Missouri River.[24] Here Emil and Green bought some onions and about 30 bu. of potatoes from Zimmermann's. We ate dinner there too. It was pretty cold on the home trip. Green staid for supper. Wrote a long letter to Ma and went to bed at 11 o'clock. Beautiful scenery along river.

---

[24] The badlands of the Little Missouri River were situated fewer than five miles south of Emil's cabin. The prairie dropped off sharply to the river below. Coal and trees for firewood could be found here, and various large ranches were located along the river. In 1916, trees were rare on the prairie, probably due to range fires in the past.

Saturday November 27

We got up late (8:00). I helped Emil water the horses. Then he drove over to Green's to get some coal, while I hitched up Rex and 3 year old Jack and drove to Table Butte. Stopped at Berg and mailed a letter to Ma and to Watford Guide. Did not get lost; had to face a bitter wind all the way. Got to Jore's at 4:00. Helped with chores; met Clarence Jore[25]

Sunday November 28

The sun came out bright this morn; but a keen wind was blowing, which increased to a storm by noon. I preached to 22 souls in Jore's kitchen and ate a "cafeteria" dinner there. Although a heavy snow was falling and the wind cut icily, I pushed on to Res. Cor. where 14 people awaited me. Spent the night at Bob Janssen's because Mrs. Draegert was sick. Mr. Janssen is very talkative and somewhat of a braggard.

Monday November 29

Got up at 8. Pan-cakes for breakfast; wrote my report to Rev. Hilgendorf[26] in fore- noon and talked a great deal. After dinner I prepared my confirmation lesson. Had Minnie Harms, W. Draegert and one Janssen boy. Got through fine. Talked a good deal in eve. and went to bed at 11:00. A fine, sunny day. Had a miserable cot to sleep in, but managed some-how.

Tuesday November 30

Left Janssen's at 9:00. Stopped at Berg to mail my letter and get some groceries. It was very cold with a heavy wind, which luckily was not directly in my face. Drove to Catlin, where I had 9 letters. Emil was not home, and there was no coal oil in the house; the lantern burnt out at 8:00, so I went to bed. Had no supper, because I expected Emil and Howard back.

---

[25] This is Clarence Jore, brother of Ole. Clarence's son Don resides in Montana today and contributed useful information for editing this journal.

[26] Reverend R. Hilgendorf was Superintendent of Missions for the state of North Dakota. RCJ wrote monthly reports to him.

CHAPTER 3

MEETING THE CATLIN CONGREGATION

Wednesday December 1

Got up at 7:00, tended to the horses and then sat down and wrote a complete sermon for next Sunday on John 1:14. Bucked part of it in the afternoon.
Had bread and cheese for dinner.
Howard and Emil came home at 6:00.
Emil's black mare (Belle) had taken
sick and he left her at Lilly-bridges.
We loaded up 40 bu. of wheat for Mr.
Howard to take to Watford.

Thursday December 2

We got up at 3:30. Howard left by
4:30- Emil and I were so tired that we
went back to bed and slept till 8:30-
then we made dinner and drove over
to Howard's. Emil fixed up the door
and table for her, while I had a very
interesting conversation. We got back
home before dark and had a late supper. I had intended to study, but was
too sleepy.

Figure 16: *Clarence and Marit Jore, with Selmer (son) and Hazel, about 1911. Photo courtesy of Don Jore.*

Friday December 3

Got up very late. Helped Emil to haul hay and did not leave for Schafer till 2:00 PM.[27] It was a nice day and not very cold, but it was pretty dark when I got to Schafer. Bought some groceries and got a huge armful of packages etc. from the P.O. Ma sent me a bathrobe etc. It was very dark before I got my team put up at home. I did not do much studying, but went to bed early.

Saturday December 4

Got up at 9:00. Breakfast: Grapenuts, crackers. Hitched up and drove to Watford, where I got a hair-cut and bought some necessities. Met Howard on the road. Emil's mare is doing fine, but his other horses are getting sick. Filled my "straw-bag" and made a mattress. Bucked my sermon and looked up hymns etc. in eve. Am very short of coal and hay. Went to bed at 10:30.

Sunday December 5

I got up leisurely and drove over to Schafer where I preached on John 1:14. Got thru well, thou I had not studied much. Ate dinner at Randall's and drove to Watford in PM- In spite of the fact that I had advertised the services, nobody was there. Felt pretty disgusted. Wrote several letters in evening.

Monday December 6

It rained this morning and in early afternoon. Another instance of our changeable weather. Wrote a letter to Dietze and drove to Schafer for some groceries and my mail. Went to Alex's where I paid my laundry and fetched out another batch. Borrowed a sack of coal from them. – Wrote several more letters in evening and went to bed at 10:45.

Tuesday December 7

Got up at 8:00 packed my things away, cleaned up the house and then hitched up and drove to Catlin. The roads were very icy, so that "Rex" fell

---

[27] On Sundays when RCJ was scheduled to preach in Schafer and Watford City, he would plan to spend the night in Frey's house at Schafer. Services would take place at 11 a.m. in Schafer and 2 p.m. in Watford City.

twice. Stopped at Catlin for Emil's mail, and got to his place at 5:00- Drove over to Green's with him and had a late supper. Played checkers all evening. Went to bed at 1:10.[28]

Wednesday December 8

Got up very late. Drove to Catlin for groceries and went to Mrs. Howard for bread, butter etc. Ate dinner there. Drove over to Lilly-bridges, where Emil's sick horse was. Helped with chores and ate supper there. Took a box of records home with us and played phonograph. Emil and I crawled out of bed again and played 7½ because we could not sleep. Went to bed again at 3:30 and got up at 11AM.

Thursday December 9

Played 7½ till we had the dishwater heated, and then washed dishes. After supper I sat down and wrote a complete sermon on Philippians 4:4-7. Got thru at 11:00. Emil and I smoked and talked till late and finally "hit the hay". Drank a lot of "Hupner".

Friday December 10

Got up at 10:15. after tending to the horses we had a combined breakfast and dinner. Wrote 3 letters in PM. Emil took them to Catlin, while I stayed home and bucked my sermon. I finished the introduction and first part. Played a lot of 7½ in evening and some casino. After a mid-night lunch we went to bed (1:30 AM)

Saturday December 11

Got up close to dinner. Had a combination meal (Breakfast and Dinner) in fact, we have been having only 2 meals a day for a long time. We did not do anything all day. By evening I knew my German sermon, excepting the close. I got tired of studying, so we played cards till very late. Ate a mid-night lunch again and went to bed very late.

---

[28] He is staying at the Frey house for the night. He probably spent the night at a hotel in Watford City the evening before.

Sunday December 12

My audience at Veeder's School-house consisted of Emil and Kummers (Lorenz). I distributed contribution envelopes for Xmas and preached in English only on John 1:14. I was glad of this, for I did not know my German sermon[29] very well. In the evening I wrote out a lot of letters to people around Catlin, enclosing envelopes. Also wrote to Jack, Monk Hartenberger. Also sent for a new diary to the St. Paul Sta. Co.[30]

Figure 17: *Emil Bellin's barn. From this picture, the barn appears to have been a sturdy structure, well able to withstand McKenzie County winds and weather.*

---

[29] In several of his preaching posts, RCJ was expected to preach one sermon in English and another in German. This was common in most Lutheran Church-Missouri Synod (LC-MS) parishes at the time. Later, as pastor of First Lutheran Church in Chattanooga, Tennessee (1925-1950), he preached English and German sermons up until World War II.

[30] The 1916 diary would give RCJ considerably more room to write each day than his 1915 edition.

Monday December 13

We had planned to clean out the barn, go to Catlin, Howard's and Lilly-Bridges, and fetch home a load of hay. We got up so late though, that we only got to Croffs (Catlin) and Howard's. Did not wait for mail at Croffs, because the days are too ding- busted short for that, but I am going to try to stay next Wed. at Howard's. We got some bread, went to- bed at...

Tuesday December 14

Got up a little earlier than usual (8:00). Had breakfast and dinner at 11:15- Lloyd Buell was over for a few minutes. Talked and played phonograph till late PM, then we cleaned out the barn and got a load of oats straw (had run out of hay). I made up an order of some phonograph records and played a lot on the machine in eve. Went to bed at 12:35.

Wednesday December 15

Got up at noon. I wrote a letter to Otto (about moving house) and dropped a card to the "Watford Guide"[31] and to Daddy Roettger. "Shorty" was here for about an hour. Drove to Croffs where I mailed the order to S.P. and Co. It had snowed a great deal yesterday and last night, so the mail stage did not get thru; consequently I did not get my mail. – wrote introduction to Xmas sermon in eve.

Thursday December 16

Got up at 7:00 AM and by ten I had the sermon completely written out. "Wienie" Wehrle was here for dinner. Emil drove over to Howard's in afternoon; during that time I bucked a little more than half of my sermon. After he came home we had a late supper (10:00) and then we played casino till late.

---

[31] The weekly newspaper, published at Watford City. RCJ usually announced the location of his services for the upcoming month in this paper and the Schafer Record.

Friday December 17

We got up quite late. I read around a great deal, then we played casino for a while. At about 2:00 we cleaned out the barn and hauled in some straw. Emil then drove to Croffs for the mail. I got a letter from Ruth, Bill Medo and some wristlets from ma, also a check for 30.00 from the Mission board. Wrote to Ruth in eve, telling her that I would gladly be sponsor.[32]

Saturday December 18

Prof. Metzger's Birthday; Got up at 8:00, studied sermon for a while. It was the coldest day we had so far, and I had to drive to F. Buck's, a distance of 20 mi. I had never been there before, but I inquired my way at Keogh's ranch and at Eltins. Mrs. Harry Buck is staying with the old people. Had a good supper and talked a long time. Slept with Mr. Buck. Bed at 11:00.

Sunday December 19

Helen's Birthday - Sunday 26th. Although I had announced services for 11 o'clock the people came so late, that I did not start till 12:15. Preached on Luke 2, 10 -13. Got thru nicely, tho I hadn't studied much. After a "cafeteria" dinner I drove to Res. Corner, where I preached in English only. Ate supper at "Bob" Janssen's and also spent the night there. Had an argument on Lord's supper.

Monday December 20

A year ago today I began this diary. I began it in Room 111 at the Seminary and to-day I am writing at Robert Janssen's, Charlson, N. Dak. Slept till 9:00. Ate oatmeal and a cracker for breakfast. At about 3:00 PM I went to Harm's where I had confirmation lessons. The kids are not very bright, but I might pull them thru. Wrote a letter to Ma in the evening. Talked with Bob till 10:30.

---

[32] Ruth was the wife of RCJ's older brother, Jack. She had just had a new baby.

Tuesday December 21

Got up at 8:00; had breakfast and got ready to leave. During early part of day a brisk north wind was blowing and I was rather chilled when I got to Berg, where I mailed Ma's letter. "Whitie" broke a single-tree hook, and it took me a long time to fix it. Drove to Emil's place via Catlin, where I got a letter from Ma. Ate a meager supper and went to-bed at 9:15.

Wednesday December 22

Got up at 8:00- Fed the horses- Grand larceny "imagines" Jo.- had fried onions, ham etc for dinner.[33] Emil came home at about 4:00. He bought a box of apples etc along, and we hopped to it. Heard evangelist Sherman Chapin in eve. at Leon Veeder's Sch. House. Drove to Howard's after that for bread and milk. Got back home at about 12 AM.

Thursday December 23

Slept till nine. After a cold meal we watered the horses and then drove to Billy Bellin's place[34] for some hay. Had four horses on the sleigh. I drove out. We put on a big load and upset twice. The second time we broke the rack and let the hay lay. Took half of it home. Wrote to Helen and Jack in the eve. Bed at 12:00.

Friday December 24

We could not find Rex and Babe, so Emil hitched Mable with Whitefoot. Got to Veeder's schoolhouse at 2:30 and I preached to a good audience. In the evening I drove to Howard's; Lloyd and Mrs. Buell were there. Saw the Xmas tree and toys; played whist. Ate a good lunch. Played phonograph till late at night.

---

[33] The Editors are not sure what RCJ meant by this phrase.

[34] Billy Bellin was Emil's older brother who had come to McKenzie County in 1910. He homesteaded 1.5 miles south of Johnson Corners. Billy died of pneumonia in 1914, and Emil farmed his land for many years thereafter. Emil's homestead was about three miles east of Billy's.

Saturday December 25

Emil had caught Rex last night. I hitched him to Whitey and drove to Scha-fer. Stopped at Croffs for mail. Had to face a heavy snow-fall all the way; luckily it was wet and not blizzardly. To my joy Hofman had not moved my kitchen. Emil had sent coal and wood along and I soon had a good fire. Wrote several letters and ate .25 worth of chocolates.

Sunday December 26

It was bitter cold with a strong north wind. Had half a mind to stay home but finally drove in to Schafer. Found 6 people there. Ate dinner at the Cherry View hotel and then drove in to Watford. Again there was nobody there. Felt very disappointed. Got a jumper full of straw and after supper I wrote a report to Hilgendorf.

Monday December 27

I happened to wake up at 5:00 this morning. It was 9:30 before I left for Schafer. There I got a big box of goodies from Dora and some groceries from Stevens. Drove via Croffs, where I got Emil's mail. Emil was home, being prevented from going to Watford because Howard did not show up. Played casino.

Tuesday December 28

We slept pretty late. Harry Howard was here in PM. Played phonograph and talked a great deal. Mr. A. Oderman came over in eve and asked about his kid, which he had baptized. I reassured him and he left greatly relieved.[35] Young Lillybridge was also here. I stayed up till 2:15 writing letters and Emil could not sleep so he got out of bed. We played casino. He got up again at 4:00, but I was so sleepy that I crawled back into bed.

---

[35] The Odermann homestead was three miles west, a half mile south of Billy Bellin's. The Odermann baby had been born a few days earlier but was doing poorly. Mr. Odermann came to RCJ with questions about the child's eternal security. The Lutheran Church - Missouri Synod took the position that the act of baptism saves a person. This is still taught today by many LC-MS pastors.

Figure 18: *Emil Bellin's jumper. This was used to travel over snow.*

Wednesday December 29

After Emil had left, Howard came over and dumped me out of bed. I crawled in again and slept till noon. Watered the horses at 3:00 and doctored Jack and Rex. Made an attempt at milking. Wrote a letter to Art Behn.

Thursday December 30

Slept late. Made myself a good dinner, consisting of beans, potatoes, fried ham etc. I attempted to write my sermon for next Sunday, but I did not get beyond the introduction. I was just riding the horses to the spring when Emil got home. He fetched the 6 records etc along, that I had ordered. Ray Catlin was here in eve and we played thru the entire selection of records (48) before he left. It was after 1:30-

Friday December 31

On the last day of 1915 we ate only 2 meals as usual. Eggers and Alton were here looking for horses and ate dinner with us. Howard was after a load of hay and jerked Emil out of bed. Rex had a bad attack of colic in PM, but was nearly better in eve. Last year I celebrated by boozing, this year Emil and I played casino, and at 12:00 I was in the barn milking the cow. A year ago I would not have imagined such a thing possible.

Saturday January 1, 1916

Went to bed at 2:00 this morning and arose with great dignity at about 10:00. Emil and I washed dishes before we could eat any supper. I tried to buck a german sermon, which I had written some time before Xmas, while Emil rode the Pinto to Croffs for the mail. Had a letter from Monk and Deke, who enclosed $10.00 as a Xmas present. Read the papers and smoked a lot in eve.

"Billy" Bellin's Homestead, Catlin, N. Dak. (8x12 ft; 3 men lived here for years)

Figure 19: *Billy Bellin's 8'x12' shack and barn on his homestead, about three miles from Emil's house. RCJ wrote on the photo that "three men lived here for years." Billy died in 1914, and Emil used his shack for a barn. Later, when he married Leta Kummer in 1920, Emil moved this structure to his place and attached it to the back of his cabin. It was the couple's bedroom until 1955.*

Weather Record
❧ Schafer, North Dakota ❦

Nov. 7th- first snowfall, strong wind, drifting. Cold winds are a characteristic of this part of the state. For days the wind will blow steadily from some certain quarter with unabating fury. Evening in Nov. the thermometer sank to 25-35 below zero. I did not suffer much, because I was always dressed warmly. We had a heavy snow-fall Nov. 24th, but it melted away again so that sleigh-riding was impossible in places. – The weather in this part of the state is very changeable. After all the wet weather of November, December began with a series of warm, sunny days. It was so warm that it rained on Dec. 6th.

Had a heavy snowfall towards middle of December. The weather was extremely unpleasant, cloudy and windy. It snowed again on the 16th and 17th, but cleared up on 18th. It was pretty clear on 19th, but both days were very cold. Winter opened with a slight west-wind, which died down towards eve, making it very warm. We had a lot of snow towards the close of the year. 1915 ended with a snow-fall, and in the eve it cleared up, the thermometer sinking to -10 degrees.

Wea.　　　FRI. MAY 26, 1916　　　Ther.

I wished to start for home very early, but Kinau-
nook and Wrav kept assuring me that I had plenty
time, so that I did not get started till about 9.00
o'clock. Had a great deal of trouble in finding the
Cradle Springs. First I followed an old pony trail
for several miles, before I noticed that I was on the
wrong trail. For a while I was so completely lost
in the crazy Blue Buttes, that I began to get
genuinely scared. At last I heard the sharp crack
of a 30-30 rifle to my left, and I galloped towards
the place as fast as I could. To my immense joy
I ran upon Frank Keough, of the Keough ranch,
who had been trying to pull a bogged cow from
a water-hole, and had finally shot the exhausted
animal. His way led him past Cradle Springs
and we rode that far in company. I declined
his invitation for dinner, since the ranch buildings lie towards Berg, and would take me
too far out of my way. Instead I rested my horse
at the springs, and let her graze for an hour,
while I ate some dried beef, which Kinanook's
squaw had given me. At 2.30 I mounted a-
gain, and since I was well acquainted with
the trail from the springs, I found home
without difficulty. I struck the shack before
8.00, and put my tired pinto in the barn. I
hate to think of the long trip to Schafer to-morrow.

Wea.　　　SATURDAY 27　　　Ther.
Violent wind-storm.

There was a terrible windstorm
to-day. I had to face the wind for over
thirty miles (having taken the north road)
At Schafer I fed "Whitie" and stopped for
dinner and a session with the barber.

While I was being shaved Harry
Howard came in with two of the girls. He
was taking a load of grain to town, and
the girls wanted to see the famous show at
the Watford City opera house.

It did not take much persuasion to get
the girls to accompany me for the rest of the
way. I took them into Lundin's restaurant
and filled them up with ice-cream. Then I
secured rooms at the Watford hotel for our
party. We ate at the world-renowned restaurant
of the Viking cafe, and then took in the show, an
emotional drama called "East Lynne."

PART II: 1916

"The Preacher" in his den.

Figure 20: *RCJ writing letters in Emil Bellin's cabin. The cabinet behind him still survives and was owned by Arno Bellin. Note the phonograph at upper left.*

Figure 21: *RCJ dressed in winter garb in front of Emil's cabin. Note the tarpaper above the logs.*

CHAPTER 4

WOLF ATTACK AND LA GRIPPE

Saturday January 1, 1916 Catlin, N. Dak.

Wea. Cloudy   Ther. 8 above 0

When I look at my diary for 1915, which I have just laid aside, I cannot help but contrast the differences in my environments between now and a year ago to-day. Jan. 1, 1915 I was in St. Louis, in a city of nearly 900,000 inhabitants, while the entire state of N. Dakota at present has only 577,000 people living in it. A year ago to-day I ushered in the new year with a lot of booze; This year E. Bellin & I had neglected to do our chores, and 12:00 AM found me in the barn, engaged in the highly amusing and exciting task of milking a cow.

Emil rode the little pinto to Croff's[36] for the mail, while I attempted to rustle up a sermon. I had a letter from Mr. Deke, with a check for $10.00, and a highly interesting epistle from "Monk" Hartenberger.

Sunday January 2

I did not know a thing about my sermon, as I set the alarm on 8:00, (we had stayed up til 12:30) but when the alarm went off, I merely poked up the fire and reset the clock on 9:00. Then I finally dressed and worked out a new introduction and closing to my sermon before Emil got up.

After a hasty dinner we hitched "Whitie & Babe" to the jumper and pulled out for Veeder schoolhouse. Although we were just 1 hr. late, nobody was

---

[36] For many years the Croff family maintained a post office and small general store, a common occurrence in North Dakota that saved many miles of riding for local residents who needed to resupply with basic goods and pick up their mail. These stores also provided an opportunity for the person, often a homesteader himself, to make a little extra cash to improve his financial condition. Wallace Croff ran the family farm in McKenzie County until 1975.

Veeder's School house, Catlin, N. Dak.
(One of Jim's Preaching Posts)

Figure 22: *Veeder's School, located close to Bellin's cabin. These schools were moved periodically to be close to where children were more concentrated.*

there. Emil & I waited however, until Kummers,[37] who had seen us pass, came. I preached in German on Phil 4:4-7. When we got home we watered the horses, hauled a load of straw with Babe and Whitie and then ate a cold supper. It was dark (no moon) but still we drove over to Howards. Got off the trail several times, but got there and back safely. Got some coal oil, bread, butter, and meat there. Bed at 2:15.

---

[37] Although there were numerous Kummer families in McKenzie County at this time, all related in some fashion and originating from Sauk Center, Minnesota, this was likely the Lawrence and Minne Kummer household on the "section line road" between Emil Bellin's cabin and the Veeder School.

Monday January 3

Wea. Cloudy; light snowfall in eve   Ther. +4

This was one of my "lazy days". Emil and I had planned to drive to his brother's claim and fetch a load of hay. But in the first place, we slept till noon, and then we fooled around so long that it got too late. There was a very strong East wind, which swept through the many chink holes in the shack and kept it very cold inside. We had a roaring fire in the heater, but it was too windy for the shack to get warm. For a part of the afternoon Emil & I slept, but I finally woke up to get some coal, and then we walked down to the spring to water the horses. I hitched "Beauty and Mac" to the bob-sleigh and got a load of straw. We had steak for supper. Emil threw back the table-cover and pounded the steak with an ax. It got nice and tender too. I found a fantastic book, treating of AD 2000, of which I read 175 pages.[38] Went to bed at 1:30.

Tuesday January 4

Wea. Clear; severe east wind   Ther. −4, +8; -22

For several weeks Emil and I have had only two meals per day; we rarely get up before 10:30 and while Emil tends to the horses I usually sweep the shanty, make the beds and get the dishes ready. We then eat some cereal, in lieu of breakfast, and have potatoes & meat. Often it is 2:00 PM before we eat. We usually have supper at 4:00.

---

[38] This is almost certainly *Looking Backward* by Edward Bellamy (1888). This popular book told the fictional story of a Boston man, Julian West, who was sleeping in a deep chamber underneath his house in 1887. The house burned and by some means West was completely preserved in the ground until he was rediscovered alive in the year 2000. West found that all American citizens were working collectively toward the common good of the nation. Those future citizens had given up their individualism. Gone was the boundless enthusiasm and entrepreneurial spirit found in turn-of-the-century America. No vision could have been further out of character in McKenzie County in 1916 than this one.

Geo. Taylor, 1st Range Rider for "◇C◇" Ranch
Near Emil Bollin's Cabin

Figure 23: *George Taylor riding up to Emil's cabin. He was a First Range Rider for the Diamond 'C' Ranch and visited RCJ and Emil often. His homestead was adjacent to Emil's.*

To-day we expected to get some hay, but we postponed it again. George Taylor[39] was over here, looking for his horses, and finally rode "Babe" in search of them. Emil and I talked around all afternoon and fed and watered the horses just before dark. The spring has about 2ft. of ice of in it now, and Emil told me that he generally had to let his dipping pail thru the ice by a rope before spring. I began a letter to Reese, but did not finish it. Swapped yarns about the "bus" and played casino till 3:15 AM. It was -22 degrees at that time.

Wednesday January 5

Wea. Sunny but very cold   Ther. −22, +2, -18

Emil got up about 10:00 and raised cane with me. Tied me down on the bed with a rope and leaned my cot up against the wall. We had dinner at 2:00. I had made up my mind to ride "Babe" over to Croff's for the mail, and for this reason I wrote part of a letter to Reese in the afternoon. Later on I considered that I could not finish all the letters that I expected to write, so I dropped postals to Mr. Deke, "Bill Medo," and "Monk." Just as I was ready, Emil came driving up to the shack with the rack, which he had hastily repaired. I quickly made up my mind to help him instead of going to the post office, so I dressed and went along to the Cleveland flat where we got some of Howard's hay,[40] it being too late to go to Emil's stacks. It was −10 and I froze considerably. While Emil watered the horse, I unloaded the hay into the barn. We ate supper at 10:00 and went to bed at 3:00.

Thursday January 6

Wea. Sunny and warmer   Ther. −20, +48, -?

Emil and I were still in bed at noon. Suddenly we heard some sleigh-bells close by, and we had barely jumped out of bed when Howard burst into the door, expecting to dump us out. He talked a while, and then drove off with his rack to fetch some hay. We ate a hearty breakfast-dinner and then drove

---

[39] George Taylor homesteaded immediately north of the Bellin claim. He worked at the Diamond 'C' ranch, where he was First Range Rider.

[40] Cleveland's flat was a swampy, marginal field, just on the other (west) side of the school section from the Bellin claim. It was owned by A. Kleveland. Harry Howard apparently rented it for hay.

to Croff's. To my surprise there were no letters for me. (My magazines, packages, in fact, all but the 1st class mail is held at Schafer). I selected a lot of photos of scenery in McKenzie Co., but Emil paid for the lot.[41] I mailed an order for some warm clothing to-day. Mr. Howard had invited us for the evening, so we quick watered the horses, ate a hearty supper, and left at about 2:00. It was pretty dark then, but I drove "Whitie" and "Babe" over alright. At Howard's we played several games of Whist (I won) and a game of "chanticleer." We had a nice time and got a substantial Midnight lunch. We got home at 12:00 and went to bed at 2:15.

Friday, January 7

Wea. Warmer; slight west wind   Ther. −17, +50, -8

Howard stopped in again for his mail. After dinner, Emil and I fooled around til after 4:00. Emil has the habit of killing time by shooting at a picture of some calves, which is hanging on the west wall of his cabin. He sits down near the table and fires at anything in the house that takes his fancy. We shot up all the bullets to-day at some tin-cans hanging on the fence. We simply shot at them through the open door of the shack.

At about 4:00 we got ready to fix the fence around the hay corral. Emil had fetched some woven wire along, and we put that around the posts and three strands of barb-wire on top of that. Fixing fences in January is a rather cold proposition, but it had to be done, for the range cattle will break through most anything. In the evening I played my old favorite pieces on the phonagraph (Miserele, Anvil Chorus, Traumerei, etc.) We had an 8:00 supper, and then I worked out a sort of a shema[42] for Sunday's sermon. Bed at 12:00.

---

[41] Jahn's good friend Emil Bellin undoubtedly paid for some of the photographs featured in this publication. Some of these scenery pictures were taken by the Watford City photographer, Redding.

[42] RCJ undoubtedly meant to use the word "schema" in reference to his sermon preparation.

Saturday January 8

Wea. Cloudy

By about 1:00 P.M. I was ready for the trip. It was not very cold, and I had as good a trip as could be expected in winter. Emil drove ahead as far as Billy Bellin's place; he was after a load of hay. From there I had to break the road for 17 miles to Ole Jore's. I was supposed to have services at Clarence Jore's, but Mrs. Jore was sick, so she could not have the people. Ole was riding to Berg, and told me this. So I decided to spend the night at Jore's.

I drove "Whitie and Babe," and they surely are a fast team. "Rex" is not feeling very well. Last winter Mr. Jore boarded the school teacher, and the latter left the majority of his books. I read around in them a great deal in the evening. Was especially pleased with a work on political economy and on morality. Was not much impressed by Chadman's Encyclopedia of Law, though it is a very good work for the layman. - Slept in a room which was curtained off with calico. Mr and Mrs. Jore slept on the other side of the curtain, which was rather transparent. It turned very cold during the night.

Sunday, January 9

Wea. "Blizzardy"   Ther. −32, -2, -18

During the forenoon a fine snow, powdered fog, began to blow, driven by a sharp East wind. There were no services, of course. I spent the morning in conversation with Mr. Jore, who is a splendid man. By noon the wind had shifted due north. I was convinced that nobody would come to Reservation Corner for services, because it looked too much like a blizzard. Still, it is my duty to go to my stations whenever there is the slightest chance for me to break thru, so I left Jore's against his advice, and started the nine- mile trip at about 2:00.

Words fail me when I attempt to describe this journey. I got to a deep coulee just north of the mighty Table Top,[43] which had drifted full of snow. For a while I drove around aimlessly, trying to find a better crossing, but I could not find it and the only alternative was to turn back. I have a goodly share of "bull-headedness" in me, a lot of grit, and so I whipped up the horses and

---

[43] Table Butte.

Figure 24: *Ole Jore and Jessie Buck Jore in December, 1903. RCJ found Ole to be a "splendid man." Jessie was "perfectly deaf" but was an excellent lip-reader. Photo courtesy of Don Jore.*

plunged them thru. Whitie cut a hole in his front leg with his sharp calks, but I pushed him on. When I rounded the Butte, the wind struck me square in the face and the snow blinded me. The trail was entirely obliterated, but I had a good idea of the location of the buttes, and at times they were visible to me. I shaped my course according to them and had to chase my poor team through knee deep snow. With the utmost relief, I finally found Larsen's place, and from there on I was safe. It took me over 3 hours to make the trip. Got to Janssen's at 6:17. Was badly chilled. Bed at 11:00.

Table Butte near Berg, N.D.

Figure 25: *Table Butte. Ole Jore's house was near its foot, and it was a convenient landmark for the traveler.*

❧1916❧

Monday January 10

Wea. Extremely cold; strong wind   Ther. –39, +1, -22

I slept pretty long this morning. After breakfast I read around in a well-thumbed copy of the "Arabian Nights." I remember, that just when the stories were getting interesting the rest was torn away.

According to my usual schedule, I was to instruct my confirmation class to-day.[44] I sent Karl Janssen over to Harm's, but they were butchering and could not spare Minna. So, at the request of Mr. Janssen, I took his two boys privately. They did not know their lessons very well, so I told them to buck it over again. It was very cold to-day but not as bad as the rest of the week proved to be.

Tuesday January 11

Wea. Very stormy and cold   Ther. –61 at Watford

I had expected to go back to Catlin to-day, but the weather was so bad that I accepted Bob's invitation to hug the stove. There was a heavy fog in the morning, which was dispelled by a fierce Northwest wind and a fine, sand-like snow fell, but there was no blizzard. We had bean-soup for dinner.

Though Janssens are rather "unsanitary", the soup was really good. I spent the afternoon by reading a work on Logics, which I afterwards packed up with my books. Then I stepped out before supper and sawed some wood for Mrs. Janssen. By evening it got a little quieter and it cleared up. It got very, very cold tonight (at Watford the thermometer registered 61 below zero, as I subsequently learned). I had to sleep on a miserable cot, without a mattress or straw-bag, and it was so uncomfortable that I could not sleep; in fact, I have never slept over here at Janssens. In the same room in which I slept the boys were drying some skins, and numerous odds and ends of junk were flying around. Probatum est.

---

[44] These were lessons in Luther's Small Catechism. Upon completion, the student would become "confirmed" and eligible to take the Lord's Supper.

Wednesday, January 12

Wea. Clear, very cold (the coldest day in ND since 1882---33 yrs)

Ther. −64, -41, -50

This was just about the coldest day of the year, but since it was nice and sunny I decided to drive home to Catlin. I am willing to admit that I did not know how cold it really was, until I finally landed at Bellin's else I never would have attempted to drive across. As it is, I froze my nose badly while I watered the horses and harnessed them. I went up to the house, thawed my nose out, and got a good blaze started in my carriage heater. I put on my new overcoat and Daddy's fur coat, a pair of woolen mittens over which I drew my sheepskin mittens, and Mrs. Janssen tied my woolen shawl around my face up to the eyes. To this shawl I owe a great deal, for it saved my entire face from freezing.

The heavy storms of the last few days had caused a lot of bad drifts in the trails. In addition to this I had to break the road all the way, and so travel was necessarily slow. There was a very slight wind from the west but it was sufficient to cause me the most excruciating agony whenever I was compelled to face it. I got to Berg at 9:30, having spent nearly 5 hours in making the 15 miles. My nose, forehead and upper part of my cheeks were frozen again. I thawed it all out, bought some groceries and tobacco and drove on. My carriage heater worked fine, and kept my feet warm but my heels were cold. When I got in the coulee between Billy Bellin's and Sawyers shacks I found that it had drifted completely full, so I slid down to the bottom where I passed thru. Cut across from Odermanns, and got home at 6:30.

OBITUARY

Hertwig W. Odermann was born August 12, 1885 in Naugatuck, N. J. At the age of 20 he went west and spent several years in Montana and southern Canada. In 1907 he came to North Dakota where he was employed by various ranchers, finally accepting a position as cow-puncher for the <C>ranch.

January 12, 1916 he was attacked by a band of timberwolves,[45] who mangled him so terribly, that help arrived too late to save his life.[46] During his dying moments he was attended by the undersigned, but circumstances prevented him from conducting funeral services, since another death case intervened.[47] Interment took place January 15th on the butte east of the "NT" ranch.

"Peace to his ashes!" - Rich. C. Jahn

Age 29 years, 5 months.

---

[45] The wolves that killed this young cowpuncher were likely prairie wolves, which used to follow the buffalo herds before the buffalo were decimated. Wolves were becoming more rare, but there were still sightings and reports of them being killed during these early settler days of McKenzie County.

[46] This is an extremely rare documented account of a human being killed by wolves in America. RCJ recalled late in his life that the cowboy had been riding on horseback with others during a snowstorm when he got off to walk his horse through the snow. The others went on ahead of him. A pack of wolves attacked him, and his horse bolted, leaving him without his rifle. By the time help arrived, the wolves had badly mangled Odermann, and he was taken to his bunkhouse. George Taylor must have known RCJ was in the area. The young minister arrived at the bunkhouse about an hour before Odermann died. He was able, although nervously, to share the Gospel with Odermann, who seemed very comforted by the message. It was the first time RCJ had witnessed to a dying person.

[47] There seems to be no relation between Hertwig Odermann and the Odermann child who died on the same day.

Wed., Jan 12ᵗ, 1916 — 65° below zero!
Watford City N. Dak.

Figure 26: *Watford City on January 12, 1916. RCJ reports it was 65° below zero.*

Thursday January 13

Wea. Rather windy   Ther. −38, −18, −27

Since I began this diary Emil Bellin and I have never cooked more than two meals per day. We have no reason to get up sooner mornings, although I could often make good use of the morning hours.

After a very "neutral" dinner Emil and I tossed around on the bed and joshed each other till it was time to do chores. I had just put on my "arctics" when Mr. Ambrosius Odermann came over. After warming up a bit, he asked me to conduct the funeral of his little boy, who had been born on the 24th of December, 1915, and died on the 12th-inst. I gladly agreed to deliver the address, in spite of the fact that Mr. Odermann was Roman Catholic. I "meditated" over a suitable text while Emil drove to Howards for some bread and butter.[48]

---

[48] Much to do with religious dogma was forgotten in the sparsely settled McKenzie County. Men of "the cloth" were not plentiful and in situations such as this funeral, religious differences would be overlooked.

Friday January 14

Wea. Quiet but very cold   Ther. –40, -24, -35

Emil drove to Croff to-day for the mail and some groceries. In the mean time I sat down and wrote out the address for tomorrow's funeral. I selected Job 1:21 ("The Lord gave, the Lord hath taken away, etc") and used the disposition on that text in Groz' Auxiliarium. I dwelt especially on the fact that the child had been rightly baptized and was therefore saved.

I finished writing the address at 5:30 PM. Then I sat down on my hind-legs, and by 12:00 I knew it fairly well. I am not used to bucking a sermon on such a short notice, and felt rather shaky about to-morrow.

Saturday January 15

Wea. Bad blizzard   Ther. Temp dropped to –48
(The temperature at Pembina, N.D., dropped to 48 below.)

The funeral was scheduled at 1:00, but it was nearly that late before we were ready to leave our shack. The weather was so stormy that I felt like the ceremony would be post-poned. Emil was to drive the coffin, so we hitched Mabel and my cayoose Whitie, to the big bob-sleigh and started out. I wore my heavy overcoat in addition to the fur-coat and put on two pair of woolen socks. A lot of people had expected to come, but the weather was so bad that only Jim Catlins, Paul Odermann, Veeders, Kummers, etc. were present. In my little "Taschen Agende" the funeral service is not given entirely; just a few prayers. So I had two songs and a prayer "ex corde" besides my address. I got thru without a hitch, only I was bothered a little because the women and Mr. Odermann were crying. After the service we dressed up warmly and I tied my woolen shawl around my face. The cemetery was about 8 miles away, and I never made such a trip in my life before.[49] Mr. Veeder (Herb), Mr. Odermann, Emil and myself constituted the guard. We danced and jigged around in the sleigh in order to keep warm. The snow-drifts were so deep that our horses were just about foundered in some places. We roused out

---

[49]This is the present-day Union Cemetery, home to a small temporary marker for the Odermann baby. This would have been a formidable trip from Catlin in open sleds during a blizzard. RCJ's records indicate that he baptized Ambrosious and Emma Odermann on this same day, probably after the funeral. He also indicated that the child was named Friederich Karl Odermann.

Mr. White, who lives near the cemetery, and buried the child in the blinding snow-storm. The grave was cut in solid scorio, but not very deep.[50] I cut the ceremonies very short, merely saying a prayer. On the way back, we stopped at Herb Veeders, where we had a few good drinks. We ate supper at Odermanns and got back to the shack at 11:10. It was 6 degrees in the cabin, the fires having gone down. With the aid of a quart of oil we soon had a roaring fire, however.

Sunday January 16

Wea. Very windy   Ther. −12, -2, -20

I was supposed to preach in Schafer and Watford to-day. As a rule I leave on the previous Saturday when I make a trip of this kind, but I could not go yesterday because of the funeral. I was determined to-day to reach Watford in time for services, so I set the alarm on 6:00, although I did not get to bed til 1:00. When the alarm went off, there was a terrible wind howling outside. The snow was drifting through the cracks in the wall, and I knew from yesterday what the roads would be like, for there were no trails broken through the drifts. I am not so very anxious to commit suicide, so I shut off the alarm and crawled back into bed where I stayed till noon. We had "dinner" at 3:30 this afternoon. Then we piled on the bed and scrapped and wrestled around till nearly 6:00 so that we had to water the horses while it was getting dark. Some of the horses and the cow had no water for 3 days, so they were rather dry. The spring was gradually running dry; that is, it is freezing deeper all the time, and may cause serious trouble before long. We use snow- water for cooking and drinking since Emil's well-water is of a very poor quality, being black and of an unpleasant taste. Besides, his well is very shallow and holds scarcely enough water for our own use.[51]

---

[50] "Scorio," more correctly called scoria, is a soft red rock formed by moist clay beds that were heated by burning coal veins. With the constituency of soft pottery, this red or "pink" rock covers the surface of many roads in rural McKenzie County. It absorbs water and therefore can be dug even in extreme frost conditions as it breaks up. This undoubtedly allowed gravediggers to prepare the child's final resting place even in the extreme weather conditions. It was not uncommon for bodies to be "cold stored" until the frost gave way in the spring and a grave could be dug.

[51] Creating water wells posed a real problem in McKenzie County until the advent of rigs capable of drilling deeper wells and equipment that could lift the water to the surface with something other than a bucket and a rope. Emil's water probably turned black as it came off a shallow coal vein. Natural springs or manmade springs that flowed year-round, even in the harsh North Dakota winters, were valuable commodities and remain so today. Emil's well was abandoned soon after 1916, and, until he died in 1970, he never had running water on his property.

❧1916❧

Monday January 17

Wea. Very windy   Ther. −12, -8, -16

As usual, we got up very late. For over a week there has been a steady Northwest wind, which makes it very disagreeable outside. The loose snow has all been piled up in drifts, so that there is not much danger of a blizzard.

We had to get some straw for the horses today, so we hitched up "Mac" and "Beauty" to the rack. After watering them we drove up to the straw pile at the eastern end of Bellin's land. The snowdrifts were so deep that we could not drive close to the stack, and the wind was so that I froze my nose again. Freezing my face is becoming an everyday affair, and causes only mild interest for me. I wrote letters to Ban Johnson and Bob Janssen, also an order to Davis for Altar wine.

Tuesday January 18

Wea. Bad NW wind   Ther. −8, 4, -7

We drove to Croff's store this afternoon for our mail. I got a letter from Helen and ma, also a package from Chicago with my sheep skin boots, etc. Now I am able to dress up better for the N. Dak. weather.

From Catlin we drove to Howards to fetch their mail over and to get some bread. Howard used our team to get his kids from school, while we played his new phonograph records. When we got home, I rode "Beauty" to the spring for water and did the chores, while Emil chiseled the ice out of the spring.[52] We played some 2-minute records of Howard's, which he had sent along. There, we played several games of casino before feeding oats and milking the cow. Went to bed at 2:00 A.M.

---

[52] This water source, known as Clark's Spring, was several hundred yards east of Emil's cabin. It actually bubbled up in the bottom of the large coulee that continues in the direction of Ole Skaar's home. Its water was strongly alkaline and not fit for human consumption, but animals would drink it. Years later, Cameron Dodge and John Kirkland dug out the mouth of the spring to form a deeper pool.

1916

Wednesday January 19

Wea. NW wind   Ther. −8, +2, -5

This was one of my periodical gloomy days. I felt disgusted with everything. Yesterday I sent "Ban Johnson" a check for $5.00, and those fellows will have a good old time on me, while I am forced to hang around here in this ding busted hole. In addition my check from the Mission Board for December is long overdue. I am sorely missing the money and have been forced to borrow from Emil. The poor fellow is always willing to help, but I know his bank roll is not very big, and I may prove to be a serious drain on his resources.

So far I have pulled thru the winter alright. I have only had one regular service, however, on the 2nd, besides the funeral at Odermanns. This was not my fault, for I have always been willing and anxious to meet the people. Either I underestimate, or else the old residents overestimate the dangers of a blizzard.

Emil has the habit of going to- bed without his underwear for the nether limbs, and I had to laugh at him tonight. He got up out of bed at about 2:00AM for a drink. There was no water in the house, so he walked outside in his bare legs, filled a can with snow, melted it, and there you are. He sure looked comical in the bright moonlight.

Thursday January 20

Wea. Remarkably clear and warm   Ther. −3, +29, 7

Mr. Odermann once told me that McKenzie Co. usually had a "January thaw" It seems as though this thaw has arrived, for it was so warm to-day that the snow on the road melted partly.[53] It also was very quiet, the terrific winds having died down some-what.

---

[53] The "thaw" referred to is known as a "Chinook." This unexpected and sudden warming is a common annual occurrence in western North Dakota and usually takes place in late January or early February, resulting in much-needed relief from the harsh weather. The Chinook is the result of warm winds blowing in from Montana and will last for a week or two before winter conditions are likely to return.

Mr. Howard came early enough to be able to jerk Emil out of bed. It being such a nice day, we attacked some work which we had been neglecting recently. To begin with we cleaned out the barn, first turning loose most of the horses, we hauled out 7 double wagon-boxes, before we had the barn in presentable condition. Then we went after a load of straw. A hayrack is a dangerous vehicle in North Dakota at this time of the year. I remember that Emil and I tipped over twice not very long ago. It began to get colder, so that I froze my left hand; it was so warm that I hadn't dressed up decently.

Emil induced me to take several chews of "Peerlys" to-day. Mr. Howard told us that Mrs. Howard, who had an attack of pneumonia, is not much better. There is a lot of la Grippe[54] in the country, otherwise everything is OK.

Friday January 21

Wea. Bad blizzard in Eve.   Ther. −3,+ 25, -20

We got up much earlier to-day than usual (9:00). Emil wished to repair the partitions in the barn which the horses had kicked down, so we decided to drive to Croffs after the mail and some groceries and nails. Just as we had hitched up Mr. Howard came over. He has a bad attack of the La Grippe, and asked Emil to get Mrs. Johnson to act as nurse for Mrs. Howard. Mrs. Buell, who had been doing the work so far, wished to go home.[55] Emil drove off immediately. I helped Mr. Howard unhitch and took him to the house. He knew I was going to Watford to-morrow, if possible, so he asked me to fetch some groceries along for him, leaving me a blank check.

Emil returned at 2:15 with Mrs. Johnson. After she had warmed up a bit, Mr. Howard drove off with her. Emil and I went down to the spring to water the horses and then cut across the flat for Croffs. The wind was rising gradually, making things very unpleasant outside. I had no letters at Croffs, but got a number of newspapers from Dora.

---

[54]Influenza. This is not the deadly strain that would affect the entire nation in 1918.

[55]The text gives an excellent account of neighbor women stepping into the role of doctor or nurse when their neighbors were suffering from illness and needed help. This spirit is common in western North Dakota today. When a neighbor is in dire need due to a medical condition, there is no shortage of volunteers to pitch in and help out.

We were short of bread, and besides we were not sure whether Mr. Howard could do the chores or not. I stayed home, while Emil drove over. While he was gone a fierce blizzard came up, causing the shack to groan and creak. I felt kind of lonesome for a while, but the storm soon blew over, and Emil came home after all.

Saturday January 22

Wea. Strong wind   Ther. −24, -11, -11

I really did not feel much like going to Schafer to-day, but I felt it my duty to try at least. Emil left for Howard's early in the morning. I hitched up Whitie and Rex and left the shack at 1:00 PM. Mr. Ahlmstad was here with Emil's threshing bill. At Croffs I had a letter with a check for $40.00 from the Mission-Board. This cheered me up a little, for I was running mighty short of funds. From Hartholds I took the grain-hauler trail to Schafer.[56] I did not like this trail very much, because I had to get out three times to open gates. At Schafer, where I landed at 6:00, I put up my team at the livery barn and spent the night at Steven's Hotel (Boyd, mgr.) In my mail was the box Room 67 had sent me.

Sunday January 23

Wea. Cloudy but warm   Ther. −4,+ 20, -2

This was an exceptionally nice day. It was so warm that the snow thawed in sheltered places. I had not announced services in Schafer, so I drove over to my shack in the morning to see how things looked there. I found that Hoffmann had not moved my kitchen yet, although he had swiped a lot of things (kettles, dishes, etc.)

---

[56]Farmers and ranchers worked long days from spring through fall, leaving no time to haul grain. This was a common winter activity when conditions permitted. The trails were frozen hard, so the load would not sink into soft soil. The Watford Guide of February 17, 1916 noted that "Ole Score (sic)" of Catlin was at Monday's market with a load of grain. Ole said that he counted 18 teams in a string on their way to Watford.

Incidentally, I celebrated my advent to manhood. I was 21 years old to-day. So I indulged in a regular blow-out by eating a can of strawberries and crackers, and a jar of olives. I got late start for Watford, but I reached the town before dark. Had to break the road down to Starlings.[57]

I put up at the Watford Hotel and put my team in the livery barn across the street. In the evening I attended the movies (3 reels for 25 cents). Came back to the hotel at 11:30 and went to bed.

Monday January 24

Wea. Very stormy; light snowfall   Ther. −30, -18, -35

McKenzie Co. lived up to its reputation in regard to the changeability of weather, for it was a perfect fright outside. I had a package of books at the station, and I walked down there to get it. When I got back, a man stopped me at the Zeller Hardware store and thawed up my nose for me. Everybody advised me to stay in Watford to-day, because they claimed no man could live thru the 30-mile trip to Catlin. I had promised to fetch some quinine for Howards, however, so I made up my mind to risk it. I bought a lot of groceries and things, and got my hair trimmed. The barber strongly urged a shave, but I did not care for a chapped face, so I declined. At Schafer I had a long talk with Mr. Graham, the editor of the "Record,"[58] and then I beat it for Catlin. I met a man near the big school and he thawed up my left cheek and nose, which had frozen again. It certainly was cold, and I suffered terribly. Got stuck in a snowdrift at "Bobby" Morrisons, and broke the tongue of my jumper. Got home at 2:00 and cooked a hearty supper. Emil came home later.

---

[57]Dr. Harry L. Starling was a dentist with an office in Watford City. His farm was located across the road from the present-day Schafer Cemetery, approximately three miles east of Watford City.

[58]The Schafer Record of Jan. 27, 1916 duly notes that, "Reverend John (sic) of near Catlin passed through town on Monday en-route home from a journey to Watford."

Figure 27: *Dr. Starling's house. It was located about halfway between Watford and Schafer, across the road from the present Schafer Cemetery.*

Figure 28: *A team trying to pull a load of lignite coal in Watford City.*

Tuesday January 25

Wea. Breezy, snowfall   Ther. −19, -14, -17

The Howard family is still sick, Mr. Howard is forced to hug the bed too, having a bad attack of the grippe. So Emil went over there again this morning. I swept the shack, got a box full of coal, etc. And then I hitched Beauty and Mac to the rack, tied the faithful old cow behind, and drove out for a load of straw. Got stuck in the coulee and had to shovel the team, rack, and cow out. Watered the whole bunch at the spring, which I chiseled out nicely, and then drove up to the straw pile. There were such enormous snow drifts near the stack, that I could not get very close, and had to pitch all the straw twice, first near the rack, and then on to it. Of course I had to shovel several feet of snow off the stack first.

I suffered a great deal from the cold, but I finally got a fair sized load and got to the barn without upsetting (Quite a feat, considering the treacherous drifts and coulees.) Put the team and cow up in the barn and chased the rest of the horses out for water, riding "Babe". The pinto was feeling good and set off at a furious gallop. I had no saddle or bridle on her, merely the halter rope, but I managed to keep my head. Froze my nose again.

Wednesday January 26

Wea. Heavy snowfall   Ther. −29, -9, -11

This was one of my lazy days. I kept a good fire after Emil had left, and read "Cedlurs", "Metropolitan" and the new "Morgan Robertson" books I got last Monday. Then I shoveled out the coulee near the house, so that the horses could get thru, and made a preliminary trip to the spring by riding Beauty down and leading Mac. I have to keep these horses separate, because they are shod and very apt to kick. After I got these "cranked up" I turned the rest of the dingbats loose, and followed them on "Babe". Some of the horses did not want to go in the barn, and I had a lively time chasing them with the pinto. She wheeled so fast in a coulee that she pitched me off into the snow. It was a soft fall and did not hurt. Got the horses chased in all right and then I thawed up my nose, which had frozen again. Emil came home late and we stayed up till 2:45 AM.

Thursday January 27

Wea. Heavy snow fall
Ther. −17, -8, -35

This was a mighty cold day again. After Emil left I did the housework and then wrote the greater part of my sermon for next Sunday. Towards evening I rode Mac and Beauty to the spring, chiseled a big hole in the ice and watered them. Then I turned out the rest of the horses, and had a great time later on, when I had to round them up. Although I had a heavy woolen shawl wrapped around my face, I froze my nose as usual.

After Emil came home we put some wet lignite[59] into the heater, and nearly put the fire out. The temperature within the shack sank lower and lower, until it hovered around 20 degrees. It was a funny sight, however to see Emil sit in front of the stove, with a poker in one hand and a tin can full of oil in the other. With monotonous regularity he would poke the fire and dump in some oil. Altogether he used up over a gallon of kerosene. We stayed up till 5:30 in the morning, just for devilry.

Figure 29: *Emil Bellin at the cook stove in his cabin. The calendar shows it is August, 1916.*

[59] Lignite coal is common throughout western North Dakota, with small surface mines utilized by many local people. There was eventually one underground mine in McKenzie County as well.

Friday January 28

Wea. Very breezy(N.W. wind) snow. Ther. −22, -17, -30

Emil left for Howards as usual. I put the shack in order, set up a pot of beans to boil, and then shoveled out the coulee east of the house, so I could pass through with the horses. Then I hitched Mac and Beauty to the rack (for we had run short on straw again), tied the old bossy behind, and away we went for the spring. I had a lot of chopping and chiseling to do before I could get any water. The poor old cow only gets water once every two days, and she drank without much coaxing. Then I turned her loose, and tried to find my way to the straw pile. This was no easy matter, for there was a blinding snow-fall. I froze my nose repeatedly and my right cheek once. My nose feels like a piece of leather. Had to do an enormous amount of scooping before I got to the straw pile, but I managed to fill the basket which was all the horses could pull in the drifts. After unloading the straw I watered the rest of the horses. Spent over 8 hours in the open air, working around. Wrote several letters in evening.

Saturday January 29

Wea. Very stormy Ther. −20, -16, -37

There was a very sharp West- wind to-day, and this, combined with the low temperature, made it extremely unpleasant outside. Emil was not feeling well to-day, and besides, the weather was too bad, so he did not go to Howards. Mr. Howard, according to the last reports, is able to do his work alone now.

I had quite a time in rounding up the horses tonight. They did not care to face the wind, so they were hard to drive. I froze the lower part of my nose again, having frozen my nose every day in the past week. Bucked my sermon in evening and stayed up till 3:15. It was terribly cold then, but I poked up the fires and kept the shack warm.[60]

---

[60] One not familiar with the living conditions at the time might wonder why these two young men were such "night owls." Because of the poorly insulated shacks these homesteaders lived in, the fierce cold and wind, and the small cook stoves utilized for heat, it was not uncommon to stay up into the wee hours or even all night to tend to the fire to keep warm. It was still cold during the day, but the sun's heating power made it easier to stay warm.

Sunday January 30

Wea. Blizzard   Ther. −35, -20, -27

I had set the alarm clock for 7:00 but when the old beast roused me from my peaceful slumbers, I merely shut it off, poked up the fire, and crawled back into the cot. For there was the old familiar roar of a nice young blizzard outside, and a blizzard means: No Church!

I got up again at 1:30, and rustled up some food. Emil is down with the Grippe and only got up for a few hours to-day. I watered the horses during a lull in the storm and merely froze my right cheek. Wrote my monthly report for the Mission Board and letters to Marc and Helen in eve. Went to bed at 12:00.

Monday January 31

Wea. N.W. Wind, as usual   Ther. −18, -20, -37

These ding-busted McKenzie Co. winds get my goat. So far there has hardly been a day on which we did not have a storm. We are running mighty short of hay, and if this weather doesn't let up soon, our horses will be up against it. In spite of the storm, Harold Lillibridge[61] was over to-day. He had gone out to fetch the mail, but he did not dare to turn back home, so he drifted along with the storm until he struck our shack. His visit was a pleasing break in the monotony of the winter days, so he received a hearty welcome. Towards evening the wind died down, as usual, so Harold went home, and I chased the horses to the spring. Emil is feeling pretty bum, but he was up again to-day. I stayed up late trying to get the cabin warm, before I hit the hay.

Tuesday February 1

Wea. NW wind, not quite so stormy   Ther. −25, -14, -37

When I woke up it was only 10 degrees in the shack. I dressed with some speed, went out and chopped up some wood and proceeded to make the old heater hum. After I had raised the temperature to 100 degrees, Emil got up and insisted on helping me get some straw for the horses.

---

[61] The Lillibridge family still resides in the area today.

After scooping through a huge snowdrift we managed to get close enough to the stack to load up. Although we only filled the rack basket, because of the wind, we very nearly got stuck.

While Emil unloaded, I hitched up "Whitie and Mabel" and dashed over to Howards. We had been out of bread for several days, and in addition Howards were still sick when Emil last was there, and we naturally were anxious to know how they were getting on. I had a lot of drifts to climb, but by 2:00 I was back home again. Howards were still "kicking". Mr. H was engaged in digging a tunnel to the barn, in order to see how the stock was getting along. He had not been there for some time, because of the snow. After I came home I thawed up my nose, and ate a good supper.

Wednesday February 2

Wea. Snow, N.W. wind   Ther. −38, -22, -49

Last night Emil and I were just looking at some pictures, when we suddenly heard a noise outside and in came Ed Green, Swiggum,[62] Ray Catlin and Chester Alton, for a whist party. They came after nightfall, and had quite a time in finding here. A whist party in this country always means an all night affair. So we filled the lamps and lanterns, moved the table to the middle of the room, and rustled up some chairs etc. for seats.

During the first part of the night I was pretty lucky, winning all the games, but later on I had Ray Catlin as partner, and he lost most of the games, being a very poor hand at it. We had a midnight lunch, consisting of fried ham, bread and coffee, and we played all the records of the phonograph, considerably over 50 of them. The crowd left after daylight. We cleaned up the shack, fed the stock, cooked a good breakfast, and layed down for a nap at about 11:30. At a little after 1:00 a rapping on the door woke me up and I admitted Ole Skaar,[63] who sat around and gabbed till late in the PM! He finally stated his business, namely that I should baptize his kid. Then Emil hiked over to Croffs for the mail and groceries, while I watered the horses.

---

[62] This was probably Andrew Swiggum, who later married Alex and Chester Alton's sister, Alma.

[63] Relatives of the Skaar family still reside in McKenzie County. Ole Skaar's homestead was about a half mile east of the cabin.

Thursday February 3

Wea. Very windy   Ther. −14, -7, -48

We are running low on feed again, but could not get straw to-day because of the terrible wind. It was enormously cold this morning when I got up, but I managed to get things warmed up. I am not feeling very well my-self; probably going to get the Grippe.

Last night I got a letter from Helen in my mail, also a group picture which contains her face. Got a dandy letter from Bill Medo and Paul.

We had to wash dishes to-day, a job that bachelors hate like poison. But every dish in the house was dirty, and we had been eating potatoes etc. directly out of the pan. Then we had a general house cleaning. Emil cooked several towels etc. and washed them, besides washing the dishes. I did not feel very nice to-day; am afraid I'll get the Grippe.

Friday February 4

Wea. Unusually quiet   Ther. −28, -14, -33

For the first time in many, many days the wind has died down to a mere whisper. I have a bad attack of the Grippe, but I made up my mind to stay out of bed as long and as much as possible. So I accompanied Emil on a straw hauling expedition. I felt so weak and dizzy that I could hardly move, but still I began to shovel away the snow drift on the south side of the stack, so that we could get there with the rack. Emil had loaded up before I was finished. After that I stayed home, while he got another load. Then I went back to the barn and filled the cribs during the time he watered the horses. We are out of coal oil at present, but there was some [oil] left in the lantern tonight.

Saturday February 5

Wea. Pretty quiet   Ther. −49, -37, -20

Although it was very cold, it was reasonably quiet again to-day. I felt miserable due to the hateful Grippe, but I got up early nevertheless. Emil went to Howards for some bread etc.; we have been out of bread and butter several days. He was gone till nearly 4:00, and in the mean time I wrote a pile of letters (To ma, Dietz, Deke, Buddy). Emil came back without any bread; Mrs. Howard was just getting ready to bake when he got there, and he did not want to wait, for he was going to get some coal to-day yet. He put it off however, and so he also neglected to get kerosene. Figured on going to Howards again to-morrow and also to Mathesteads[64] after some coal. We had some oil left in an old can; enough for to-night.

Figure 30: *Helene Burmeister, seated, and her brothers and sisters. They resided in Lyons, Nebraska. She was RCJ's first cousin.*

---

[64]This would be the Mathistad family, some of whom still live in McKenzie County. Their homestead was a mile east of Emil's.

Sunday February 6

Wea. NW storm again   Ther. –47, -16, -39

We woke up to the tune of a fearfully cold NW wind again. Emil has the habit of running around barefooted and poking up the fire; then he crawls back into bed until the shack is warmed up. This morning I suddenly heard him let out a yell, and when I solicitously inquired about his trouble, he showed me where a red-hot cinder had dropped between his toes. I felt sick as a dog, but I had to laugh till my sides ached.

I had not announced services for to-day, because of the Grippe. I was supposed to preach at the Reservation Corner, but I have made up my mind to stick to Catlin, unless a radical change takes place in the weather and the roads.

Emil's plan of getting some coal to-day had to be abandoned. It was blizzarding fearfully outside again, and no dog could have weathered this storm. We still have enough coal left to last us for about a week. I did not help with watering the horses, for I hated to take a chance and let the Grippe settle on my lungs; have not been forced to take to bed as yet; may not get a bad attack.

Monday February 7

Wea. Very strong E wind   Ther. –25, -16, -40

It was quite windy still when we got up. Since Emil had to use the wagon-box for hauling coal, I unloaded the rack, which was filled with straw and mounted on a bob- sleigh. While I was unloading, a strong E. Wind came up. It certainly was not pleasant outside with this low temperature.

Emil left at about noon and got the lower box of his wagon filled. Green lignite does not burn very well, so we are putting it in the oven of the range to dry out. We piled it up close to the shack this time, for the cows have been eating all the flax-straw away from the shed, and the coal we had put in there last fall is exposed to the snow and air.

Emil drove to Howards to-day and got some bread. He also fetched some beef stew along, which Mrs. Howard had sent for me. It sure tasted fine. I felt strong enough to water the horses to-day.

Tuesday February 8

Wea. Snow, slight wind   Ther. −22, 8, -9

For the first time in many days the weather was such, that we could risk the attempt to go to the post-office. I had just six letters to mail, and we needed some groceries. But there was not the faintest trace of a trail, and we were perilously close to getting stuck at times. But we just managed it, without having to resort to the shovel.

I got a letter from Ban, telling me of a serious fire at the Sem. on Jan 24th. The entire north wing of the good old coop has been destroyed. I naturally felt a little bum about this, since I have grown to love the place.[65] [Jahn later inserted: "This was a story cooked up by the boys (at the seminary)."]

Rev. Hilgendorf notified me of some Lutherans around Mary, ND, who wished me to look them up. Since that is about 50 mi. from here, I decided to wait till spring. Harry Howard was here to-day and stayed for supper.

Wednesday February 9

Wea. Good E. Wind   Ther. −49, -31, -51

This was an exceptionally cold day again. We got up early, but fooled around till noon before either one of us felt like leaving the shack. Emil went to the barn to feed the horses and to nail up some feed-boxes. I stayed in the cabin and poked up the fire, and carried out the ashes.

Read several articles in the last "Metropolitan" in PM. Was especially impressed by a plea for preparedness (A Reuterdahl).

While I was watering the horses to-night, Bobby Morrison came over and got his steer. He rode through the west coulee, but he did not dare to go back that way, on account of the snow.

---

[65] Ban Johnson's letter of Jan. 25 survives. Johnson spun a longer yarn about the fire than RCJ indicates. This seven-page letter described the boys having "opened the door and nearly being choked by the clouds of smoke." He went into such detail as to include, "The nearby stores, businesses, and houses were given over to us for the night to store what belongings were retrieved from the building."

I was riding the pinto, as usual, and I had the draw-rope, with which we lift the water out of the spring. Unthinkingly I swung it around my head, while chasing the horses and I scared the nervous little pinto. She picked up her little legs, and I don't think I ever traveled that fast in my life. When I got to the barn I finally got her cooled down.

Thursday February 10

Wea. Stormy: E. wind   Ther. −41, -12, -22

This was one of our lazy days. We had made up our minds to get some straw etc., but the wind was roaring so bad, that I merely poked up the fires and crawled back into my snug little cot. There I staid till Emil yelled from his cot, that it was past 1:00 PM. Then we finally got up and had a 3:00 o'clock dinner.

I am suffering from a severe cold, the after-effects of my attack of La Grippe, so I flopped around on the bed, scrapping with Emil. We fooled around till it was time to water the horses. The wind had died down somewhat, and it looked as though we might expect decent weather. Played casino till late at night.

Friday February 11

Wea. Gentle east wind, fine snow   Ther. −20, +6, -1

For the first time in many days the Thermometer registered above zero. There was a mild E. Wind, and a fine snow, but we did not bother about that, since we had some long neglected work to tend to. I had set the alarm at 6:30, and roused Emil out of bed then, despite his protests. It was still dark; I had to use the lantern in the barn.

After breakfast we harnessed up Belle and Mac and proceeded to clean out the barn. We had not done this for a long time, so we filled seven double wagon boxes before we were finished. One of the "Fuzzy-Tail" colts suddenly took sick, so we doctored it up with "15 drops" and liniment, and one of us always stayed in the barn and watched the Ding bat, while the other unloaded. Emil broke a good trail across the coulee by fastening a heavy chain between and underneath the two rear runners of the sleigh. This broke the hard crusty snow in the middle of the roadbed. After cleaning the barn we hauled up a load of straw and thus closed a good days work.

Wea.   MONDAY 29   Ther.
Pleasant.

There was a very sad accident in our
neighborhood to-day, which affected me especially.
Young Einar Dahl, a Norwegian bachelor who
lives a few miles north of us, came walking
over in search of his horses. ~~I loaned~~ him
the pinto, and watched him ride away in an
easterly direction. After a few hours the pinto
returned, minus its rider. Emil caught it up
and led it into the barn. We discovered several
whip-marks and a bloody flank, where a
spur had been dug into her side. To my horror
I also noted that the hoofs were matted with
blood, although there were no wounds. So Emil
hastily saddled his pony and I climbed the
pinto, who bucked terribly, and we rode in
search of poor Dahl. After riding for several
miles we suddenly came upon the body.
The neck was broken, and the head had
doubled under the body. The left arm was
also broken, and the furious pinto had smashed
nearly all the ribs, and fairly trampled
the corpse into the ground. We carried the
corpse up to the shack and later removed it
to Dahl's deserted claim shack.

CHAPTER 5

PERILS OF THE BADLANDS

Saturday February 12

Wea. Very nice and quiet   Ther. –7, +28, -4

This was beyond question the finest day that we had in 1916. It not only was quiet, but it even thawed in sheltered places.

Emil's big red cow chose this day to give birth to a bouncing little calf. Probably she had waited for this day, so that the calf might have a chance to get used to the N. Dakota climate gradually. For there certainly will be some more bad weather before spring. I was in the barn at the time and had to play an unwilling, tho successful accoucheur.[66]

We hauled a final load of straw from the stack and then set fire to the remainder. We did not do this in a spirit of wastefulness, but because, in the first place, there was hardly any straw left, and because the stack was drifted in so terribly that we had to unhitch the horses and drag the rack in by a chain. Since it was still early in the day, we struck out for Ole Skaar's straw pile, but at first we met with much disaster. We got stuck in a coulee near the stack and had an awful time with the horses, but we finally got thru. After loading up we chose a round- about way and got home without mishap. The rest of the horses had been out all day, so I jumped on the baby pinto and rounded them up. Then we harnessed Rex and Whitie, and drove to Howard's, leading Mac and Beauty. Howards were not home, but that did not worry us. We played the phonograph, took some bread and a dozen records, piled an immense chunk of lignite against the door and went home. Howard has 50-foot tunnel through a snow-drift to his barn.

---

[66]A person who assists in childbirth, especially an obstetrician or midwife.

[67]Leaving a house unlocked was common, not just because there was trust among neighbors, but in severe weather an empty but unlocked home might provide necessary refuge for a traveler suddenly caught in it. Practical jokes and humorous antics added some fun to the rugged homesteader life. Harry Howard was a favorite target.

Sunday February 13

Wea. Breezy (E. Wind)   Ther. −9, +34, -7

It was a little windy to-day, otherwise it was nice and warm. A somewhat unusual, but quite natural thing happened to Emil and myself. We got mixed up in out dates, and did not know whether it was Saturday or Sunday to-day. I had not filled out my diary, so we could not get any information from that source. We were still arguing over this question, when the dog began to bark, and we saw a man crossing the "school-section" leading his pony on account of the deep snow. This man turned out to be Isham Spence, alias "Moonshine Ike", alias "Right Smart", who was on his way to the Christiensen Ranch.[68] He stopped at our shack to feed his horse and himself. He informed us that it was Sunday.

I did not have any services to-day. The weather was so bad in the beginning of this week, that I did not think it worthwhile to invite the people; besides I had a terrible cold and could not have preached a full sermon.
We dug out the well to-day; it had been drifted under snow since December.

Monday February 14

Wea. Slight breeze, much warmer   Ther. −4, +38, -2

In the morning I was so sleepy that I did not rouse Emil sufficiently, and so we slept blissfully till 1:15 PM. Then we cooked up a hurried meal and I turned the horses loose and galloped down to the spring with the pinto and watered them. Then I went to the coulee NW of the farm, which Emil had begun to dig out. We are very short of oats and we have to get to Billy Bellin's homestead for a fresh supply, hence this snow shoveling business. The coulee was unexpectedly badly drifted in. In places it was filled with 6 ft and more of snow, and it was a very arduous job trying to scoop it out. However, we succeeded and were finished by 5:30. After a slight rest I rounded up the horses and chased them into the barn. In the mean time Mr. Howard came over, and stayed for supper. After the meal he talked a while and then talked about leaving. First he suggested a game of "Rum-Dum", however and ....

---

[68]"Christiensen Ranch" probably refers to the ranch located south and east in the badlands.

Tuesday February 15

Wea. Windy   Ther. 30, 34, 7

... so it was daylight (8:30 A.M.) before he made his departure. We had arranged a trip to the Badlands for some fresh coal, for Emil and I were running pretty short, and so we cooked up a good breakfast, turned all the horses we could not use, loose, and left with a four-horse team. Howard met us at Croffs. He has no tongue in his sleigh, and that causes it to slide along rather independent of the horses. I took the seat beside him and we got to the "Breaks" at about 5:00. The wonderful, almost weird shapes of the buttes, the gigantic boulders and steep slopes made a great impression on me. I could look up over hundreds of sections and the fantastic groupings of the peaks made a spectacle that I never shall forget. We mined the coal from a dry mine about half way up the slope of a butte. We let the lignite roll down to the foot of the slope, where we loaded it on the sleds. After a lunch with the owner of the mine (Jim Callaway), who has a very dirty little shack, we struck for home. Howard and I nearly got killed sliding down one of the steep hills. Without a tongue the horses could not keep the sleigh back and it crashed on top of them and they smashed up the box badly. I was thrown several feet, but escaped with a few bruises. Got home at sundown.[69]

Wednesday February 16

Wea. West wind; surprisingly warm   Ther. -1, +48, +20

Ed Green met us at the shack last night and stayed till nearly eleven o'clock. Emil and I were so sleepy that we "hit the hay" immediately after he was gone, and we slept till noon to-day.

There was nothing of importance to-day. Emil and I fooled around the shack most of the day. I rode around with my pinto and shot several jack-rabbits; chased up a coyote, but could not get within range. Howard had invited us over for a game of whist tonight. He had fetched us some bread to Croff's, but we forgot it there, of course, now we had to go for more.

---

[69]Lignite mining was hazardous, and RCJ understates the dangers in this account. Howard's sleigh, lacking a tongue, was not the right equipment for the job. Noted author Erling Rolfsrud was from McKenzie County and grew up in the 1920s near Berg (present-day Keene). His father had suffered a badly broken hip while mining lignite and was crippled for the rest of his life.

After some time young Veeder[70] and a friend came over, and we settled down to what proved to be an all-night game of "Rum-dum". Mrs. Howard got us a mid-night lunch, and after putting up our horses and poking up the fires it was nearly 9 o'clock.

View of the McKenzie Co. Bad lands near Callaway's lignite mine.

Figure 31: *View of the badlands near Calloway's lignite mine.*

Thursday February 17

Wea. Warm again   Ther. +4, +37, +5

We were very sleepy, of course, so we fixed up our cots and turned in for a few hours sleep. Then I chased the horses down to the spring while Emil cleaned out a big barrel, and then we cut up our pork and salted it down. It was too warm for us to try to freeze it. I saddled Babe, put the rifle in its scabbard and rode around the prairie hunting for game. I killed several jacks, and a porcupine. Jack-rabbits are very plentiful out here. Coyotes are very scary, so that I managed to kill only one of them so-far. In the "Breaks" or Bad Lands there are a lot of Timber wolves, beavers, some deer, etc. But these animals rarely leave the shelter that the fantastic buttes give. They have plenty of food there, and there is no reason why they should change their home.

[70]The Veeder family lived north of Emil Bellin's shack. Family members still live there today.

We stayed up late and played several games of "Rum-Dum". In fact, we have made it a habit to sleep long mornings and remain awake late in the night.

The last end of U.S. mail hauled from Williston to Schafer, no. 28, '12, distance is 150 miles. Feb. 9, '16.

Figure 32: *A fully packed mail sled headed to Schafer. The photo, not taken by RCJ, is dated February 14, 1916. RCJ wrote on it that it was the last mail sled from Williston, although this fact has not been verified.*

Friday February 18

Wea. Warm; west wind   Ther. +20, +58, +31

We were still in bed when Harry Howard came over. He was riding, so he sneaked up without waking us. I saved myself by jumping out of the cot, but he managed to dump Emil. It was nearly eleven o'clock by this time.

Howard stayed for dinner and after playing several selections on the phonograph we settled down to a game of "Rum-Dum", which I lost. While we were playing a man drove over and asked for me. He introduced himself as Mr. F.J. Otto, an elder of the Schafer congregation,[71] and asked me to come

[71]F. J. Otto was one of the elders who signed the original call. Apparently, Otto had not attended any of RCJ's services in the previous four months.

down to-morrow and baptize his kid (John Raymond). I promised, and later on Emil decided to join me in the trip, since he had some business in Schafer and Watford. We hit the hay at 10:00, since we wanted an early start.

Saturday February 19

Wea. Very warm; spring like   Ther. +25, +60, +14

We got up before 5:00, watered the horses and ate a hasty breakfast. By 6:00 we were on the road. The moon was shining brightly by and we expected a dandy trip. Since the trail near Morrisons was covered deeply with snow, we decided to go a mile out of our way and drive past "Winie" Werhle's.[72] All unsuspecting we drove into his coulee and got stuck. There was a strong, deep current of water running thru the coulee and our jumper settled down nicely. My suitcase began to float away, so I grabbed it and put it on the seat, which stayed out of the water. We crawled onto the backs of the horses and unhitched them. By dint of much coaxing and a liberal use of the whip we succeeded in getting "Rex" out. "Whitie" however, had broken thru the hard crust of snow and his foot was sucked down by the slush underneath, so that he was helpless. Emil roused Wherles out of bed and obtained a shovel, with which we managed to dig Whitie out. Emil tied all the remaining straps available to the pole and pulled the jumper out. Before we reached Croffs we were downed again in a similar manner so that I felt like giving up the trip. Still we pushed on, found Ottos. I baptized the kid while Emil acted as one sponsor.[73] We then drove on to Watford and spent the night at my shack.[74]

---

[72]The Werhle homestead was located southeast of Emil's cabin.

[73]The child had been born on Feb. 3, 1916. The other witness was Ms. Ida Mergenthal.

[74]It was about 13 miles from Emil's cabin to Schafer. It is hard to imagine how arduous it was to travel in McKenzie County in the winter in 1916. The iced-over coulees were major obstacles to horses and wagons, as this account aptly describes.

Sunday February 20

Wea. Very warm, no wind   Ther. 4, 47, 17

Sleeping on my cot was rather crowded, but I put in a good night, staying in bed till sun-up. There were a lot of things to tend to; I locked my quilts and things away in my trunk, swept the three rooms and straightened up a bit. Then I helped Emil wash the dishes; we had grape nuts, peanut butter and crackers for breakfast. It was noon before we left the shack and we stopped in Schafer for about ½ hr. Got some groceries at Steven's and then we beat it for home. There was not a cloud in the sky and it was a beautiful day. Only the snow is melting so fast that the roads are showing big bare spots, and are getting very mushy and muddy. The water was rushing thru every coulee, but none of them were so deep as to bother us much. From Richardsons we took the old mail-road, which wound around among the hills and finally landed us near Odermanns. From there we broke a trail through the School-section,[75] where the snow was dreadfully deep, and we finally landed home, after crossing the coulee where we had scooped it out. Howard had wired up our door and piled up our furniture.[76] It was so warm that we did not start a fire in our heater.

Monday February 21

Wea. Very warm, slight west wind   Ther. +20, +58, +30

We are getting so short of oats, that it was absolutely necessary for us to obtain a fresh supply. Emil has his deceased brother's shack filled with oats, so we made up our minds to buck through the dreadful school section and Cleveland's flat. We selected the heaviest and strongest horses and took two shovels along. However we managed to plunge through without causing mishap until we struck the coulee east of Billies place. Here we stopped our team, picked up our shovels, and made the snow fly for about half an hour until we had completed a nice trench through which the horses could easily make their way. We had to load the oats with a bucket, since they were piled

---

[75]A section is a square of land one mile long on each side. Every sixteenth section in McKenzie County was designated as a "School Section." It was owned by the local school board, and income from this land was used to support the school system. One such section was located a few hundred feet to the north of Emil's cabin. In winter, deep snow built up through this land, making it difficult for Emil and RCJ to traverse in that direction.

[76]Here Harry Howard repays the practical joke described on Feb. 12.

high under the eaves of the house. We had quite a hard pull in some places on the way home. In the school section the snow was so deep that our horses could just break through, while near our shack there was no snow whatever. Ed Greene came riding up just as we drove on to the place, and he stayed for supper. He got his shotgun, which we had had all winter and brought two letters for Nettie Green Howard,[77] which had been put into his mailbox. Shortly after he left Mr. Howard came over. He has shaven his entire beard, and I hardly recognized him. He stayed till about 3:30 AM, playing Rumdum.

Tuesday February 22

Wea. Very pleasant, no wind   Ther. +12, +59, +10

After Howard left we turned in and slept till noon. It was a beautiful day, a day that one generally only expects and finds in early May. I often feel exasperated at the changeability of the McKenzie Co. weather; compared with the furious storms and the bitter cold of the previous part of the winter, this is certainly grand.

We chased all the horses out excepting Belle and Nancy. These we hitched to the rack and drove to Ole Skaar's straw pile for a fresh supply of the "golden hay". We did not have as much hard luck as on the 12th inst., when we got stuck several times. Emil stopped on the way and showed me a peculiarly shaped mound, which was covered with petrified stumps of some huge trees. Some of the stumps were fully seven feet across. The smaller ones showed the marks of axes very plainly. This must have been some religious place of the Indians, for we found rings and figures carved in the stones; the stones were also set together to form curious, tho pretty patterns. I picked up a handful of arrowheads.[78]

We got two loads of straw. The horses did not come home tonight. While I was writing a letter I heard them outside. My pinto was neighing at the door. I mounted her and chased in the rest of the horses, it was 1:30 AM.

---

[77]Her name was actually Nettie Green. She was Delia Howard's daughter from her prior marriage. Nettie, Eva and Lucille Green, Delia's daughters, are mentioned frequently in this diary.

[78] The description indicates a "religious" site for the native peoples. However, often these sites are not associated with the Indians who currently live in the area, but another group that lived here at one time and migrated elsewhere. Petrified stumps are fairly common in McKenzie County.

Chapter 6

Socializing Through Snow and Ice

Wednesday February 23

Wea. Heavy NW wind, blinding snow fall   Ther. +12, +37, +30

The weather, which has been so extremely pleasant during the past week, finally changed for the worse. It was quite windy in the morning. Towards noon the violence of the wind increased and a flinty sort of a snow came whizzing through the air. It was impossible to face the storm.

I stayed home to write letters and buck my sermon, while Emil went to Billy's place after a load of oats. The storm broke loose just before he got here. I helped him unhitch and then we sought refuge in the house where we were confined for the rest of the evening. I wrote eleven letters while I coaxed Emil to write four.

Thursday February 24

Wea. Chilly, usual wind   Ther. −4, +20, -3

Winter is by no means over; old King Boreas seems to have some big trump cards up his sleeve, and he is playing them out with a generous hand, with a sort of reckless abandon.

We got up leisurely and made a flying trip to Croffs. Rex had his second wind and we just hit the high spots in the trail, that's all. I had a package of books from Paul and a carton of "Omars" from Ban Johnson. They certainly tasted good, for I had been deprived of Turkish cigarettes for nigh onto four months. Also got a rollicking good letter from Paul, and a sweet little missive from Helen.

I rounded up the horses on "Whitie" tonight. The pinto was out on the prairie with the other cayutes. We were out of bread again, so we hiked over to Howards just before nightfall. We met Harry on the road to Leon Veeders, where he was expecting to play cards. He waited till we got our bread and things, and then he rode along with us. It was pitch dark when we got to Veeders, and an ugly wind, coupled with a nasty snowfall came up during the night. I never cease to wonder at the McKenzie Co. storms. I expected the roof to go at any moment.

Leon treated us to a good supper and as a substantial midnight lunch. We played cards and discussed ranch life. I bought a dandy little

Friday February 25

Iver Johnson .410 gauge (.44 calibre) gun from him, together with a hundred wicked - looking cartridges. The storm abated a little towards 4 o'clock AM and we decided to go home. Leon went to the creek crossing with a lantern, so that we would not miss the ford. The coulee is filled with about 8ft. of water, and missing the ford would mean drowning the team. As it is, Rex refused to go across and tore a single-tree hook before we whipped him over.

We turned in when we got home and slept till very late. After a hearty meal we practiced shooting my "410 gauge". I found the rifle to be a hard hitter and a very straight shooter. The rest of the afternoon I spent in reading "Mr. Pratt" by Joseph Lincoln, one of the books Paul sent me. I consider it a very amusing story; Mr. Pratt's quaint humor, his persistency in using nautical phrases on all sorts of occasions interested and greatly appealed to me. I finished the book during the afternoon.

We washed dishes again to-day and had pancakes for super. Dish washing is very prosaic work, no matter how it is viewed, and I am perfectly willing to consign it to my future wife, should I ever marry.[79]

---

[79]The Werhle homestead was located southeast of Emil's cabin.

Saturday February 26

Wea. Cool very quiet   Ther. −1, +12, -4

Yesterday we had one of the worst blizzards of this season. The out buildings, the familiar coulee, everything vanished from sight, was swallowed up, as it were, in a sort of a "White darkness". The snow was sticky and wet. Luckily we had plenty of straw and oats in the barn. The horses had no water, however. In yesterday's report I mentioned that we tried out my rifle. We did so by sitting on a chair in the doorway and shooting at anything convenient in sight.

Changeability is the chief characteristic of McKenzie Co. weather. To-day, tho cold, was quiet and fair. Towards evening the dog began to bark and I saw Mr. Howard riding towards the east coulee. I yelled to him to stop since the coulee was drifted shut to a depth of about 10ft. He left his horse on the other side and walked across the crusty snow.

It seems that a neighbor of Howards, Ericsen, had recently plunged into the pool of matrimony, and Howard invited us to join the shivaree lunch. We ate a hurry-up supper, consisting of a can of raspberries and cookies, and then I slung the carbine strap of my gun across my shoulder, loaded my pocket with shells and mounted "Whitie", while Emil straddled "Rex". We met the rest of the gang at Leon Veeders, where we left our horses, and then we put in about a 12-mile walk. Ericsen was finally located at a friend's house and we proceeded to give him a grand ovation. He treated us to whiskey and cigars.

Sunday February 27

Wea. Windy, snow towards evening   Ther. −12, +17, -18

Several members of our bunch nearly got pickled last night. In the first place, we had four glasses full of whiskey a-piece, and in the second place most of the fellows did not smell booze for many months. Our bunch got back to Veeders alright, and from there Emil and I rode home. "Whitie" bucked a great deal at the start. I had no saddle on him. I did not give up though, but made him come to trim. Felt greatly flattered when I heard "Winie" Werhle remark: "That preacher is a game devil, isn't he?"

We set up our cots and turned in at 6:00. It was past 1:00 when a knock on the door woke me and "Muchy" McLune came in. Muchy was after some calks for horseshoes. Emil got up despite the cold and walked around the shack, dressed in nothing but a shirt and a smile. Later on Howard came over, per agreement, and got Emil's sleighs. He expects to haul a load of flax in to-morrow.[80] He had dinner with us before he left.

The ice on the watercourses in the coulees is not yet strong enough to bear the weight of a team, for this reason I did not go to Schafer, as per agreement.

Monday February 28

Wea. Much colder; East wind   Ther. −19, +2, -21

The usual wind form McKenzie Co. comes from the Northwest. To-day however, we had a breeze from exactly the other quarter. The chinks and cracks are especially numerous on the east side of my 14x16 log shack, and the wind whistles merrily into the room. I placed the thermometer on the inside east wall where it registered 4 below zero, and this with a raging fire in the heater. But no fire could avail against such a wind, coupled with such a temperature. The snows came drifting in on the floor, where it piled up in ridges under the table and bed. We have never had the floor warm enough to thaw things all winter, excepting during the week of thawing. In order to protect ourselves from the cold we hung horse blankets on the east wall.

Emil and I put up a board along the entire North wall, which is to serve as a shelf. We also cleaned off the top of the cupboard etc. Chester Alton came over and invited us to a dance at Ed Greens. Later Emil left for Howards to do their chores, while I watered the stock and gave them straw. Froze my nose again, something that has not happened to me for quite a while. We washed dishes tonight and I spent nearly the entire night reading "Hopalong Cassidy". Went to bed at 2:30. Covered up with fur coats.

---

[80]Despite the adverse weather conditions, an optimistic mood was prevalent at the time in McKenzie County. Most everyone believed that they would prosper. At a farmer's conference in Watford City on Feb. 14, J.G. Haney told the group, "The man that will get four cows and feed them properly can make a living, and the man that can get ten cows and give them the proper care will get rich." (Watford Guide, Feb.16, 1916).

Tuesday February 29

Wea. SE wind, stronger than yesterday   Ther. −24, -9, -27

Emil left for Howards while I was still in bed. I got up at about 12:30 and monkeyed around with the stove till I had it roaring nicely. It takes an immense fire to keep the shack warm with this east wind, hope it blows over soon. I suppose this is a sample, a beginning of the March winds, which everybody seems to dread so much.

I cooked up a big dinner and then proceeded to devour "Hopalong Cassidy", never ceasing till I had the book finished. It is a western novel, full of gunplay etc., but it is a novel of the better sort, well calculated to make its time fly. What makes a book of this nature especially interesting to me is the fact that conditions here in McKenzie Co. are very similar to those described by Mr. Mulford, the author. Of course, the cowboys no longer carry revolvers; in summer they wear overalls etc, instead of the picturesque chaperayos, but the conditions of the country, the absence of decent highways, the unsettled condition of the land, and the wild mesas, buttes and coulees are here.

The wind interfered considerable with the chores. I was thoroughly chilled while rounding up the horses. Emil came home rather late, he having driven the kids[81] over from school, etc.

Wednesday March 1

Wea. Strong wind, NW   Ther. −34, -20, -31

It does not take much of a wind to chill a person when the temperature is down to zero, but a wind of the N. Dakota variety, coupled with 4 degrees below zero is a combination that is hard to beat. I suppose that I am guessing a great deal about the winds out here, but since they are the most distinguishing feature of McKenzie Co. I might as well give them due space. A cyclone, such as we frequently met with in Oklahoma, Kansas and Nebraska, is practically unknown out here. The wind is simply a steady, ever-increasing hurricane that blows from the same quarter hour after hour without diminishing in violence. At Charlson[82] it blew over the church recently, and it often turns the simple claim shacks end over end.

[81]This would be Nettie, Eva, and Lucile Green, Delia Howard's kids.

[82]A small village now nearly abandoned, located in the northeastern part of McKenzie County.

Emil left for Howard's again this morning. We expected Harry back tonight, but Lloyd Buell told Emil that Harry was going to spend tonight at Lillibridges, and that he was going to take in a load of Emil's wheat from Billies shack. While this arrangement saves Emil the monotonous trip to Town, it also makes it necessary for him to go to Howard's again tomorrow and Friday.

I busied myself with some letters today. Did not spend much time on my meals, but I washed the dishes, the most hateful of all household duties. I'm glad I am not a woman and doomed to a lifelong of ever recurring dishwashing.

Thursday March 2

Wea. Wind shifting to east   Ther. −24, -14, -19

March came in a roaring, that is, the wind picked up fearfully early yesterday morning, and the thermometer showed 34 degrees. If the old saying has any foundation in truth, this month ought to go out like a lamb.

I was hungry today, had not cooked myself anything decent to eat for several days. So I prepared an elaborate menu, even making Jello for dessert.

I now have finished 5 of the six novels Paul sent me; am going to save up the last one for a while. My little pinto was feeling the oats tonight and nearly bucked me off. She refused to slow down to a walk, and when a horse bucks at full gallop, you sort of have to hang on tight, especially when riding bare backed.

Friday March 3

Wea. Very cold, blizzardy   Ther. −18, -22, -31

This was a trying day for an innocent young bachelor. Emil did not come home to-night because of the storm, and at about 6:00 PM along came Ole Skaar's two sisters, begging me to keep them overnight. Ole only lives a mile from here, but it is quite a winding trail, twisting around the buttes as it does, and nobody has any business on the trail after dark, during a blizzard.

Since it was out of the question to take the girls home, I made the best of it, and it is not so very trying to accommodate two blushing young damsels.

While I tended to their horses and did the rest of the chores, they made themselves at home in the shack in true western style. I had swept the floor, but my blankets and things were all topsy turvy, so the girls tidied everything up nicely. Then I fetched in a huge amount of coal, for it was very cold, and also a bucket full of wood-scraps. Then we cooked supper in company; the girls baked up some delicious biscuits, while I peeled the potatoes and sliced up the bacon. Then they chased me away from the stove and say, I did not enjoy a meal so much in all my life. After supper we washed dishes and then we played the phonograph and talked till after eleven o'clock. Then I stretched a curtain around my bed and told the girls to crawl in while I made up a bunk on the floor. They did not hesitate very long about undressing.[83]

Saturday March 4

Wea. Cold west wind   Ther. −20, -4, -18

The girls left early in the morning, and shortly after they were gone Emil came home. We turned all horses except Whitie and Babe loose this morning. Emil had to wait till after dinner to get his sleigh from Howards, for Harry is taking Mrs. Emmerson's stuff to her place. I decided to go to Croff's while Emil was gone, so I mounted Whitie and, after a few preliminary bucks, I rode off in search of Rex. Caught the latter on the run and made the trip to Croff's in a hurry. Had a letter and a package from Ruth, a letter from Ma and Ban.

When Emil got back, it was past 7:00 o'clock and too late to get any straw. The horses had to do without to-night. Emil fetched "Mac" along, because Mac is sharply shod. We put shoes on Bell to-day. Hit the straw at 12:30.

Sunday March 5

Wea. Cold east wind, snow during night   Ther. −19, -3, +22

In spite of the fact that we had much to do, we slept pretty late this morning. This was largely due to the fact that the wind was setting up a most dismal howl, and it was whistling thru the chinks between the logs, so that we could hardly get the shack warmed up.

---

[83]McKenzie County was still quite Victorian in 1916, and this would have been a memorable evening. Ole Skaar was then about 29, so his sisters were probably in their 20s.

We got a big load of straw from Ole Skaar's straw-pile, in spite of the wind. Then Emil took a hearty bath in the wash-basin (sponge-bath), after which he hitched up and drove to Howards. He had arranged to take a load of flax to town for Harry, and expects to load up to-night and leave to-morrow morning. I am to do Howard's chores in the mean time, for Harry is also going to town.

I wrote a letter to Rev. Frey and "Ban Johnson" in eve. We had a nice snow-fall. Hit the hay at 1:30.

Monday March 6

Wea. Blizzardy, bad drifting   Ther. −9, -12, +1

I had expected to get to Howards early enough, so as to take the girls to school. But the howling wind outside was the sweetest lullaby imaginable, especially since I had been up so late, and so I slept blissfully on. What is more, my alarm clock failed to turn loose at 6:30; the wires had become disarranged.

I was awakened by hearing a well- known step crunching out-side, and Emil came walking into the shack. The storm had looked so bad, that he and Howard had decided to wait till to-morrow about going to town.

Emil helped me to get dinner and then we washed dishes and read novels till late in the day. Emil had come over on "George", Mrs. Emmerson's vicious bronc, and he dared me to ride him. Of course, I was fool enough to accept, and for about 5 minutes we evolved about a hundred different pinwheels, but I finally got the "hinge-back" cooled down and rounded up the horses on him. Then Emil rode back to Howards. I stayed up to read for a while. Went to bed at 12:30. Alex Alton fetched seven horses into our barn, his having caved in.

Tuesday March 7

Wea. Strong cold wind   Ther. −1, +20, -3

In accordance with my arrangements which I had communicated to Mrs. Howard thru Emil, I did not drive over till late in the afternoon. First I went to Croffs for some necessary groceries, and then I drove over to H's, taking a parcel along for Mrs. Howard. I watered Beauty and George, then chased them into the barn and fed them. Then I rounded up the cows on George, watered them and put'em up in the barn also. I had not unhitched any horses, so I simply jerked off their blankets and drove to the school; there I got the girls.[84] Failed to get a glimpse of the school marm.

Having gotten the girls safely home, I immediately went back to the shack to do the chores. Mr. Alton came over to water his horses. He did not quite have his barn fixed up, so we decided to leave the horses in Emil's barn tonight also. I put up our horses before Alton left and we noticed that Jack was showing symptoms of the colic. I dozed him twice, and was preparing to leave the barn after Alton had gone, when I noticed that Jack was rapidly becoming worse. I ran to the house for a lantern, my sheepskin, fountain pen filler, and blankets. I hung my watch on a nail, and regularly every 15 minutes I gave Jack a filler of "F". He was very ill and I sat up with him till 5 AM, before I dared to leave him. Was very sleepy and cold, so I cooked some coffee and then hit the hay.

Wednesday March 8

Wea. Very warm, west wind   Ther. −1, +38, +33

An unexpected warm wind arose when I woke up at 10:30, and in a short time the snow surely began to sizzle away. Water was running all over when I went to the barn, and great patches of brown grass were appearing in the most unexpected places.

I turned the horses loose, except Jack whom I still regarded somewhat doubtfully, and then I fried an enormous quantity of pancakes, eating them as fast as they were fried. When I finally got ready to leave for Howard's it was 2:30 PM. To my surprise I met Harry at Leon Veeder's. He and Emil had come through without stopping for dinner. After talking with him for a while, I turned around and drove back to the shack, where I found Emil busily unharnessing his team. He had brought my magazines etc. along from Schafer, including several dozen Synodical-Berichte from the Publ. house of the North Dakota and Montana District. He also had brought several hundred shells for our several cannon.

---

[84]This again would be Nettie, Lucile, and Eva Green, Mrs. Howard's daughters.

We experienced a lot of uneasiness when Nancy failed to turn up with the rest of the horses. The most careful search with the pinto failed to find her. But at about 10:00 I heard a soft whinny, and there she was just as spruce and sassy as ever. The north lights were beautiful tonight. Alton got his horses this morning.

Thursday March 9

Wea. Medium N wind   Ther. +2, +28, +18

There was no thawing going on to-day. It was so chilly that a fur coat was right welcome. I managed to pull Emil out of bed at 7:00, inspite of his hearty and vociferous protests. We had breakfast, after which I picked up a magazine and read around till noon. Emil took the opportunity to doze off to sleep again and I let him sleep till noon. Then we lunched a bit and got ready to get a load of straw. I rounded up the horses and chased them down to the spring while Emil went down with the rack. He took his revolver along and proceeded to demonstrate his marksmanship by shooting a bird off a post.

We put on a fair size load and came home around about 3:00 PM. A bachelor has not the faintest regards for the "ethics" of his home. Emil for instance, put a .22 shell on the table, and we used it for a rifle target. What mattered it that I, for instance, cut a nice groove thru its oil cloth table cover and onto the table? What mattered it, that Emil once struck the plaster between the logs, thus opening the way for some more ventilation? All we cared about is that I hit the bullet twice out of 5 shots, and Emil hit it four times out of the same number of chances.

Emil left for Howard's tonight. He expects to take in a load of flax for Harry to-morrow.

Friday March 10

Wea. Quiet till eve.   Ther +9, +54, +30

For a change there was hardly any wind to-day. The thermometer gradually climbed up to 54 degrees, but since there was no wind, the snow did not melt very fast. Nevertheless it got pretty muddy in places.

After watering the stock I cooked a huge dinner and then I went at the hateful job of washing dishes. Nearly everything was soiled and I spent several hours at the job. Practiced shooting with Emil's "Colt". It certainly is a powerful weapon, for I put a bullet completely thru a fencepost from a distance of about 2 rods.

My pet cat managed to get into the cupboard and proceeded to help herself to the eatables. She tackled nearly every exposed food I had in there, and I had to throw it all away. She sailed out of the door in company with the baked beans.

Wrote a letter to Art Behn in eve. Looked thru my diary before I went to bed. Hit the hay at 11 PM.

Saturday March 11

Wea. Warm   Ther. +28, +43, +33

Water is beginning to run underneath the snow in the coulees. Our well, which consists of a 22 ft. hole about five feet square, is rapidly filling with snow water. It is merely boarded over, and we get our water by snapping a rope to a bucket and lowering it into the well.

Shortly after I had turned the horses loose, Ed Green and Alex Alton came over to invite us to Bert Catlin's shivaree. They stayed till evening. During the afternoon they gave an exhibition of western shooting. Some of their stunts were truly marvelous. Alex Alton shot at little chunks of lignite that I tossed in the air, and every shot of his revolver was a hit. Then Ed Green took his "Colt 45" and shot empty .22 shells off the top of a post. Ed Green shot a bird, on the wind, with his "32-30" rifle. This is the only time I have ever saw the feat accomplished. I doubt if the average hunter would have bagged the bird with a shotgun.

Towards 3:00 o'clock Emil came back from Watford. He reported bare ground most of the way, and the water in the creeks is touching wagon boxes. He did not have any dinner, so I peeled a few extra potatoes and cooked up a square meal for the four of us.

Quite naturally the unexpected happened again, and we got company. A Russian Jew clothes peddler begged us to keep him over night and we finally consented. We had to cook a special supper for him, and listed to his uncouth gibberish half the night.

Sunday March 12

Wea. Warm east wind   Ther. +17, +8, +21

To-day the snow went with a rush. The coulees of course are still filled; some of them contain 30ft of snow, and that won't melt very fast. The north slopes of the buttes are also still covered with deep snow, but on the levels and flats the white mantel has disappeared.

Emil manufactured two elaborate windmills this morning, which he tacked onto the two gable ends of the shack roof. He purposely constructed the mills very loosely, so they would give the maximum amount of noise. I busied myself by constructing an intricate canal system with the water, which is flowing in the old buffalo trail right south of the shack. I used our ash pile for material with which to construct dams, and it was great fun to see the rushing water eat away through this flimsy material. Kids play? Why certainly, but it was great sport just the same.

Ray Catlin, the Indian, came over on his pinto and chatted for some time.[85] He shot at some of our pictures with his "45" and tore the plaster out of the chinks between the logs.

We played several games of casino in evening and hit the hay at 1:30 o'clock.

---

[85] A group of Catlins had settled two miles south of Johnson Corners about 10 years before. This is how the area got its name. The Catlins built a store with a post office in a log building. Nettie Catlin was the first postmistress. W.B. Croff bought the cabin in about 1910 and moved it southward about three miles. RCJ visited this same store frequently, although Mr. Croff enlarged it substantially.

Monday March 13

Wea. Colder, north wind   Ther. −4, +12, -2

There was a decided change in the temperature to-day. A fine, feathery snow had fallen all night and things had assumed their usual whiteness again this morning. Wee overslept again as usual., Instead of cleaning the barn, as we had intended to do, we just did the things that were absolutely necessary. I drove to Howard's while Emil got a load of "golden hay". We had been out of bread for several days and so I hitched Whitie and Rex to the jumper and started. Our winter trail to Howard's angled across Clark's flat.[86] I had to choose a different route today, for the flat was completely inundated. After circling around in the buttes, I finally struck "Winie" Wehrle's coulee, only a few feet from the spot where Emil and I had been stuck on the 19th of February. The water was rushing worse than on that day, but I noticed that there was solid ice underneath, so I whipped the horses into it and crossed it safely. After draining the water out of the jumper I proceeded to Howard's, where I got bread and some turpentine for Nancy, who was kicked by some sharp shod horse last Sunday. There was a great deal of bare ground and my jumper didn't slide along very easily. Played several games of mill in eve. Lost most of them. Bed at 1:30.

Tuesday March 14

Wea. Cold NW wind, snow   Ther. −18, -4, -9

In spite of the severe cold I roused Emil out of bed at 7:00 AM, and cooked breakfast, while he did the chores. Then we proceeded to clean out the barn. Quite an undertaking, since we have allowed the manure to accumulate for many weeks. However, we succeeded in removing the excrement by about 1:00 PM. Just as we were ready to sit down to our noon meal, along came Ole Skaar, for one of his periodical visits.

He ate along with us and then sat around all afternoon. I thought that he would probably ask me to come over and baptize his kid that night, since he had indefinitely asked me once before. However, he did not mention one word about that. Emil took him home in the jumper and fetched a keg full of water along, for drinking purposes. Our own well is full of a sort of brownish

---

[86] This was a long, flat field located east of the cabin.

liquid and not fit to drink out of. It caved in in one place, and a lot of dirt etc. washed into it with the snow water.

We played several games of casino in eve. I attempted to write a few letters, but did not succeed.

Wednesday March 15

Wea. Cold east wind   Ther. −21, -9, -24

It was unusually chilly to-day, due, no doubt, to the fierce east wind. As usual, this wind whistled into our shack to such an extreme that we could not keep it warm. Emil is figuring on coating the outside walls with cement this summer. This will make a great difference in the temperature.

Mr. Howard was an early caller, routing us out of bed. He objected strenuously to the noise our windmills were making on the shack roof, so he crawled up and jerked one of them off. Later on he took it along for his kids to play with. We played two games of "Rum Dum", I being the loser by a narrow margin in both games. After Mr. Howard left, I cooked up supper and then we began to do the chores. On such windy days it is impossible to carry hay or straw into the barn; one has to push it along the ground. We had quite a time with Nancy in dressing her wound. We were finally forced to tie one of her hind legs up, so that she would stand still. In spite of this, she tore around fearfully, and nearly worked her foot loose.

We went to bed at 12:15 tonight.

Thursday March 16

Wea. Bad east wind; looks like snow   Ther. −27, -14, -31

It seems to be getting colder every day, just as if winter were coming back. In such chilly, windy mornings bed appeals very strongly to a person, so we stayed in bed till 10:30. While Emil did the chores, I swept the shack and cooked breakfast on the heater. I set a covered pan full of potatoes on top of the stove, and another pan full of baked beans on top of this first pan. The coffee-pot went right into the blaze, of course.

Although the weather looked very threatening it did not snow. On the contrary, it cleared up somewhat towards evening, and the night was intensely cold.

I wrote a letter to Helen and Ban. I had already written one to Art Behn some time ago, but did not have a chance to mail it as yet.

During the afternoon I cleaned the guns and sorted over the ammunition. We are running short of shells for my .410; Croff does not sell cartridges.

In the evening we played several games of Casino and checkers. Bed at 1:15.

Friday March 17

Wea. Much warmer   Ther. −14, +37, +16

This is North Dakota! My impression of the Northwest always was that the temperature was not very constant; that it would gradually get cold in Autumn, stay intensely cold all winter, gradually get warm again in spring and stay warm. Instead this part of the North West is more changeable and fickle in regard to the thermometer than a woman.

It thawed nicely to-day for a while. The water began to rush down the old buffalo trail, disappeared under the snow on the North Slope of the coulee, and reappeared again in the bottom of the ravine. I opened numerous ditches to drain off the gumbo[87] as rapidly as possible. After trying to walk across a patch of muddy gumbo, I learned to avoid the stuff like poison.

Emil cleaned the cellar to-day. I carted away several bushels of refuse. In cold days, we had the habit of sweeping all the dirt, etc. right thru the trap-door of the cellar, and this had piled up considerably. We also sorted over the potatoes, throwing the frozen and spoilt tubers away.

The horses enjoyed the chance of roaming around on the prairie and did not come back till late to-night.

---

[87]Gumbo is a local name for clay that, when wet, is slippery but builds up on shoes, tires or anything that walks or drives through it.

Saturday March 18

Wea. Warm; snow melting   Ther. Slight east wind

For about a week I haven't been to the post office and am rather anxious for
my mail. Inspite of the water, which was rushing in the coulees, I persuaded
Emil to accompany me to Croff's. We left early in the afternoon in the jumper. The jumper's days seem to be numbered however, for there was only very
little snow left. Most of the time we were dragging along on the bare ground.
We managed to cross all the coulee's successfully. The one in the Morrison's
lane near Catlin, was the worst. I had my foot on the edge of the jumper-box;
still I got my foot wet and we shipped a good deal of water.

To my dismay I had only one letter; a frantic appeal for a loan from Ban. Rev.
Frey sent us a joint letter. It appears that the mail has not been able to cross
the river lately.

We got some straw again to-day.

Sunday March 19th

Wea. Warm, no appreciable wind   Ther. +28, +48, +30

It was nice and warm again today. It usually freezes nights until about the
middle of April, I am told. But the thin veneer of ice on the rivulets soon
melted away.

There is quite a current of water washing down the Old Buffalo Trail immediately south of the shack. Emil and I slipped on our "rubbers" and shoveled
and dug away the snow in the coulee, so that the water would have a struc-
tured passage. In the course of this work I stepped through the crusty snow
into the slush underneath and got both feet badly soaked. Emil also was
compelled to change his clothes.

We had the horses out all day. We do not need to bother about watering
them on days like this. I hope this nice weather will continue for some time,
although the roads are impassible on account of the water in the coulees.

Monday March 20th

Wea. Warm west wind   Ther. +29, +38, +28

Mr. Howard caught us in bed again this morning. He dumped me out; Emil escaped in time. Harry was going to get his wagon truck. He fetched us some food and ate dinner with us.

It had been my intention to go to Croff's today. In the first place, I am expecting some important mail, and in the second place I would like to announce services in Schafer for next Sunday. But the water was filling in the coulees so fast that, that the mail-man can't get to Schafer anymore, much less I.

I spent the afternoon with shooting and digging trenches for the snow-water. Emil repaired his wagon seat. I helped and constructed a water mill. Played several games of mill and checkers in the evening.

Tuesday March 21st

Wea. Snow-storm   Ther. −1, +20, +7

It is, of course, self evident that a good thing can't last forever. After the nice sunny days we are getting another good taste of winter weather. And it seems as tho McKenzie Co. is anxious to make up for lost time, and as if it had crowded 15 blizzards in one day.

We had intended to go to Croff's today, but we had to abandon our project, of course. We stayed in bed till nearly noon, when the insistent demand of our "tummies" drove us up. I waited till Emil had started a good fire in the heater before I got up. We cooked breakfast on the heater and then I read for some time and filled out this diary. Emil fitted a new handle onto the ax and then I helped him change two pipes on the stove. The old ones had burned thru. This happens pretty often, since we have no chimney in the cabin; the stovepipe runs straight up from the stove thru the roof. Since we had a good fire in the heater, changing the pipes was quite an unpleasant task.

The chores were a hateful job to-night, but it had to be done. Most McKenzie Co. barns have no hayloft; we have to carry the junk in from the outside. The stock got no water to-day.

Wednesday March 22nd

Wea. Blizzard   Ther. −2, +11, -7

About two inches of snow had fallen by this morning, and white feathers are still falling. Of course, the flakes do not come down so big and gentle as in Missouri or Nebraska. It always resembles sleet more than a real snowfall. "Un affaire d'amour sale". Homo agricola sub papyrum videt.[88]

I am beginning to feel apprehensive about my long-delayed Schafer trip. I am supposed to send a permission signed by the elders of the Schafer congregation to the mission board, authorizing the latter to call a minister from among the candidates next spring. Since the "Verteilnugs-Kommission" will meet soon, it is imperative that I send the call in soon.

Emil and I manufactured a rattle mill to day. We mounted a rattle in the frame work of the mill, and the revolving wheel operates the rattle to perfection. The noise, while not excessively loud, was so penetrating that we could hear it quite plainly in the barn. We had to dismantle the mill from the roof of the cabin before we turned in to sleep. The ice is becoming quite thick on the coulees and we are running short of coal. Read till after twelve to-night.

Thursday March 23rd

Wea. Very windy; more snow   Ther. −8, +3, -11

Before this last spell of bad weather, most of the ground was free of snow. Now everything is covered again by a white mantle. The old jumper will have to be pressed back into service again.

It was bad as ever today and the lowering sky does not give any promise of better weather. I hope we will be able to get to the post-office soon, but probably the mail stage is not coming thru either. Last Tuesday was election day, and I would like to see the results.

We cooked our breakfast on (and in) the heater this morning. Since we are running very low on fuel, we decided to cut up a huge log of oak, which Emil had hauled up last Fall to serve as fuel in the wood-stove. We sawed the log

---

[88]Seminary students were expected to read, write, and understand Latin, Greek, and Hebrew, in addition to being fluent in English and German.

into 18 chunks, and then split the blocks into pieces small enough to fit into the heater.

While engaged in this highly amusing occupation I had the misfortune to have the ax-handle split on me so that it became practically useless. What makes matters worse is the fact that one would have to drive to Watford City for a new handle.

It was mighty cold today. After a taste of spring it is rather hard to grow accustomed to another spell of real winter weather.

Friday March 24th

Wea. Blizzardy; N.W. wind with snow   Ther. -18, -7, -23

The storm is continuing with unabated fury. Emil predicts a change tomorrow, and I fervently hope that his prophecy may come true. He is experienced in the ways of this country and might be right.

I was introduced to Mr. William Lillibridge today. He had walked from his house to the mail trail, to see whether the stage has been thru lately, and he did not care to face the wind back again, so he walked over to our place. He is a great friend of Emil's and Howard's; used to be Emil's neighbor when the latter was staying on Billy Bellin's place.

The weather was so bad that Mr. Lillilbridge stayed and spent the night with us. We were completely out of straw for the horses, so we had to drive to Ole Skaar's stack with the rack. The stack was covered with ice, except on the N.W. corner, so that we had to pitch against the wind. We did not succeed in hauling more than just enough for one feed.

In the evening we played several games of "Rum Dum", I being the victim in every instance. Hit the hay about 2:30 A.M.

Saturday March 25th

Wea. Slight east wind; warmer   Ther. +2, +37, +21

Emil's prediction came true! The temperature rose high enough to melt the snow a little and caused some water to run. There must be between 4-6 inches of snow in the level, however, and that will last for some time.

Mr. Lillibridge walked back home at about 10:00 o'clock. Ole Skaar's straw is getting pretty small, so Emil and I decided to tackle Emil's own wheat-stack. He has not fed any of it so far, because some of the straw is a little rusty. The stack is close by, not a quarter of a mile away, but there is an ugly coulee between it and the farm. We walked around the ice covering the coulee, looking for a suitable crossing, but the ice was too thin. Emil followed the coulee down cutting holes in the ice to gauge its thickness, while I busied myself with my ".410". The cats accompanied me on my hunting trip and devoured the birds as fast as I shot them. I looked in vain for a coyote or even a jack-rabbit. Saw one bald eagle, but could not get within range.

Emil finally found a crossing and we managed to get at the straw pile after going a mile out of the way. We hauled one load, which will last us till Monday.

Sunday March 26th

Wea. Slight east wind, warmer   Ther. +3, +60, +18

The warm weather has its drawbacks too. The gumbo, which surrounds this place with great generosity, is bottomless again and one can only cross it with the utmost difficulty; for stickiness, gumbo has the best Missouri clay beat seven ways from new year.

We are out of bread again. Emil has been baking biscuits lately and we had expected to hit Howard's to-day. Harry and his family came sailing past this morning, however, evidently bound for the Lillibridge's, so we had to postpone our visit.

To relieve the monotony, we decided to hitch up a 2 year old colt (Fanny, black). We loaded the water keg on the jumper, hitched Jack with the colt and drove to Ole Skaar's. I manipulated the "strings; the colt showed very little tendency to raise cain. After filling the keg, I drove the colt back. We cannot use the water in our well because it has partly caved in and dirtied the water considerably. Played checkers in eve.

CHAPTER 7

OBSTACLES: COULEES AND CHERRY CREEK

Monday March 27th

Wea. Warm west wind   Ther. +23, +58, +30

It froze a little last night, but to-day was warm again, with a hint of rain. I absolutely had to get to the post-office, so I persuaded Emil to ride along with me. Using the jumper was altogether out of the question, there being hardly any snow left on the flats. I rode the bronco (Whitie), but he did not buck much today. At Croff's I had my check for February ($60.00), a letter from Monk, Rev. Hilgendorf, Ma and Dora. I mailed Ban a postal money order for $50.00 with the promise of loaning him another '50' if possible. The mail had been unable to cross the River[89] for 10 days on account of the high water.

We had quite a time on the way home. Our horses had to swim one coulee and needless to say, we got drenched. Emil rode Jack to Howard's in order to get some bread. In the mean time I did the chores, rounded up the cattle and cooked myself a good supper. Emil came home late. He had a hard time crossing "Winie" Wehrle's coulee because of an ice jam. The water in our east coulee is running above the fence post in the coulee.

Tuesday March 28th

Wea. Somewhat colder; little snow   Ther. +12. +34. +21

It is rather uncomfortable to-day. We got up early, because we expected Mr. Howard, who is intending to clean his flax with Emil's grader. Emil repaired the grader sieves, while I cooked breakfast. Mr. Howard came along at 9:00 A.M. While he and Emil were working in the barn, I intended to write my

---

[89]Missouri River

sermon for the next Sunday; I have announced services for Schafer in spite of the warning that Cherry Creek would be impassible. The Creek washed a buggy along the other day, but the driver escaped.

I was too cold to sit quietly at work, so I got a good fire started, then proceeded to wash the dishes, all of which were dirty again, of course. While engaged in this humorous job, I cooked dinner and composed a new pirate song to relieve my feelings.

Chester Alton hailed me from across the coulee while Emil was getting a load of straw. He invited us to a card party at his shack. Emil rode over, I staid home on account of my sermon.

Wednesday March 29th

Wea. Bad blizzard   Ther. +12, +21, +3

Most likely I will have to postpone my trip to Schafer again. The blizzard we are having today will cause the water to rise higher than ever. As it is, Schafer is inundated; the entire flat is covered with from 1 – 6 ft. of water and Cherry Creek is a violent stream. The only way to cross it is per rowboat. I would have to leave my team on this side, and it would not be easy to find adequate shelter for it. Then too, I could not fool around in Schafer without a horse, I could not possibly move around there. Besides, none of my members would be there, so the trip would be in vain. Rev. Hilgendorf, the Superintendent of Missions, wanted me to send in the call from Schafer in March; he will be lucky if he gets it in April.

Emil came home around 11:00 A.M. They had consumed a gallon of whiskey and several of the guys got drunk. Emil has his oats stored in his deceased brothers shack. As he was riding past there he noticed that the range horses had kicked in one of the lower panels to the door, thus allowing the oats to escape. He figures that he lost over 100 bushels. He slept nearly all day. I read one of the books that Paul sent me (C. Mulford's "The Orphans") and poked up the fire to keep the shack warm.

Figure 33: *View of Schafer in the distance. Note the proximity of Cherry Creek to the town. Various wagon trails can be seen at left and right in the picture. The only structure still standing today is the jail.*

Figure 34: *Cherry Creek. In late March, 1916 it flooded, as RCJ describes.*

Thursday March 30th

Wea. Warmer; slight wind   Ther. +18, +34, +22

The storm had ceased by morning. I seized the opportunity presented by the fair weather to take a trip to Croff's. Emil chiseled his buggy out of the ice which held the wheels. The buggy pole, which we put on the jumper last fall, has a broken circle and is useless, so we put the shafts on the buggy and drove Whitie singly. There was a lot of water running in the coulee, but we made it alright. I mailed a hurry-up letter to the Monk and got some mail including a dandy letter from "Daddy" Roettger who is vicaring in Gardena, N. Dak. Daddy expects to return to the city[90] by Easter. Lucky Dog!

The north-lights are still very much in evidence. They were especially brilliant tonight, lighting up the heavens with a soft glow. There is something indescribably weird and mysterious about these lights that keeps me spell-bound. I sat outside till late at night, smoking and watching the ever-shifting radiance.

Friday March 31st

Wea. Warm Chinook wind   Ther. +30, +47, +29

For the first time in my life I was privileged to see an avalanche; incidentally I narrowly escaped from being crushed to death. I was riding along "Many Dead Chief's" trail looking up some prospective people from the Catlin Community. As I was riding along the northern shoulder of "Seven Mile" Butte I suddenly heard a roaring, shrieking noise high up on the summit. My pinto shied violently, nearly throwing me. Then it seemed to me as if all the thousands of tons of snow on the northern slope were loosened at once, and only the nimble feet of my pinto saved my skin. A rock the size of a man's head came whizzing past me, missing me by only a few feet. The avalanche crashed into Seven Mile Creek, and blocked the water for several hours.

Ole Skaar, our nearest neighbor to the East, came over and asked me to baptize his kid tomorrow night.[91] The little girl is nearly a year old.

---

[90]This would no doubt be St. Louis, back to the Seminary. Roettger was in RCJ's 1914 high school class and was serving as a supply pastor in Gardena. He must have started his service in early 1915.

[91]His daughter's name was Edna May Skaar, born April 19, 1915.

I made an extremely lucky shot with Emil's revolver to-day, killing a big black cat from a distance of about 1 rod. The shot went neatly thru her head. I could never duplicate this feat in a thousand years.

Figure 35: *Old homesteader's dugout near Seven Mile Creek.*

Saturday April 1st

Wea. Warm; Prospects for rain or snow   Ther. +20, +48, +19

This is the famous day, which has been sacred to Fools since time immemorial. As a rule I get stung several hundred times on April 1st, but I was wary to-day and escaped completely.

We cleaned out the barn again to-day. This was quite necessary, because we hauled out seven double box loads. To begin with, we manufactured a reach for the wagon-truck out of a slender ash-pole; it held splendidly.

Towards evening we dressed up, ready for the visit to the Skaars. The cayooses were still on the prairie. So we were forced to hitch up "Belle." Belle and Mack are being kept in the barn because they are sharp-shod and would cause much damage with their hind legs. We had quite a pleasant time at Skaar's. Some neighbors came over for the ceremony and I had four witnesses to the act.[92] Mrs. Skaar prepared us a dandy supper and I had a highly interesting talk with a student of the state normal school, of Valparaiso Ind. We stayed till 2:30 A.M. before we got hitched up, Mr. Skaar handed me a check for $5.00.

Sunday April 2nd

Wea. Pleasant, Chinook wind   Ther. +29, +58, +4

The rather primitive conditions of McKenzie Co. and the extremes of the western hospitality are well illustrated by this incident. When we came home about 3:00 A.M this morning, I was startled to see a bright light blazing from the window of our cabin. When we went to the house for the lantern, we found Ed Green rolled up in my blankets and sleeping full speed. He awoke when he heard my dog bark and explained that Mr. Howard and he had come over for a visit. Not finding us home they had waited till about 10:00 P.M. at which time Mr. Howard rode back home, while Ed decided to stay. He left the light burning to guide us should we come home during the night (there being no moon).

We pulled all up in our blankets and slept till 9:00 A.M. Mr. Green rode off about 3:00 P.M., after I had an interesting talk with him. He has traveled very extensively over the northwest, and is a pioneer who has had many unusual and exciting experiences.

Emil was gone for a great part of the afternoon searching for a colt (Fanny) which had strayed away. He found her in George Taylor's drove of horses. Ed Green informed me that one of Howard's horses was recently kicked in the stifle, but he did not know the extent of the injury.

I wrote a long letter to "Daddy" Roettger in eve.

---

[92]According to RCJ's records, the witnesses were Mr. and Mrs. Syvert Mathistad, Ms. Elinore Hildremeyer and Emil Bellin.

Monday April 3rd

Wea. Blizzard   Ther. +9, +31, +3

For many days the sky has been overcast, and threatening. It "sleeted" off and on this morning and during the greater part of the afternoon there was a heavy snow-fall, which was whipped along by a strong north wind. I had expected to drive or ride to Croff's this afternoon, but gave up the project.

During a lull in the storm Emil busied himself in shoveling out a crossing in the coulee west of the barn. Floating ice jammed in among the mesquite[93] and chaparral in the coulee, obstructing the flow of water. Emil got a bad ducking while he was trying to break the jam. He changed clothing and then I dug a channel in the coulee back up the drive way.

Alex Alton came over to borrow some coal oil while I was working in the coulee.

I wrote a letter to Dora in the P.M. Read some old copies of the "North's Companion" in the evening.

Tuesday April 4th

Wea. Very chilly; east wind   Ther. +37, +18, +9

It was nice and sunny this morning, but the sky became rapidly overcast during the remainder of the day.

Harry Howard came over this morning and asked us to help him butcher. Incidentally, I had expected to drive to Schafer tomorrow, and since my buggy was over at Howard's, Emil and I threw the harness on Rex and Whitie and prepared to ride them over. Harry had left his pony on the far side of the coulee. I swung myself onto Whitie, but he bucked me off before I was firmly seated. On my second attempt to mount him, he threw me squarely on my left shoulder, I felt the most excruciating agony in my left thumb, and found it was dislocated. "Whitie" evidently objected to the harness, for he had never managed to throw me before.

---

[93]Mesquite is a misnomer, as it does not grow in North Dakota. Very likely this reference came from the "Hopalong Cassidy" books the Reverend had recently read. In all probability it was sagebrush.

Harry set the thumb for me, then he climbed Whitie and cooled him down while I rode Harry's horse. We butchered three hogs and stayed for dinner. We hitched up the buggy, and on the way home we noticed that one of Alex Alton's horses had foundered, so Emil went over and notified him. They helped the horse to his feet by means of a pulley and Alton stayed for supper. He notified me that I could not cross Cherry Creek, so I could not go to Schafer.

Wednesday April 5th

Wea. Sunny, west wind   Ther. +14, +41, +20

I was mighty sore because I could not get to Schafer, although I have a lot of business to tend to. For instance, we are out of lard, running low on coffee, out of breakfast food, no coal oil, and lots of other things. Croff, the Catlin merchant, is "out" of all of these articles himself. Besides, I still have to tend to that call for a missionary. But as long as Cherry Creek is impassible, I may as well not make the attempt at all.

Emil left with the rack, attempting to get a load of hay. I explained the situation to Rev. Hilgendorf in a long letter and then hitched up and drove to Croff's. They told me that the mail had been unable to cross the River on account of the flood, so no letters came through since last Thursday. I had a letter from Helen, however.

The roads were terribly muddy, so that I had to drive slowly all the way. As an illustration of how strange the farming conditions are out here, I might mention that Bobby Morrison was threshing to-day. His grain snowed in on him last fall, so he had to delay threshing till now.

Emil managed to get a load of hay, and came home about 6:00; he got stuck once.

Thursday April 6th

Wea. Hail, sleet and snow   Ther. +4, +13, +19

Instead of the April showers which must now be visiting Missouri, we are getting April snows out here. It looked pretty nice this morning; we got up at

5:00 A. M. and while I cooked breakfast, Emil harnessed and fed the horses, and then drove to his brother's claim to clean seed wheat. It was so chilly I got a roaring fire started in the heater, but the terrible wind kept the temperature down.

Later in the day, we had a violent hail storm, which turned into sleet and then into snow. The wind was so heavy however, that it swept most of the snow into the coulees.

I busied myself with the fires and took a nap in the afternoon. Alex Alton came over to get the ropes and pulley, his horse having floundered again, I offered to assist him, but he had three men to help him. I stayed home and opened up channels in the coulee so that the water would run faster. Since it always freezes nights, there is a great deal of ice in the coulee.

Emil came home around 6:30. We had not washed the dishes for a long time, except just enough for each meal, so we cleaned them to-night.

Friday April 7th

Wea. Warmer

Ed Green came over and asked us to go hunting with him. Since we had nothing else to do, we gladly accepted this opportunity to break the monotony.

I rode the pinto and selected my .410 high power rifle. Emil and Ed had 12 gauge shot guns. We rode out into the "Breaks". I did not manage to shoot anything before dinner. Ed shot two prairie chickens, although it is unlawful to kill them at this season, and we cooked them over an open fire. The long ride in the keen air had given us a fair appetite.

I was pretty lucky in the afternoon. Ed shot a coyote, but the shot gun could not take effect on the animal, so I unslung my rifle and managed to hit the beast just back of the shoulder; the bullet went clear thru.

We saw many deer and some beaver, but the strict game laws kept us from taking a shot at them. I killed another coyote before dark. Also two sand hill cranes.

We camped in the open air, rolling up our saddle blankets and using a saddle for a pillow. It was pretty cool during the night, but we were sheltered by an overhanging cliff and the wind could not strike us. I slept very soundly; the long ride had wearied me.

Saturday April 8th

Wea. Warm and pleasant   Ther. +20, +36, +20

We slept very late. It was nearly ten o'clock before I roused myself sufficiently from the arms of King Morpheus to get up. Ed rode straight home; Emil and I went to the cabin.

After dinner Emil announced that he expected to drive to Croff's and Howard's so I quick wrote a long letter to Helen and accompanied him to the store. Here I learnt that the first class mail was being brought across the river per rowboat, while the papers, parcels and packages are being held up. I had a letter from "Hux" Mueller and Art Behn, with a postal from Jack. Jack seems to expect to continue in the ministry, although he wrote once that he intended to resign this Easter – Croff did not have any butter or lard, ingredients of which we are sorely in need. I learned that he had driven into Watford to-day.

I stayed at the shack, while Emil drove to Howard's for bread. In the meantime Ed Green and Mr. Lillibridge came over. They ate supper with us and then we settled down to an all night session of whist. Ed Green and I were partners most of the time. I had a fair run of luck but I certainly was caught during the very last hand this morning. I had "granded" on a good playing hand, but Emil took every trick on me.

Sunday April 9th

Wea. Very Pleasant; Chinook wind

This certainly is a beautiful day. There was a steady "Chinook" wind blowing, that famous west wind which is peculiar to the North West and which often licks up every trace of snow in January. Mssrs. Green and Lillibridge left at 8:00 after breakfast. Emil and I, although sleepy, did not go to bed right away. We busied ourselves in the west coulee prying cakes of ice loose and opening fresh channels for the pent up water to escape. We succeeded in raising the torrent of the water fully a foot.

While I was still working in the coulee, Emil went to the shack and slept. When I came in I could not lie down because my cot was folded up and thrown on top of Emil's bed, and he was on top of the cot. I managed to wake him at last and sleep till 4:00.

We did not begin to do chores till after dark, went to bed very early. The Chinook continued all night and the roar of the water in the coulee could be heard distinctly.

Monday April 10th

Wea. Very warm; shiny N.W. wind   Ther. +30, +68, +21

Howard came over and asked Emil to accompany him to Watford City. The Cherry Creek is very high of course, but Ole Skaar crossed it yesterday, and claimed it was safe. Harry did not want to go alone because Lucas, an older rancher, got drowned last Thursday, trying to cross the creek with a big wagon. The team was also killed.[94]

Much as I hated it, I washed dishes to-day, for everything was soiled. We dip our water for cooking, drinking, washing etc. directly out of the coulee. This is rather unsanitary, of course, since an incredible amount of refuse, dead animals etc. is being washed along. However, we cannot use the water out of the well, because the latter has caved in and is very dirty.

I cooked a dandy supper, consisting of fish balls, fried potatoes, biscuits etc.

---

[94]This news was partially correct. James McLucas drowned when crossing Cherry Creek with his team of horses and wagon, but the team survived. When he left the wagon seat to make an adjustment on the harness or wagon, one of the horses kicked him, rendering him unconscious. He fell into the creek and drowned. He left behind a wife and young children, including this editor's (Johnson) aunt.

Recently I ordered Monson's, 'The Difference' from Concordia Publ. House. The work is admirable although more suited for the layman than for clerical use. It does not go into detail enough. But as Rev. Monson states in the introduction, it is intended primarily for the Christian household than for ministers. I read around in this work tonight.

Tuesday April 11th

Wea. Rainy; cloudy; heavy rain   Ther. +22, +57, + 20

I got up at 6:45 – for the first time in 1916 we had a shower of rain; till now it has always sleeted or snowed. The rain did not continue for very long; however, and the fierce East wind soon dried off the ground again.

We are almost entirely out of oats, so I chased the horses out without feeding them. I kept Rex and Whitie in the barn at first, intending to drive out to Croff's, but I changed my mind and turned them loose later on.

I was surprised at the diminished current of water in the coulee; the flood has receded several feet at least. There is still an enormous amount of snow in the East coulee.

A little bit after 6:00 Mr. Howard and Emil returned from Watford City. They had a frightful trip. Cherry Creek is on the rampage again. They had to cross into Schafer by boat and afterwards they followed the creek down for miles before they found a bridge on which they could cross. They returned via the North Road and Emil picked up a strange dog near Billie's shack. The new dog has such a wistful expression that I want to call her "Poverty", but Emil insisted on naming her "Bobby", she having her tail bobbed off very short.

Wednesday April 12th

Wea. Rainy; East wind   Ther. +29, +37, +81

This was an extremely dismal dreary day. It was raining violently when we got up, and it continued to rain fits and starts throughout the day. Emil told me that it always rained in McKenzie Co. whenever rain was undesirable and not needed. During summer this is usually a very dry country. This is borne out by the fact that the prairie grass is very short. It can be cut for hay only every other year, since it would quickly die out, and give place to sagebrush and chaparral, unless it is permitted to grow seed.

Ed Green came over during a lull in the rain and stayed all day. He had a pair of shoes, which Emil half soled for him.

For the first time in many months we used water out of the well. We have been dipping our drinking water out of the coulee, but decided it was too unsanitary, besides being unpalatable. The well water is not much better, but at least it has a better taste. We have no oats left for the horses, and fed the last bit of straw and hay to-night. To-morrow will be a very busy day for us provided the weather is decent.

Thursday April 13th

Wea. Cloudy and cold in A.M.; sunny in P.M.   Ther. +17, +44

We slept longer than we intended to, it was after 9:00 o'clock before we had hitched to the rack and drove to Billy's place after a load of hay. The west coulee is still so full of snow that we had to drive miles out of our way. We drove past George Taylor's place and then swung north of Parley Catlin's and Ed Green's shacks. It did not take us long to load up, and the horses pulled the load easily, in spite of the soft prairie.

Harold Lillibridge came over shortly after our return for the purpose of exchanging phonograph records. We were practicing with the rifle, and the shots scared "Mose", Harold's horse, so badly that it broke a shaft.

We did not have any bread, and rather than bake ourselves, I drove to Howard's. I also returned some harness parts that we had borrowed from Harry, and brought Emil's coulter shank and pail of Sauer-Kraut[95] back with me.

I ate supper at Howard's and came home before night-fall.

---

[95]RCJ was surrounded by families of German descent. Homemade sauerkraut allowed them to store cabbage though the winter.

Wea.   SUN. MAY 28, 1916   **Ther.**

Slight rain after dinner, else pleasant.

Howard's party left for Catlin early this morning. I drove as far as Schafer, where I expected to conduct services. There was, however, an interdenominational meeting of ministers who were discussing Sunday-School work. I was invited by Rev. Cowgill to attend, but I refused, explaining our Lutheran view of the federation of churches. Since the Revs were expecting to use the Community-Hall all day, I could not hold services there, so I drove straight over to my shack 2 miles south of town. An old lumber-jack by the name of Renell had established himself there, and fixed up the rooms fine. Mr. Hoffmann has finaly removed the kitchen of my shack. The cellar-hole is immediately in front of the house proper. — I drove over to Watford shortly after dinner and preached in the Skandinavian Lutheran Church to a nice audience. Then I drove back to my shack, where I bunked with Mr. Renell. Sent a set of views of my shack to Rev. Frey at Jordan, Minn., and also to "Daddy" Roettger. Pd. Rev. Frey the loan I made last Fall, while I visited him.

CHAPTER 8

A WHITE EASTER

Friday April 14th

Wea. Chinook wind; very warm   Ther. +39, +80

Spring work starts

To my surprise the thermometer crawled to 80 above zero today. This temperature compares very favorably with that of Nebraska or Missouri at this season. The only disagreeable feature of it is, that it won't last.

Emil drove over to Billy's place with a four- horse team and got an 80 bu. load of oats. I staid at home, tidied up the shack and attempted unsuccessfully to write some letters. Seemed to lack the inspiration somehow.

After Emil returned we got the plow in running order and got the horses ready. Emil rigged a serviceable harness for "Jack" out of an old ox-harness, with ropes for tugs. Then he hitched on to the breaker and turned over about eight rounds of sod. I drove around once, more or less unsuccessfully, so that I could claim the distinction of having "turned over" the virgin prairie. We had quite a time to get the six horses working in close harmony, but they pulled nicely towards the end.

Had to wash dishes again to-night.

Saturday April 15th

Wea. Cooler; froze solid to-night   Ther. +33, +60, +4

It was much cooler to-day due to a protracted north wind. Emil and I sawed down an ash tree in the east coulee, and he manufactured another whiffle tree out of the lower part of the trunk.

After dinner he hitched to the breaker again, driving the 6 horses 3 abreast. I threw the saddle blanket on the pinto, grabbed a grain sack in which to stow the mail and groceries, and galloped off to the store. First, I had to subdue the pinto, however, as she was showing a violent disposition to buck. I had letters from Ma, Hux Mueller, Ban Johnson and Dietz. Ban acknowledged the receipt of 50 bucks which I had loaned him, he taking 25 and Bill Medo the same. Dietz wanted me to vicar another year, but I declined. Am getting too rusty on my Hebrew, and would have a hard time to re-learn it.

Sunday April 16th Palm Sunday

Wea. Warm; North wind

This is Palm Sunday! I did not get a single one of my classes far enough for confirmation purposes. I did not even preach to-day, having announced services in Schafer, and being unable to get there on account of the floods.

We fooled around, doing nothing all day. I attempted to write several letters during the afternoon, but with negative results. So finally we decided to give the barn a much needed cleaning, and hitched up Jack and Nance for that purpose. Isham Spence was here attempting to rent his farm to Emil; Emil however, has his hands full and declined the offer. I stayed up till after 1 A.M. writing to Ma and Bill Dietz.

Monday April 17th

Wea. Warm then cooler   Ther. +55, +36

At 5:00 A.M. the alarm roused me from the arms of King Morpheus. I had a hard time waking Emil, but finally succeeded in routing him out. Emil did the chores while I cooked breakfast and did the housework. Emil finished the patch of prairie directly east of the shack by noon. George Taylor rode up to him and asked him for the loan of a plow or disc or harrow, it being immaterial to him what particular tool he got. Such is farming in McKenzie Co!

I wrote a hurried letter to Ban and an order to "Savages" for Emil. Then I mounted the pinto, who bucked viciously again, and set off for Catlin's, accompanied by two dogs, "Shep" and "Misery". Had a letter from Bill Medo and a check for $64.00 from the Mission Board. Bill was indignant because I had sent him a postal instead of answering his epistle with a letter. So I im-mediately wrote him another postal. We went to bed much earlier than usual, hitting the hay at 9:00.

Tuesday April 18th

Wea. Rain in morning; sultry in P.M.   Ther. +39, +78. +26

We got up at 5:00 A.M. It rained quite hard while Emil was doing his chores. I ran out and fetched in an armful of wood so that my cooking would not be interrupted. After breakfast Emil suddenly decided to attend Ole Berg's sale at Berg P.O. instead of plowing. I agreed to accompany him, and so we turned out all the horses except "Whitie" and Rex. While I was lead-ing Whitie to the coulee for water, Emil let Rex go, expecting him to follow Whitie. But Rex was rather ambitious, so he proceeded to run away. Since we were afoot it took us several hours to catch him. In the mean time Ole Skaar came over, also for the same purpose of going to the sale. I then de-cided to stay here, so the two of them left around 9:00.

After dinner, I took Emil's rifle and went out hunting. I took a pot-shot at a coyote, but I must have miscalculated the range, for the beast got away, although wounded. Jack Rabbits are getting scarce in our neighborhood, so I finally began shooting crows. Killed three and missed about a dozen. Crows are hard to "get".

Emil came home about 8:00 P.M. He said that most of the articles fetched a prohibitive price at the sale, so he came away without buying anything.[96] We went to bed very early again.

Wednesday April 19th

Wea. Rain and snow   Ther. +37, +30

A very heavy mist was obscuring everything when the alarm pulled us out at 4:00 A. M. While we were eating breakfast it began to rain, gradually at first, but with ever increasing force, until there was a steady down pour. Not knowing how bad the weather was, Emil climbed my pinto and rode to George Taylor's on some mysterious errand; I hope he got soaked.

[96] The Watford Guide of April 27, 1916 reported that, "The O.I. Berg sale, according to auctioneer Ellingson, brought a total of $4,945.40. One team of horses sold for $500.00."

Towards noon the rain turned into snow. At first it melted away upon striking the ground, but gradually it began to accumulate, until there were a good three inches of snow by evening. The prairie has again assumed the familiar white look it had all last winter. Indications are that this weather will keep up for some time.

Emil came home at 7:00. He was wet all over, and the pinto looked a fright, she had been standing outside all day. We turned the horses and cows out for water. They did not stay out longer than they had to.

When we went to bed it was still snowing.

Thursday April 20th

Wea. Snow; strong N. wind   Ther. +3, +7, +7

Winter seems to have returned in full force. It not only is extremely cold but we also had a steady snow fall all day. The strong north wind built up a considerable drift near the shack.

The last time Emil was to Watford City he fetched 500 shells along for his rifle, and these helped us greatly in whiling away an otherwise tedious day. We shot at various tin cans and blazed at a boulder on the other side of the west coulee. Most of the bullets struck the boulder at an angle, and we could distinctly hear the angry whine of the ricocheting shells.

We were very low on bread, and since it was not exactly blizzarding outside Emil hitched up and drove over to Howard's for a new supply. While he was gone I did the chores, getting drenched to the skin from flying snow, which persisted in crawling down my neck. When Emil came home he had only been able to secure one and a half loaves of bread, enough for a few days however. In spite of our fuel shortage I kept a fire all day.

Friday April 21st

Wea. Occasional showers   Ther. +27, +39, +30

Good Friday

We were disgusted with the rotten weather of the last few days, so we stayed in bed till nearly noon. The chief cause was that Emil had forgotten to turn on the switch of the alarm.

We probably would have slept later yet but two punchers from the <C> came loping up and pulled us out, passing all sorts of sarcastic remarks about laziness etc. Later on it developed that they themselves had been caught in bed at 2:00 P.M. last winter by Chester Alton, who came riding up a few minutes later with Herb Wright. The other two punchers were George Taylor and Alex Alton.

They ate dinner with us, and since we only have one chair and two stools, Emil got some of his "parlor" furniture from the attic, said furniture consisting of some apple crates.

After the cowboys left, we got a load of straw from across the coulee, it being too late to go for hay. Since the coulee still contained several feet of snow and ice, it was quite a job to cross it. I found a strange cat on the straw pile and took it along home.

Saturday April 22nd

Wea. Warm in P.M. Rain in early morning   Ther. +19, +58, +37

People have been crossing Cherry creek in the beginning of this week. I did not think that the recent snow and rains had raised the creek much, so I got ready very early for the trip to Schafer. At Croffs I found a huge box of goodies from dear old Dora. I settled down for the 36-mile trip. I encountered a great deal of mud and bottomless gumbo, so that the going was naturally impeded. Never-the-less, I struck Schafer or rather Cherry Creek, as early as noon.

To my extreme disgust I discovered that all the bridges had been carried away again last night so that it was impossible to get across with a team. I tied my sturdy little horses to a stake, after watering them out of the creek, and gave them a good feed of oats from the sack I had carried along with me (There are no oats at my Schafer cabin). Then I crossed the creek by means of boat, paying 10 cents to the ferryman, and got a gunny sack full of provisions from Steven's. Ate dinner at the Cherry View Hotel and also got a most needed hair cut from the hotelkeeper. – There was nothing left for me to do but go back to Catlin, much as I dreaded the long journey. I reached the cabin again at 7:45 P.M. – 72 miles.

Sunday April 23rd (Easter Sunday)

Wea. Cool and cloudy   Ther. +30, +40, +21

Since I prepared a sermon for today, and since an Easter sermon cannot be used any other time of the year, I climbed the pinto early this morning and rounded up all the people I could find in the neighborhood. We had services at Veeder's school house near Catlin, and I had a pretty fair sized crowd. Got through nicely.

It snowed a little this morning. While the middle of the day was comparatively warmer, the wind picked up again in the afternoon, and it got much colder. A "white Easter" is a new experience for me, but I know that there will be more snow than this before I leave McKenzie Co.

Since I contemplated a visit to the <C> and Lazy S ranches to-morrow, I got everything ready to-night, and went to bed early for a good night's sleep.

Monday April 24th

Wea. Warm, very pleasant

I got a very early start and by 10:30 I was already on the hill which overlooks the <C> buildings. I saw a huge cloud of dust by the third corral, and rode over there. "Sid" Alton, Geo. Taylor, Ben Wright and some other punchers were engaged in "breaking" a pair of broncos for a Norwegian farmer, who had bought them off Mr. Henderson,[97] the owner. The broncos were ex-

---

[97]The Henderson ranches were east of Emil's cabin, past Ole Skaar's place. The Hendersons were known for years for the fine horses they raised. Some of them still farm and ranch in the locale.

tremely indignant and gave vent to their rage by biting and kicking at every-thing in sight. Young Wright's pinto caught the fever and raised him out of the saddle with a sudden buck. Wright was not thrown, however; he regained his seat and proceeded to teach his pinto more. I ate dinner with the boys, and at the request of Mr. Henderson, I preached my Easter sermon. Then I rode onto the "Lazy S" where I ate supper and slept in the bunkhouse. I also preached here in the evening.

Figure 36: *George Taylor at a Diamond <C> Bunk House. RCJ says it is in Montana.*

Tuesday April 25th

Wea. Cloudy, but pleasantly warm

At the request of Mr. Signalness I rode out of my way a bit on the way home and followed the trail to "Baldy" Preston's shack. "Baldy" hadn't shown up there for two weeks. I took his mail and some groceries along, and promised to return for help if anything had happened to him. My failure to return meant that everything was alright.

I found "Baldy" in a very cheerful frame of mind, A Lazy S puncher had left him two quarts of "Tanglefoot" in return for "Baldy's" services in setting a broken arm, and Baldy had therefore shamefully neglected his duty as an outrider of the "Lazy S" and proceeded to devour the demon rum. Since these men get whiskey only very rarely, a small amount goes a long way.

After eating lunch with Mr. Preston I rode straight back home where I arrived just after sundown. Did not get a shot at a single coyote during these two days.

Figure 37: *View of Baldy Preston's shack. It is visible in the distance, center of photo. RCJ marked an X above it. This photo was taken from the cable ferry on the Little Missouri River.*

Figure 38: *The cable ferry across the Little Missouri River, south of Watford City, with car waiting.*

Figure 39: *Another view of cars waiting on the ferry in the badlands.*

Wednesday April 26th

Wea. Warm

Shortly after Emil had gone to his plowing, I hunted up a grain sack, climbed the pinto and rode to Croff's. The pinto naturally was extremely disgusted at the prospect of a seven-mile trip, and she showed her displeasure by some hearty and vigorous bucking. I know her disposition, however, and I succeeded in keeping my seat.

I got a dandy box from Helen, containing some of her delicious cookies, smoked beef and sausages. Emil's goods (underwear etc) from Savages also arrived. In addition I got a dandy letter from "Monk" Hartenberger and Helen, also a letter from Dora. I dropped a letter to Rev. Frey and invited the people for services at Veeder's schoolhouse next Sunday. I have not started a sermon as yet.

After galloping home I prepared dinner.

Thursday April 27th

Wea. Clo. & windy

We got up before 5:00 A.M. again. Emil plowed this morning while I worked out and wrote a complete sermon on Romans 1:16. I have preached on this text before, but I followed a totally different outline, and the contents of the sermon are radically different from the other ones.

Since we are out of hay again, Emil hitched up Nancy and Jack and went after a load. I plowed all afternoon, and did enjoy the work very much. Plowing is my favorite bit of all farm work. I drove "Belle" although she is very high with foal.

Emil came back shortly after I had put the horses in the barn. He had purchased some eggs at Purley Catlins who used to run the local Post Office and still had sort of a store.

Friday April 28th

Wea. Extremely windy & colder

The population of this farm was enlarged today, Belle giving birth to a bouncing baby colt. It had just been born when Emil entered the barn for the purposes of doing the morning chores, and naturally he was delighted that everything passed off so satisfactorily.

One of Ole Skaar's marcs had a colt last night. Since he has not enough horses left to run his gangplow, he turned it over to Emil. He is using Emil's sulkey.

I bucked about half of my sermon during the day, leaving the remainder for to-morrow. Emil was hardly recognizable from the dust which the wind had generously deposited on him.

Figure 40: *Group of unidentified but proper ladies pulling into Schafer with their team.*

Saturday April 29th

Wea. Cloudy; snow   Ther. +12, +30, +22

Although it is nearly May, we had quite a heavy snowfall. This seems rather strange to a person who is accustomed to the heat which must now prevail in the south, but it does not seem out of place in McKenzie Co.

I studied the remainder of my sermon today; and selected the hymns etc. In spite of the snow Emil continued to plow, for the ground did not freeze up sufficiently to prevent that. I cooked dinner and supper and gathered a lot of dead wood from the coulee. Also practiced rifle shooting and cleaned up my shotgun.

Sunday April 30th

Wea. Cold; light snow fall in morning   Ther. 30, +34, +39

It was so comfortable in bed that we slept longer than we should have. After breakfast we had to shave and dress and snatch a hasty dinner at 1:00 o'clock. Then I strapped up the song books, Bibles, etc. and we got to the school a little after 2:00. Mrs Omar Hart and Mrs. Wells[98] attended services for the first time. I waited till 3:00 and had just finished preaching when about a dozen people arrived. After consulting with them I decided to preach my sermon over again, for their benefit. Got through nicely both times.

George Taylor and Alex Alton had discovered some jack rabbits in our coulee and shot them. They brought the hares over with them. Upon Emil's request Alex shot poor little "Sheppie", the dog being a perfectly incorrigible and useless animal. He is now reposing peacefully in the coulee.

---

[98] Although not clearly identified as such, Mrs. Wells was the mother of Maime (Mrs. David) Crighton.

CHAPTER 9

SCOUTING TRIP TO MONTANA

Monday May 1st

Wea. Warmer[99]

Ever since last fall it had been my intention to make a sort of scouting trip through western North Dakota and left this morning.

It was out of the question for me to use a buggy, because there are mainly saddle trails in the "Breaks" so I sat the saddle on "Whitie", tied my blankets, books, etc. on, put my ".410" in its sheath and rode off. I did not intend to go beyond the <C> Ranch[100] today, so I did not leave till nearly noon.

I had an uneventful ride; saw no decent game. The punchers <C> welcomed me enthusiastically, and I conducted services there in the evening. There were 27 men and two cooks present. Also Mrs. Henderson. Slept in bunkhouse.

Tuesday May 2nd

Wea. Warm, windy

"Buckskin" had breakfast ready very early. I bade the punchers a cordial farewell. "Sid" Alton rode to the ford with me, to show me the new crossing over the Little Mo. I became confused among the towering crags and cliffs along the river and found the correct trail by the nearest accident. Among the stones and boulders it was exceedingly hard to see any paths at all. I shot

---

[99]From this point onward, RCJ didn't make as many thermometer readings.

[100]The Diamond C ranch appears to be a 4,000-acre tract near Killdeer Mountain, N.D. The Battle of the Killdeer Mountains occurred there in 1864, pitting Union troops against Sioux defenders. Following the conflict, the ranch was owned by W.L. Crosby, a law school classmate of Theodore Roosevelt. Crosby's widow sold it to Wilse Richards in 1898. The Dvirnak family purchased it from him in 1928. Since then, they have been collecting artifacts and collectibles from the battle. After accumulating many priceless artifacts, the Dvirnaks are donating the items to Dickinson State University. ("Secrets of the Land," *Bismarck Tribune*)

two sand hill cranes, but did not take the trouble to pick them up. Also took two shots at a coyote but missed both times.

Ate dinner with "Baldy" Preston in one of the "Lazy S" outposts. "Baldy" was intently pleased at having a visitor in his desolate shack, and urged me to spend the afternoon and night with him. Since I expected to preach at the "Lazy S" tonight I was forced to go on however. I was a comparative stranger to the "Lazy S" crowd, but never the less, they all gathered and listened attentively. Slept in their bunkhouse.

Wednesday May 3rd

Wea. Cloudy

After an early breakfast prepared by a Chinese cook, I struck due west and crossed the river again at the Killdeer ford. Crossed the Montana border at noon and ate a cold dinner in the shelter of an over hanging cliff, while "Whitie" grazed contentedly. After a rest of several hours, I caught Whitie with some difficulty and rode onto Killdeer,[101] where I intended to spend the night. Upon inquiry at the hotel I learned that there was no prospect of establishing a preaching station here, as there was a Presbyterian missionary in the neighborhood. When I went to bed I noticed a huge sign on the stair landings "snoring allowed but dangerous". I determined that I would not incur any danger from this source, since I am not in the habit of snoring. Montana is "wet" and there were several intoxicated persons in the bar who kept me awake for a long time.

Thursday May 4th

Wea. Warm

"Whitie" had lost one of his shoes yesterday, so I bought a new shoe and put it on him, and then I bought some provisions and rode off towards Sidney. I found a German family by the name of Burgdorfs, and ate dinner with them. They were of the Catholic faith, so my missionary efforts were useless with them.

---

[101]RCJ must be mistaken about being in Killdeer. This town is in Dunn County, N.D., south of the Little Missouri River and about 75 miles east of the Montana border. He must have spent the night in some town south of Sidney and Fairview.

From Burgdorf's I rode north leaving Sidney to my left and followed the picturesque Yellowstone River. Found some beautiful scenery, and was sorry that I had not taken my camera along. This is quite impossible, however no room in the saddle.

Did not meet a single person all afternoon, and finally decided to camp in the open air. Put the hobbles on "Whitie" and turned him loose to graze, while I gathered some dry wood and built a big fire to keep off the chill. I had no cooking utensils with me, so I ate a cold supper of beans and crackers, with some river water. Rolled up in my blankets and used my saddle as a pillow. Slept fine.

Friday May 5th

Wea. Nice and warm; cloudy in eve.

I got to Fairview in time for dinner and decided to ride back towards Schafer. The Norwegian Lutherans have a missionary here, and I was not needed. So I saddled up at about 2 o'clock and followed the railroad toward Watford City. It was dark before I reached Arnegard,[102] so I decided to sleep in the open air again, since I could not see any house in the neighborhood.

There was no shelter, so I finally put up my blankets in the coulee with running water at the bottom. Made a fire from some dry brush and had a cold supper again, like last night. The wind picked up in the evening, so I had to put the fire out for fear of starting a prairie blaze. It was rather cold during the night, but I managed to get a good sleep.

Saturday May 6th

Wea. Very warm   Ther. 85 degrees

It was actually very hot today, and I'm looking for rain. Did not stop in Arnegard but rode directly to Watford City where I ate dinner. Bought all the supplies that I could conveniently carry on my saddle pony, and then rode over to the passage two miles south of Schafer. Mr. Hoffman, who purchased Rev Frey's claim, was plowing and talked with me quite a while. I

---

[102] This town is about 40 miles east of Fairview, Montana. It is eight miles west of Watford City.

put "Whitie" in the barn and proceeded to put my shack in order. It was in a frightful condition; somebody evidently used it for a couple of days.

Read a great deal in some magazines that I had bought in Watford and cooked supper on the heater. The days are pretty long now; the sun did not set till 8:15.

Went to bed at 11:10 and slept wonderfully in my own cozy bed.

Sunday May 7th

Wea. Very stormy

There was a frightful western wind blowing today. The house creaked and groaned, and pandemonium raged in the barn where a post hole had worked loose. Never the less, I rode down to Schafer where I had announced services and found quite a crowd. Baptized a little boy for a certain Mr. Beutel who had come from Watford. He pronounces his name "Bow-tell", evidently trying to hide his German origin.[103]

There was a severe prairie fire north east of Schafer. A strip about six miles long and several miles in width burnt off, but no houses were destroyed. Owing to the high wind things looked pretty dangerous for some time. After watching the blaze for some time, I returned to my shack and cooked supper. Gave "Whitie" a generous feed of Mr. Hoffman's oats. Wrote a letter to Rev. Frey.

---

[103] The boy was Charles Elmer Beutel, son of Bruno Beutel and his wife Clara (Tank). He was born March 20, 1916. The witnesses were Mr. Elmer Tank and Mrs. Anna Kruger.

CHAPTER 10

GUMBO WEATHER

Monday May 8th

Wea. Severe winds in eve.

After breakfast I packed my personal belongings in my trunk and locked them away. Then I mounted "Whitie" and rode back to Catlin. There seemed to be another prairie fire near Schafer, but I did not stop to inquire. Got to Catlin at 2:00 P.M. and stopped for my mail. Found everything in good condition at the shack, except that Emil had neglected to wash dishes. Most likely this hateful job will develop on me again.

Emil was hauling rock off his land and dumping stones in the west coulee in order to make a wagon crossing. I had 600 rounds of shells along and shot several birds for the cat, who seemed duly grateful.

After supper I recounted my adventures to Emil and then wrote up my diary and made a report of the conditions as I had found them. Went to bed early.

Tuesday May 9th

Wea. Stormy

Emil began to plow the stubble west of the barn this morning. I took several pictures of the shack and the straw shed, which latter building had almost been completely destroyed by Sunday's high wind. After dinner Emil announced that he was going after a load of hay, and asked me to run the disk for him.

Such an afternoon! I had a patch of freshly broken prairie, about three acres in size, which I disked four times. I momentarily expected to be jarred off my seat, but I lived through it somehow. The wind assumed soaring proportions in the afternoon. Emil came home with only a small portion of his original load of hay, the remainder having been scattered all over the prairie.

Wednesday May 10th

Wea. Snow; occasional showers, very windy

When the alarm went off I looked out of the window upon a white world. There was also a high wind, so we slept till 8:00 o'clock; by that time the snow had nearly all melted away again. Emil is going to help Lillibridges plow on Billies place, and he expects to stay away for about a week. I cooked dinner for him, and he left about 11 o'clock.

I kept the pinto in the barn since it is doubtful whether I would be able to catch her later on. Carried some water for the calves and shot several birds for the clamoring cat. Spent the afternoon in maintaining a fire in the heater and with reading. With much reluctance I began the task of washing dishes at the same time as cooking my supper and preparing some Jell-o for to-morrow. It was too windy to round up the cow; she was not even milked for several days and I am afraid she will get dry. Went to bed at 11:30.

Thursday May 11th

Wea. Cloudy, slight rainfall

I slept very long this morning. Did not get up till after ten o'clock. Rode over to Croff's for my mail and then went on a long hunt. Shot a coyote, but the beast got away from me, although I found blood marks. Lost the trail in a coulee, which was so full of brush that I would not ride in it on my pinto. Had the hateful job of washing dishes when the rain forced me to come back home. Baked up a batch of biscuits for supper and kept a fire in the cook stove in order to keep the shack warmer. Did a lot of reading in the evening.

Friday May 12th

Wea. Cold and rainy

It rained a little this morning and remained quite chilly all day. I wrote several letters in the afternoon and cooked an early supper, since I expected to ride to Lillibridges in the evening in order to get one of Emil's horses for the trip to Table Butte and Reservation Corner to-morrow.

I started the ten-mile trip at 6:00 P.M. and got to Lillibridges shortly before seven. I did not stay very long, since I wished to get home before dark. Even declined an invitation to supper, although I noticed that a row of very good looking pies was on the kitchen table.

Got home shortly after 8:00 and packed up my things, so that I would have everything ready for to-morrow.

Saturday May 13th

Wea, Heavy rain all day; snow in morn.

I was prevented from making the trip by a heavy, cold rain, which continued all day. Since I have nothing but an open buggy and no raincoat it would have been decidedly foolhardy for me to travel those 20 miles to Ole Jore's.

Geo Taylor, who has been working his farm immediately north of Emil's, came tramping over through the mud and slush and spent the afternoon with me. I got so cold that we had to get a fire started in the heater, with wood which we tore from Emil's straw shed. I cooked as good a meal as I could, in order to show off. Made some soup, baked a dish of beans, and fried some meat and potatoes. Geo. went home at 7:00 and then I did up the chores. Emil did not show up tonight. Probably he expected that I would not go away to-day.

Sunday May 14th

Wea. Snow in morn.   Ther. + 30 + 48 + 40

Emil showed up just as I was getting ready to eat dinner. He fried himself some potatoes and ate along. He had hardly finished when Mr. Howard came tramping over with his two dogs, "Pepper" and "Curly". Since he had not yet eaten, I cooked up a third dinner for him.

Later in the day Geo. Taylor also came over, and we played several games of Whist, I being so fortunate as to win every game. Mr. Howard left us immediately after supper, while Taylor did not go home till dark. His partner, Alex Alton, is in Watford City, having made the long trip merely for the sake of having a tooth treated. I don't blame him. I have had some experience with aching teeth.

I did a lot of reading in the evening, also wrote several letters, including notices to the people of this neighborhood that we will have services next Sunday.

Went to bed at 12:15. Emil was sound asleep by this time.

Monday May 15th

Wea. Warm; no rain for a change

One of Howard's dogs, Curly, came rushing up this morning with a heavy cord still hanging from his tail. If he could only speak, what a sad tale could he not unfold!

Emil fooled around till noon before he returned to his brother's farm. He intends to remain there all week, in order to help Lillibridges with their work.

I grabbed a grain sack to bag my mail and groceries in, and rode over to Croff's, where I bought a quarter's worth of horrible candy, a soft of taffy that stuck so tight to my teeth that I expected to never get rid of it.

Emil left me with every dish in the house soiled. How I hate dish-washing. I had to get the mess cleared up however, so I waded in, and got things straightened out fairly well before I went to bed.

Tuesday May 16th

Wea. Rainy, a little snow

Joy reigneth supreme in the barn. The cat finally lived up to expectations by giving birth to two bouncing little babies. They struck a miserable day for their advent in this vale of tears, however, since it is just terrible outside. The prairie is fairly steaming and the gumbo spots are absolutely bottomless.

Poor "Misery" got her face sadly scratched up, she having annoyed the cat by sniffing at her babies. The cat was very friendly towards me, however, proudly showing me her kittens.

What won't a man do just to please a lady! Merely to please the cat I donned Emil's slicker and rode in search of the cow, who has not been milked for about four days. I chased her into the barn, squeezed out a bucket full of cheese-like milk and then mercilessly chased her out into the prairie again. The cat showed her appreciation of the milk by much grateful purring. After she had tanked up I gave the remainder to "Misery" and Curly.

Wednesday May 17th

Wea. Warm

When I write "warm" under the caption for weather, that does not mean the same quality or quantity of warmth as the South is now "enjoying". The thermometer nightly sinks to about 30-34, and a thin film of ice is nothing unusual mornings. The trees are budding nevertheless, and I am expecting to see leaves before June.

The pinto was furiously exasperated at being kept in the barn the greater part of several days, and she showed her indignation by biting my leg and bucking outrageously. Nevertheless, she had to carry me to Croffs, where I mailed four letters, including my semi-annual report to Rev. Hilgendorf.

Mr. Croff had returned from Watford City with a load of groceries. At last he has some coffee and tobacco again. I waited till nearly six o'clock for the mail carrier, and when he failed to show up, I finally rode back home.

Thursday May 18th

Wea. Warm, somewhat windy   Ther. +30 at 12:00A.M.

I wrote part of a sermon on Luke 19, 10 this morning. Gave it up in despair, might finish it off tonight.

I was downright hungry, so I cooked up an enormous dinner. After taking a nap to let it settle, I bridled the pinto and rode her bare back to Howard's, in search of bread. It seems to me that I am feeding her too well, for she squealed and bucked all the way to Winie Wherle's.

Mrs. Howard was not home, having gone to a ladies aid meeting at Croff's. Mr Howard with the aid of young Ericson was stringing a fence along the new quarter which he bought lately. After talking with him for a while, I swiped two loaves of bread, and ate a huge slice of cake on the sly, and rode back home, taking a guilty conscience with me.

Poor Mr. Morrison tried to round up his milch cow on foot! After watching his fruitless efforts for a while, I climbed the pinto and chased her home for him. Riding back at 11 o'clock P.M., I became completely lost in the dark, but the pinto took me home at a steady gallop, feeling her way unerringly through the prairie dog town in Clark's flat.

Friday May 19th

Wea. Very pleasant, hardly any wind

This was a mighty nice day. Having consumed a light and unusually early breakfast, I cleaned out the 30-30 rifle, filled my belt with cartridges and rode forth in search of the wild and wooly coyote. Luck smiled on me, for I was so fortunate as to "bag" two of the beasts. I "got" the first near Seven Dead Chiefs "butte". He must have been sleeping, for he started up almost under the pinto's feet, and she shied so violently that my first shot went wild. The second shot got him fairly in the neck, however. I threw the skin on the saddle and had hardly laced it tight when I saw the coyote's mate loping away across the prairie. I gave chase with the eager pinto, and when I was within a thousand ft. I dismounted, dropped the reins and shot the coyote clear through the body, just back of the shoulders. It was the longest shot I had ever made. Rode home with the two skins and ate a late dinner. Read around in the P.M.

Saturday, May 20th

Wea. Sultry & rainy   Ther. +32, +39, +31

This was a cold and disagreeable day. I finished my sermon and bucked it during the afternoon. The way the sky looks, I am thinking that there won't be any services to-morrow, but you never can tell.

Emil came home late in the evening with his remuda of horses, having finished at the Lillibridges. I was just cooking supper when he arrived, so I had to peel some extra potatoes for him.

In the evening I looked up some suitable hymns and Bible portions. The sky continued to remain overcast, and during the night we had occasional showers.

Sunday, May 21st

Wea. Rainy   Ther. +34, +39, +31

It rained steady all day, so that services were out of the question. George Taylor came over this morning and stayed all day. The weather was so unpleasant that I did not even dress up. We played several games of "Schmeer" and then abandoned this game and spent the rest of the day with talking and reading. I cooked a big supper and smoked until bedtime. George brought over some decent tobacco, thus filling a long-felt want. We hit the sack at 11:30.

"Seven Dead Chiefs" Butte, near Cuthis, n. d.

Figure 41: *RCJ's photo of Seven Dead Chief's Butte. This name is unknown today, and the butte cannot be identified with certainty. This photo does show the view one would have as a buggy rider in McKenzie County in 1916.*

CHAPTER 11

INDIAN FUNERAL
AT FORT BERTHOLD

Monday May 22nd

Wea. Cloudy but warm

"Jim" Kimanook, a young Blackfoot[104] from the Ft. Berthold Indian Reservation, came a riding up this noon, and inquired for me. I had planned a hunting trip to the prairie dog village in the Cleveland Flat, but of course, I readily abandoned this project and rode along with Jim, after we had eaten a hasty dinner. Jim borrowed Emil's saddle pony, which I was to fetch back with me. Kimanook's pinto will find home easily enough.

The object of this trip is "Mary" Chipola, Kimanook's mother, who is seriously ill and has asked for a priest or minister. On the way Kimanook told me that she had been baptized by Rev. Jacobson, a Presbyterian missionary who traveled through this country years ago.

The 52 mile trip passed without a noteworthy incident. We watered and rested out horses at Cradle Springs.[105] From here we struck off N.W., thro a country which was perfectly strange to me. I carefully studied the trail so as to be able to find back. We struck the Blackfoot settlement at 10:45.

---

[104]Reference to the Blackfoot tribe may be a mistake. However, the obituary given for Mary later in the text indicates that it is possible that she was of the Blackfoot people. Given the distance covered with Jim "Kimanook" that day, and the reference to Fort Berthold Indian Reservation, Jim was likely a Hidatsa Indian, whose mother was a Blackfoot from Montana.

[105]The location of Cradle Springs is not known.

ᔏ1916ᔓ

Tuesday May 23rd

Wea. Sultry; am looking for rain

Chipola (the sur-name "Mary" was given her in baptism) was very glad to see me. She is failing rapidly, and the crude medical appliances of the Blackfoot seem to be of little help. I had packed my English service books along, and found the "Pastor in the Sick Room" very useful. Of course I had to express myself in the very simplest language, for Chipola can only speak and understand a few broken phrases of English.

The Blackfoot settlement consists of about fifty houses, built of stone and mud, with a roof consisting of closely piled sticks and a covering of sod.[106] Now in the summer, all the cooking is being done outside. I did not see any arrangements for heating the buildings. The Indians are almost without exception stockmen. At least I did not see a sign of any farming operations.

Chipola is a widow and is living with Kimanook and his wife. I slept in the same room with the family, for the houses boast of only one room. At approximately 12:00 o'clock mountain time, Chipola passed away. I was present at her deathbed, and am certain that she had a peaceful Christian death. Kimanook immediately carried her body to an empty hut.

Wednesday May 24th

Wea. Fair

Kimanook explained his strange behavior towards the body of his deceased mother, by telling me that he was observing an ancient Blackfoot custom, which forbids the keeping of a corpse in a house. Probably this is some old heathenish rule, but it certainly is the best arrangement, for it would be very inconvenient to keep the body in a one-roomed house. Kimanook also wished to keep the body for seven days, as is customary with his tribe.[107] I told him however, that I could not remain that long, and since he desired a Christian burial, he consented to have the funeral to-morrow.

---

[106] The description of the house indicates it was an earth lodge utilized by members of the Hidatsa, Mandan and Arikara tribes, which today are the "Three Affiliated Tribes" of the Fort Berthold Indian Reservation.

[107] This custom and treatment of the body is consistent with Hidatsa Indian traditions.

I had absolutely no material with which to prepare a sermon; not a scrap of paper could be found except this diary and some old letters I had in my pocket. I put down some notes on the back of a letter from ma, and proceeded to map out an address in my mind. Luckily, a funeral address does not need to be very long.

Colt and Wrav, two of Chipola's children, came over from their joint ranch this afternoon. The Indian braves did not betray their emotions in the least, while their squaws gave vent to loud wailings.

The whole crowd remained at Kimanook's house this night. I have known cleaner people than Blackfoot Indians.

Thursday May 25th

Wea. Pleasant

I got up very early this morning, and walked away a little distance, in order to work out my sermon undisturbed. By ten o'clock I figured that I could get thru fairly well, so I turned back towards the settlement. To my surprise I found the Indians gathered in front of the deserted house, in which the body lay. They had been patiently waiting for me. I proceeded at once with my address, singing being out of the question with these half savage creatures. I got thru better than I had expected to, considering the adverse conditions.

No step was taken towards burying the body, until just before sun down, when they carefully placed the corpse on a travois and dragged it to a pleasant little burial ground, several miles west of the settlement. I spoke a short prayer "ex corde" and in a few minutes we returned to the settlement. Here we found Kimanook's pinto calmly cropping grass near Kimanook's house. Emil must have turned her loose this morning. At any rate, she found here alright.

I went to bed, that is, I crawled into my blankets rather late. Slept fitfully, because of the strange "Indian smell" which pervades the house.

> ### OBITUARY
>
> Chipola, daughter of Caloosahatchee; born before
> the Civil War on the banks of Aquokemoke creek in
> what is now Montana. She was born in summer. She
> was married to Withlacootchee when she was about
> 22 years old and had three children, Kimanook, Colt
> and Wrav, all of whom are living. After she became
> a widow (date unknown) she was baptized by Rev.
> Jacobson, a traveling Presbyterian missionary, and
> received the surname "Mary." She died of old age
> (?) on May 23rd at 12:00 A.M. and was buried May
> 25, 1916. Died in Blackfoot settlement, Ft. Berthold
> Indian Reservation, Dunn Co., N.D.

Friday May 26th

I wished to start for home very early, but Kimanook and Wrav kept insisting that I had plenty of time, so I did not get started till about 9:00 o'clock. Had a great deal of trouble in finding the Cradle Springs. First I followed an old pony trail for several miles before I noticed that I was on the wrong trail. For a while I was so completely lost in the crazy Blue Buttes that I began to get genuinely scared. At last I heard the sharp crack of a 30-30 rifle to my left, and I galloped towards the place as fast as I could. To my immense joy, I ran upon Frank Keough, of the Keough ranch,[108] who had been trying to pull a bogged cow from a water hole, and had finally shot the exhausted animal. His way led him past Cradle Springs, and we rode that far in company. I declined his invitation for dinner, since the ranch buildings lie towards Berg and would take me too far out of my way. Instead I rested my horse at the

---

[108] Frank Keogh and his brother Jack came to western McKenzie County in 1899 and located the Keogh Ranch east of what later was known as Berg, next to the Fort Berthold Indian Reservation. The Keogh Ranch operation continued in the area for slightly more than 100 years.

springs, and let her graze for an hour, while I ate some dried beef that Kima-nook's squaw had given me. At 2:30 I mounted again, and since I was well acquainted with the trail from the springs I found home without difficulty. I struck the shack before 8:00 and put my tired pinto in the barn. I hate to think of the long trip to Schafer to-morrow.

Saturday May 27th

Wea. Violent windstorm

There was a terrible windstorm to-day. I had to face the wind for over thirty miles (having taken the north road). At Schafer I fed "Whitie" and stopped for dinner and a session with the barber.

While I was being shaved Harry Howard came in with two of the girls. He was taking a load of grain to town, and the girls wanted to see the famous show at the Watford City Opera house.

It did not take much persuasion to get the girls to accompany me for the rest of the way. I took them into Lundin's restaurant[109] and filled them up with ice-cream. Then I secured rooms at the Watford hotel for our party. We ate at the world-renowned restaurant of the Viking Café, and then took in the show, an emotional drama called "East Lynne".

Sunday May 28th

Wea. Slight rain after dinner, else pleasant

Howard's party left for Catlin early this morning. I drove as far as Schafer, where I expected to conduct services. There was, however, an interdenomina-tional meeting of ministries who were discussing Sunday school work. I was invited by Rev. Cowgill to attend, but I refused, explaining our Lutheran view of the federation of churches.[110] Since the Revs. were expecting to use the

---

[109] The Lundin family eventually had a pharmacy and general merchandise store in Watford City, which operated well into the 1990s. The Lundin Ranch is still owned and operated by family members north of Shafer.

[110] This was the LC-MS view that it had determined the correct view of Biblical truth as to all relevant Christian issues. It forbade its ministers to associate with other denominations (even other Lutheran ones) in worship settings, lest some doctrinal corruption occur.

Community Hall all day, I could not hold services there, so I drove straight over to my shack 2 miles south of town. An old lumber-jack by the name of Renill[111] had established himself there, and fixed up the rooms fine. Mr. Hoffman has finally removed the kitchen of my shack.

The cellar hole is immediately in front of the house proper. – I drove over to Watford shortly after dinner and preached at the Scandinavian Lutheran Church to a nice audience. Then I drove back to my shack, where I bunked with Mr. Renill. Sent a set of views of my shack to Rev. Frey at Jordan, Minn., and also to "Daddy" Roettger. Pd. Rev. Frey the loan I made last fall while I visited him.

Figure 42: *Frey's house with the kitchen removed. The cellar is clearly visible. Reynolds has made himself at home, and RCJ must have decided to get along with him and make the best of it. The house itself was moved by August, leaving RCJ to store his things in the old claim shack downhill next to the well. See the entry for July 10.*

---

[111]His name was actually Reynolds.

CHAPTER 12

A COWBOY DIES IN CATLIN

Monday May 29th

Wea. Pleasant

There was a very sad accident in our neighborhood to-day, which affected me especially. Young Einar Dahl, a Norwegian bachelor who lives a few miles north of us, came walking over in search of his horses. I loaned him the pinto, and watched him ride away in a easterly direction. After a few hours the pinto returned minus its rider. Emil caught it up and led it into the barn. We discovered several whip marks and a bloody flank, where a spur had been dug into her side. To my horror, I also noted that the hoofs were matted with blood, although there were no wounds. So Emil hastily saddled his pony and I climbed the pinto, who bucked terribly, and we rode in search of poor Dahl. After riding for several miles we suddenly came upon the body. The neck was broken and the head had doubled under the body. The left arm was also broken, and the furious pinto had smashed nearly all the ribs, and fairly trampled the corpse into the ground. We carried the corpse up to the shack, and later removed it to Dahl's deserted claim shack.

Tuesday May 30th

Wea. Sultry

The only explanation we can give in regard to yesterday's accident is this: the pinto will not tolerate a strange rider, and often gets very balky with a stranger. She has also never been whipped or spurred. She must have bucked with young Dahl, and when he used his riding crop & spur she threw him and trampled him in her rage. – Sheriff Ellickson, who was in the neighborhood, came over when he heard of the accident. At first he demanded that I shoot the pinto, because she was a man-killer, but after I had explained the situation to him, he said I could keep on riding the horse if I had the nerve to do so. Since the pinto has always minded me and never really thrown me I decided to take the risk. Needless to say, I do not expect to use spur or whip on her.

This will not be necessary either, since she usually gallops too fast to suit me.

Arrangements are being made to conduct the funeral to-morrow. I was asked to preach the funeral address and conduct the ceremonies, so I busied myself in writing and bucking the sermon. It was hard for me to concentrate my thoughts, for I was naturally rather excited. Stayed up and worked till 1:30 A.M.

Wednesday May 31st

Wea. Rainy part of the day

It rained a little when we got up this morning, but later it cleared up and we had a beautiful day. The funeral took place at 2:00 P.M. In the morning I finished memorizing my address and writing a schedule of services, for my little "Taschen Agende" contains only meager points on this.

There was a big crowd at the Dahl place, for he was well liked. The body had been placed in a rough pine box and covered over with a sheet, for the features were very convulsed. I got through very well with my address, and after the services we all rode over to Jones' cemetery, 9 miles north east of here, were we buried the body. I was riding the man-killer, and she received a great deal of attention from the people.

After the last rites had been performed, Emil and I rode straight home. We ate a meager supper, and then rounded up the horses and turned them into the barn. Went to bed very early.

OBITUARY

Einar O. Dahl, born September 12, 1890 in Christianafjord, Norway. Was baptized and reared in the Norwegian Luth. Church. Came to America in 1909 and obtained a position as a range-rider for the <C> ranch near Catlin, McKenzie Co., N.D. Was killed by being thrown from a horse on May 29th, 1916. Syvert Dahl only surviving relative. Buried May 31, 1916 in Jones cemetery, N. E. of Catlin.

R.C.J.
Age 25 years, 8 months, 17 days.

CHAPTER 13

RIDING THE CIRCUIT: RETURN TO TABLE BUTTE

Thursday June 1st Ascension Day

Emil is nearly finished plowing the field west of the barn coulee, where he expects to sow oats. Harry Howard came over this morning and asked Emil to accompany him in getting a broncho from Chester Alton's claim. I plowed in the meantime. Shortly before dinner the two returned, having been unable to lasso the bronc without fast saddle horses. The pinto is too small for such work, being unable to hold a broncho.

Figure 43: *The pinto, looking guilty in this picture.*

I helped Howard clean flax in the afternoon, while Emil finished plowing. Harry did not stop for supper, but drove straight home. Emil unhitched at 6:30 and I had supper ready when he had his horses put up, and turned loose to graze. We had tied the pinto to a broken wagon-pole, expecting her to remain peacefully in the neighborhood, but she ran away with the heavy pole and we only succeeded in finding her after a long search. I mounted her and rounded up the horses, after which we went to bed early.

Friday June 2nd

Wea. Warm & Sunny

I had a distinct surprise this morning, Howard driving up with his wife and Mrs. Emmerson. He was going to take the flax to Odermann, who had bought 10 sacks, and while he was loading the wagon he left the ladies in the shack. I was "caught with the goods" for sure, for I had neither swept the floor that morning, nor had I cleaned off the table. Besides this every dish in the house was soiled, and there was chinaware piled on table, stove and floor.

After the party had left I rode to Croff's and fetched their mail along. They stopped over here and got it. After supper Ed Green and George Taylor came over, and stayed till about 3:00 A.M. playing whist. It was pitch dark when they left, there not being any North-Lights, and we subsequently learned that Ed stumbled and pitched into a bed of cactus, getting pretty well covered with the prickly spines.

Saturday June 3

Wea. Warm

We slept very late this morning, till almost noon. Emil planted potatoes in the afternoon, while I hitched "Whitie" to the buggy, in order to get some coal-oil from Croffs. Of course, I forgot to fetch the can along.

From Croffs I drove straight to Howards in order to get some bread. My trail led me past the Williams schoolhouse, and here I picked up Howard's little girls, who had been decorating the school with flowers, in order to prepare it for an entertainment tomorrow.

Howard invited us to come down Monday, and he would accompany us to a coulee where we could get a great deal of wood. Since we are "out" of fuel we may accept this invitation.

Sunday June 4

Wea. Sultry; slight showers   Ther. max. 84

We slept till 9:00 o'clock this morning. While Emil was doing the chores I cooked dinner and then we got ready for services at Veeder's schoolhouse. I felt terribly cramped in my "Sunday go-to-meeting" suit and linen collar. These soft shirts are spoiling me.

The meeting was very well attended; in fact, I had the largest attendance I ever had in McKenzie Co., 41 persons being present. Three punchers from the <C> came over in their picturesque garb, for Sunday suits are unknown among them. I preached in English only, on Luke 18, 10 and got through without a hitch. After services I baptized Bertha A. Kummer[112] in English. Received 1.50 for Baptism.

We drove straight home from the schoolhouse, and I changed immediately to my comfortable every-day garments. After a 7:30 supper I rounded up the horses with the pinto. She was almost ungoverable tonight, but I managed to stick to her.

Monday June 5

Wea. Rainy   Ther. +34 +47 +36

It was raining blue streaks when the alarm-clock began to ring. I yelled at Emil until he finally crawled out of his warm covers with much grumbling, and then we slept on till about ten o'clock. After dinner Emil hitched up and began to clean out the barn. This was quite a task, since the building had not been cleaned for months.

---

[112] Bertha was one of Lawrence and Minnie Kummer's children. This was a large family. Emil later married one of Bertha's sisters, Leta, and they had a son, Arno, known as Bud. This editor's (Johnson) grandmother on his mother's side was Anna Kummer, sister of Leta and Bertha.

I hitched "Rex" and "Whitie" to the buggy and drove to Croffs, where I got some coal-oil and the mail. Had a sweet little letter from the "Kid."[113] When I came back, Emil was still at work so I turned my horses loose and helped him. I got soaked on the way home, being caught in the shower. We ate a hearty supper and turned in early.

Tuesday June 6

Wea. Rain all day

This is supposed to be a dry country, but so far we have had an enormous amount of rain. It rained torrents all day again. While I cooked dinner Emil tended to his horses.

During the afternoon we had a general house-cleaning (did not wash the dishes, however). Emil packed his heater[114] away in the attic, and stuffed an old pair of overalls in the chimney. We cleaned out several bales of old and soiled clothes from underneath the bed, and cleaned away the tools etc. from in back of the stove. The shack looks very presentable now, except that the rain leaks in thru the west wall.

Towards evening Geo. Taylor came over. The pinto had torn herself loose and hiked off, but we managed to round her up with the rest of the horses. Played cards after supper.

Wednesday June 7

Wea. Cloudy, but warm. Very windy

The shack was creaking and groaning when I woke up this morning, there being a typical McKenzie Co. gale outside. Emil had forgotten to set the alarm; so we slept till about ten o'clock.

After dinner we hitched up and cleaned away the remainder of the refuse around the barn. I forget how many loads we hauled, but it was a good

---

[113] This was his faithful first cousin, Helene Burmeister.

[114] Emil used a small wood-burning stove at the opposite end of the cabin from the cook stove. This explains why there were chimneys at either end of the cabin.

amount. North of the barn, in the hay corral, we encountered a great deal of ice. Ice in June!

For one thing, I worked up an enormous appetite, and did full justice to an early supper which I cooked while Emil unloaded the last load. We spent the evening by pasting pictures in Emil's photo album.

Thursday June 8

Wea. Cloudy   Ther. +28 +90 +43

I have my sermon prepared for next Sunday, so there was nothing left for me to do. I finally made up my mind to hunt the wily coyote again. Sid Alton reported that he saw several of them playing near the Manning Ranch, so I rode south, in the hope that I might run across them.

Manning's ranch is located in the "Breaks" of the Little Mo. River. I am always a little scared of this rough country, having been lost several times in the buttes and cut-banks which abound here.

I did not see any game worth shooting until after dinner. I ate dinner with "Baldy" Preston, the lone range-rider of the Lazy S. He is always so pleased when he has company, that it is hard to get away from him. He rode along with me after dinner, and shot the first coyote we sighted without giving me a chance. I missed a sand-hill crane three times, and was so disgusted that I took only a cursory aim at an old he-coyote that loomed up above a cut-bank. I succeeded in crippling him so that my next shot fetched him low. His hide was worthless, but I secured the scalp. Got home at dark.

Friday June 9

Wea. Warm

We had a late breakfast, having overslept again. After dinner I caught up the pinto and rode over to Croff's for the mail and some groceries. Among my letters was one from Mr. Martin Kanth, who happens to be the candidate from the St. Louis Seminary who is to take active charge of the mission work in McKenzie Co. He was rather anxious to find out about this place. Rev. Frey sent a bunch of certificates of baptism which I had ordered from him.

In the evening I wrote a long letter to Mr. Kanth, which I expect to take along tomorrow for the purpose of mailing it at Berg.

Saturday June 10

Wea. Cloudy and cold

I had not been to Table Butte and the Ft. Berthold Reservation for quite a while. Several weeks ago I sent a notice to the McKenzie Co. Journal, thus letting the people know that I would be present on the 19th for the purpose of conducting services.

The days are very long now, the sun not setting till about 9:30. Consequently I fooled around at the shack, talking with Harry Howard who had come over. We had a big dinner, and at about 3:00 I got Whitie ready and galloped away towards Lillibridges and the Berg trail. I stopped at Berg for Ole Jore's mail and then rode on, finishing the 35 mile hike shortly before dark. Mrs. Jore fixed up a nice supper for me. She is perfectly deaf, but not dumb, and she can read lips with marvelous accuracy. One can converse with her as easily and readily as though she could hear.

I slept in the southern part of the bedroom which was curtained off by a calico curtain, and this wall was rather transparent!

Sunday June 11

Wea. Very cold and windy in morning

I rose early, dressed in my 'Sunday best' which had become rather wrinkled from being rolled up in my slicker and tied to the saddle. Went through my sermon carefully.

The people assembled very leisurely, and it was almost noon before I began services. The house was very crowded, and I had people sitting in back of me, which made me feel rather uncomfortable. I baptized a little girl for Mrs. Ola Helle, and then we all had dinner. Of course, there was no table big enough for us to sit at, so we all took a plate on our lap and helped ourself to whatever we pleased. This is the custom at Table Butte.

Figure 44: *Baldy Preston on right, Ole Skavanger on left. Fresh from the trail, they worked for the Lazy S ranch, not the Lazy J, the editors believe. Baldy is one of many colorful characters mentioned in the diary.*

After seeing to it that "Whitie" was properly fed and watered, I rode on between the Chimney and Table Buttes, where there is nothing but a dim pony trail, and then struck due north until I hit the Reservation trail which took me to Elvin Larsons. Instead of preaching at the schoolhouse, I staid at Larsons, baptized their baby girl, and spent the night with them. Miss Tracie Larson was one of the sponsors, and I consider her a very charming and attractive girl.

Monday June 12

Wea. Sunny and warm

I ate a hearty breakfast and then packed my clothing and books, strapped them to the saddle and mounted Whitie with some difficulty. He pitched and reared considerably, having been fed much more than his usual share of oats, but I stuck to him, and rode towards the Blue Buttes at a furious pace. I swung to the west of the Table Butte, cut across the east shoulder of the Chimney, and thus gained several miles. I had intended to get some supplies at the Berg store, but found the place locked, one of the proprietors having passed away.[115]

So I rode due south until I came to Lillibridges, from where I cut across to our shack. It is self evident that I had forgotten to mail the letter to Mr. Kanth, so I re-wrote it and rode the pinto to Croffs to mail it. Whitie was enjoying a much earned rest in the pasture. Towards evening Emil returned from the "Breaks" of the Little Mo., where he had chopped some firewood.

Tuesday June 13

Wea. Occasional rain

Mr. Pollock, who lives several miles southeast of here had a sale today, which Emil attended. I did not accompany him, because I do not expect to make any purchases anyway. I kept a good fire in the stove and washed out some dish towels, which were rather soiled. At about one o'clock three men from near Schafer drove up in search of Pollock's place. Since it was so late, and

---

[115] The deceased was actually young Johnnie Berg, son of Julius I. and Ella Berg. The funeral was at 2 p.m. on this day, according to the *Watford Guide* of June 15, 1916. Johnnie had a short illness the week before, which left him unconscious, and he died on Sat., June 10. The Guide reported that Rev. Cowgill preached the funeral service, and 200 people were present.

since it began to rain, they stayed. I gave them dinner and we played the phonograph until it cleared up a little, when they drove home again.

Emil returned towards evening. He had made an immense purchase, having bought an ax for a quarter. We ate a hearty supper, after which I rode the pinto to the spring and watered her, and then staked her out for the night.

Mabel, a white broncho mare of Emil's, had a sorrel colt Sunday night. The colt is rather poor, but it might pull through and make a good horse.

Wednesday June 14

Wea. Showers

The dish-towels having dried out sufficiently, I went at the hateful job of washing dishes. They were nearly all soiled, and I was thoroughly disgusted before I got through.

Emil plowed this forenoon. He expects to seed oats in the near future, and to cut it for hay. Prairie grass is too scanty to be relied upon for this purpose; a plot can be cut only every alternate year, for a year's time must be given to it in order to seed and grow out again. This is due to the fact that this is usually a dry country, and the grass is peculiar to this part of the state.

I wrote a long letter to Rev. Frey, giving him all the latest news, and rode to Croffs in a shower of rain. The Concordia Publ. House had sent the certificates of baptism which I had ordered. Ban Johnson sent me a postal from Missoula, Mont., near which town he intends to vicar. I had secretly hoped that Ban might change his mind and go straight thru the seminary. Now my hopes that I will ever see him again are shattered. Emil had constructed a stone boat[116] for hauling the rocks off his barn. I helped him a little.

---

[116] This apparatus was a common contraption of the time. It consisted of a platform fastened to two underlying poles that acted as skids. Heavy loads that were not to be hauled far could be placed on the platform and the entire "stone boat" pulled by a horse or a team of horses.

Thursday June 15

Wea. Cold; windy   Ther. +35 +41 +37

I had a grand "Wash-fest" today, boiling up a mess of towels, pillow casings etc. and working them up on the washboard. Of course, I had the water much too hot for my tender hands, and I actually scalded myself – but I succeeded in cleaning the towels. Work of this nature makes me more determined than ever not to batch later in the ministry. Still, you can never tell.

Our meals are rather scanty these days. Potatoes are getting less everyday; we have no meat, onions or mustard, the three stand-bys of the bachelor. I shall go to Schafer and Watford Saturday, and will fetch a new supply on my return.

Went to bed rather late. We are saving coal oil, because the days are so long now.

Friday June 16

Wea. Very sultry; occasional showers

It was terribly hot today. Emil had to rest his horses quite frequently. He has rigged up a wonderful combination harrow. He busted the draw-bar so often, that even he considered it beyond repair, so he hitched three sections of the harrow to part of the bar, and hooked the remaining two sections behind, so that he is double-harrowing his field in one operation.

Harry Howard came up just when I was beginning to cook dinner. He stayed for the meal, and then drove off in search of a scraper, with which to build a dam in his coulee. I mounted the pinto and rode to Croffs for the mail. To my intense disappointment there were no "2 cent" letters for me, and the big German pipe I had secretly ordered for Emil also has not shown up.

After cooking supper and washing up the dishes I hiked off to bed, being determined to make an early start for Schafer tomorrow.

Saturday June 17

I had expected to leave very early this morning, but I was so ding-busted sleepy that I crawled back into bed, after shutting off the alarm, and slept till Harry Howard came along with a saddle-pony and roused us out.

He wanted Emil to accompany him to Denis Moran's ranch on the "Little" River, in order to help Harry fetch up a green bronc. So Emil ate a hurry-up breakfast, mounted the pinto, and rode away.

I had quite a time, hooking the different parts of the double-driving harness together, for I had not hitched Whitie and Rex together for a long time, and I was tired of riding. I made the thirty mile hike in 4 hours, which is a pretty good figure. Stopped in Schafer for some groceries and drove straight out to my shack. Mr. Reynolds[117] (not Renell) was still occupying the shack, and using half of the barn. I shook hands with him, and after a long talk I put up my horses, went in the shack and cooked myself a cup of coffee. Mr. Reynolds continued cutting grass, but he soon unhitched, and we walked to Fr. Alex's in a shower of rain. She had baked a huge "Johnny-cake"[118] for us.

Sunday June 18

Wea. Sultry & cool

Mr. Reynolds and I overslept ourselves somewhat, and it was almost 11:00 before I got to Schafer. I put Whitie and Rex in the livery barn and hastened to the Community hall. To my intense disappointment nobody made his appearance. There must have been some misunderstanding about the date.

I ate dinner in the Cherryview Hotel and loafed around till 2:00 when I hitched up and drove to Watford City. The Norwegians were using their church, so I waited in the vestry until they were finished. Then I conducted Lutheran services in English and baptized little Daniel McMaster. After services I drove directly back to my shack. Had supper with Mr. Reynolds, and later killed a jack-rabbit with his savage 22 high power.

---

[117] Reynolds was simply squatting in the shack, as it was vacant most of the time. The kitchen was gone, but the stove must have remained with the house. In 1917, Rev. Frey complained to RCJ that Reynolds had stolen his stove without paying for it.

[118] This is a cake of cornbread.

Monday June 19

Wea. Sultry; looks like rain

Got up early and drove over to Frank Alex's where I got my laundry. From there I drove back to my shack, packed my winter clothes in my trunk, and then drove to Schafer, where I purchased some supplies for our shack. At about 10:00 I began the long drive to Emil's place. I took the south-road (the trail used by the Schafer-Berg mail-stage) because I wished to get my mail at Catlin.

When I got to the shack Howard & Emil were just getting ready to hitch up the bronco they got from old Denis Moran, preparatory to a drive to Christanson's "Figure 4" ranch.[119] I accepted their invitation to ride along and rode the pinto as far as Howards. From there I rode along in the wagon. We had the "W" on the bronc, so he did not cause any trouble. Howard paid Denis Moran at the "4" and then we drove back to Howards, stopping at Mrs. Buells. After supper Emil and I rode back to our shack.

Tuesday June 20

Wea. Rain

It was raining this morning and continued to rain all day. I spent the day in the shack, washing up the dishes that Emil had used during my absence, and otherwise tidying up the cabin.

In spite of the weather Harry Howard came over with his bronc and he and Emil hitched up the rack and drove to Johnny Budd's for hay. They had some trouble with the bronco, and had to "flop" him three times because he started to run away. Ed Green & Harold Lillibridge came over with their ponies and stayed for supper.

---

[119] The Figure 4 ranch is a large ranch in the far southeastern part of McKenzie County which stretches into Dunn County and borders the Fort Berthold Indian Reservation. It was recently purchased by the Three Affiliated Tribes.

Wednesday June 21

Wea. More rain

North Dakota does not live up to its reputation of being a "dry" country. It drizzled all day, and I am getting heartily tired of being marooned in the shack all day.

George Taylor got tired of his rainy shack as he came over and spent the day with us. His hut is very leaky, because he has shot it full of holes. He played several games of checkers and nine men Morris with Emil, and we three played several games of "Schmeer". George was out of reading material, having read his few magazines so often,that he claimed he knew the price and specifications of almost every article manufactured. I gave him a huge pile of McClures and Metropolitans, and lent him my set of Morgan Robertson. He left late at night. It was still raining and kept on all night.

Thursday June 22

Wea. Still more rain

The gumbo has softened up considerably and is now almost impassable. Emil and I slept or dozed around till almost noon.   While I was cooking dinner Emil rounded up a team, and drove to Jim Andersen's, where he succeeded in getting 110 lbs of potatoes. From there he drove to Croffs for the mail and some groceries, and then went to Howards for bread. He had bought Croff's complete stock of canned vegetables, consisting of four cans of peas. We had some for supper. Shortly before Emil came home, Jim Catlin drove past the shack and chatted awhile. He promised to come to services next Sunday.

I had a letter from Ban Johnson from Helmville, Mont. He has a place similar to mine, only he is located in the mountains.

Friday June 23

Wea. Rain all day   Ther. +41 +49 +35

It was a raw, cheerless day again. Water is beginning to rush in the coulees, and down the old buffalo trails. Emil and I slept till nearly noon, but even then the day appeared to drag along like a snail. We overhauled the rifles, giving them a thorough cleaning and oiling. Then we went to the west coulee and split out some flat slabs of rock, with which we constructed a sidewalk straight south from the shack door, across the worst gumbo, and also west, towards the barn. This makes a decided improvement. George Taylor came over again and stayed for supper.

Late in evening there began to be some rifts in the clouds, and at 11:30 I noticed that the sky had become perfectly clear. It also got very cold. Emil & I played checkers and mill till later.

Saturday June 24

Wea. Cloudy, but mostly warm

We slept till 9:30. I cooked an early dinner, and then we washed the dishes (they were nearly all soiled). By 11:30 we had the table cleared, and I began to write a sermon on Acts 16, 30-31 for tomorrow. My intention was to see whether I could make and buck a sermon in one day. I found the task much greater than I had expected.

Emil had a grand washing while I wrote the sermon. He washed three face and four dish towels, besides shirts, pillowcases, etc. He loosened up the dirt and grease by pouring borax and coil-oil into the water.

It looked very much like rain during afternoon, but it passed over. Emil drove over to Chester Alton's, where he bought and butchered a 180 lb hog. I was interrupted in bucking my sermon by Geo. Taylor. A horse of his had developed a sudden and uncontrollable flow of blood from a nostril, and nothing seemed to stop it. I was powerless to help, but Emil went over later with every remedy he could think of. I stayed home and went on bucking and teasing the cat.

Sunday June 25

Wea. Chilly, wore my heavy overcoat   Ther. +40 +51 +42

We got up very early (at 5:00), Emil because he had some business to tend to, I because Emil dumped me, and because I still had a great deal of my sermon to buck.

Emil Bellin's "shack", Catlin, N. Dak.
(Pin's home for 10 mo., 1915/1916)

Figure 45: *View of the front door of the cabin showing the new walkway.*

After breakfast Emil hitched up and drove to Croffs for some salt and to Howards for bread. As a proof he did not tarry very long on the road I will mention the fact that he was back at 9:00.

I had spent the time by taking my usual bath in the wash basin, cleaning up the shack and bucking frantically. Emil proceeded to cut up and salt down the pork he had bought yesterday. He took his bath and got ready, while I fried pork steak and cooked dinner. Although we hurried as much as we could, nevertheless we got late to Veeder's schoolhouse. There was not nearly so big a crowd as we had last time, chiefly because of the rotten condition of the roads. There were 22 people present, however.

From the schoolhouse we returned directly to the shack. Here we loaded up some fresh meat for Mrs. Howard, and then drove down to the "breaks". Mrs. Emmerson had invited us to a chicken dinner several weeks ago, and we certainly did not forget the date. I almost feel ashamed of how I hogged down the food (ate 2 hunks of lemon pie). We drove home past Jack William's old ranch houses. Mrs. Howard also was at Emmerson's.

Monday June 26

Wea. Very hot, comparatively   Ther. +49 +87 +50

I felt extremely queer all day; am afraid I upset my "tummie" terribly yesterday. Still, I'd do it again, because the meal was well worth all the pain it may cause.

Emil disced his flax stubble this afternoon. He expects to seed oats on it tomorrow morning, and to get through with his farm work by July 4th.

I had the "pleasant" task of dishwashing again. Ban Johnson wrote that Mr. Kanth, my successor, might be here by the middle of August. In that case I will have to wash dishes for only about 2 months more. Cheer up!

I rode the pinto to Croffs today. Got my check from the Mission Board for May. Mailed letters to Ban and Rev. Hilgendorf. Bought all the salt that Croff had in stock.

Tues June 27

Wea. Extremely hot   Ther. +49 +92 +87

This was an extremely hot day, at least it seemed so, compared with the cold & rainy days that have preceded it. It was a miserable day for me, because I felt extremely sick. Most likely I over ate myself last Sunday, or else the fresh meat is bothering me. We have had nothing but salt pork for a long time, and I have heard that a sudden change to fresh meat is liable to derange one's digestive system.

I had made arrangements with Mrs. Howard to give her catechetical instructions today, so I rode over shortly after dinner. The ride almost proved to be a last straw for my poor "tummie" and I was downright ill when I landed at Howards. However, I managed to keep my head up, and discussed the "Office of the Keys" and other religious topics with Mrs. Howard for several hours. I fixed up the pigpen for her shortly before supper. At supper I disregarded the warnings and protests of my stomach and ate two hunks of lemon pie. On the way home I felt so bad, that I had to get off and walk every little while. However, I am not intending to die yet.

Primary Election Day
Wednesday June 28

Wea. Rain in morning

Emil seeded another little patch of oats yesterday, and did some plowing on the remainder of his stubble ground. Of course, he does not expect to harvest a crop from this late sowing, he merely wishes to cut the oats for hay purposes. He expected to finish up today, but a little after five A.M., while we were eating breakfast, it began to rain, and it rained hard nearly all morning. I was still feeling rotten, so I crawled into my cot and slept till 11:30. Emil spread some coats and blanket on the floor and also slept.

It being out of the question to work in the field, Emil and I hitched up after dinner and drove to Croff's schoolhouse, in order to cast our votes. The assessor had failed to call on me, so I had to swear in my vote to Mr. Von Eshen.[120] I registered as a Republican and voted the ticket endorsed by the Farmer's Non Partisan League which is trying to buck the big politicians out of business. They are boosting Lynn J. Frazier for governor.

From the schoolhouse we drove to Croffs for the mail and some groceries. I had two letters, one from Joe Kanth, and one from Art Behn. Read the papers after supper and went to bed at 11:30.

Thursday June 29

Wea. Gloomy, very heavy rain & storm in eve.

Narrow Escape

We got up at 4:00 this morning, for Emil expected to take a load of grain to Watford, and he wished to make the trip in one day. I had breakfast ready very early, and he left shortly after 5:00.

---

[120] The homestead claim of this gentleman was located northwest of Emil's cabin. It was later acquired by Dennis George.

I still felt sick, but the nauseating spells had ceased, so instead of crawling back into the cot I stayed up and wrote two letters, one to Mr. Kanth, and one to mother. Judging from her last letter, she must be in Wisner now, with Jack & Ruthie.[121]

I tried to make potato salad for dinner, but gave it up in despair, and had french fried potatoes instead. Spent the afternoon with straightening out my cash account, and in reading. Later on I had my second close shave with death. The first narrow escape happened Feb. 15th, when I nearly got killed in a runaway. Today's accident was much worse. I had watered the pinto at Clark's spring, and as usual I rode her without saddle or bridle, merely had a rope around her neck. On the way home I let her run, and could not check her when I approached the steep east coulee. The pinto has the reputation to be the fastest horse in this part of the county, and she was galloping as fast as she could possibly go. Where she struck the coulie the walls are rocky and nearly perpendicular, and we both rolled over and over till we struck the bottom. I must have struck a rock somewhere, for when I regained consciousness, my left eye and cheek were covered with blood from a nasty little cut in the scalp. Also tore a gash in my right check near the mouth. Had a severe pain in my left shoulder but I soon satisfied myself that my arm was neither broken or dislocated; must have over strained some tendons. I consider my escape a miracle, for when I look at the scene of my mishap, I cannot conceive how I escaped without a broken bone, and with only bad cuts. The pinto was unhurt; there was an appalling storm in eve.

Friday June 30

The heaviest thundershower of this year broke loose last night. There was not such an enormous amount of rain, but the thunder etc. was terrible. A bolt of lightning struck a tree in the coulie, just south of the shack. The crash nearly stunned me.

---

[121] RCJ's mother would live for a few months with one of her older children, then move to the home of another. Her husband (RCJ's father), Rev. Konrad Jahn, had dementia and was in an institution in Norfolk, Nebraska. Her son Jack was a Lutheran minister living in Wisner, Nebraska at this time.

Felt queer all day, from yesterday's accident. My neck feels very stiff, and I have a dull headache. Spent the morning in writing letters to Miss Brooks and Helen. At about 2:45 I caught the pinto and rode her to Croffs, where I mailed my letters. Had a letter from ma; she seemed very excited about Paul, and also was very anxious to get news from me. I had just mailed her a letter to Jack's address at Wisner. Ma wrote that she would take Erich along, Jack having promised to pay his trip.

"Paulie,"[122] the notorious clerk at Croffs, seemed very excited about my narrow escape. My face was scratched up badly, so it was impossible to try and conceal things from him. I am in the habit of letting out every inch of speed when the pinto approaches or leaves the store, and he had always predicted that I would come to grief.

Emil hauled out some wire for Croff and got to the shack at about 5 o'clock. He had fetched out 19 prints of pictures that I had snapped; most of them turned out pretty good. I am going to have a number of prints made of those pictures that please me most, and will send them around to relatives. Emil also had bought some new oil cloth for our table.

---

[122] This was Paulie Greutzner. W.B. Croff had married a Greutzner, and Paulie was related to her, though not his son.

Catlin, N. D.
Birdseye view of the complete city.

Figure 46: *Entrance to Croff's store as RCJ and Emil would have seen it in 1916.*

Bird's eye view of the Business District
Catlin, N. Dak.

Figure 46a: *Croff's store*

CHAPTER 14

FOURTH OF JULY RODEO AT WATFORD CITY

Saturday July 1

Wea. Hot & sultry

According to my schedule I am to preach at Table Butte and the Ft. Berthold Reservation tomorrow. Emil used Rex & Whitie on the plow this morning, till about 10:00 o'clock, when he got finished. The north field is practically all gumbo, and the recent rain has softened to such an extent that drilling grain with a double disc seeder is out of the question right now. So Emil has consented to let me use both Rex & Whitie on my trip, upon the condition that I return by Monday afternoon.

I left for Berg at about 3:00 o'clock. It was still very warm, and the road was rather muddy, nevertheless I made the 25 mile trip to Ole Jore's in a little over 2 hours. At Berg I stopped for the mail for the Jore's and also for some government postals. I sent a notice to the Watford City Guide, announcing services for July 9th.

Tomorrow's services for Table Butte are supposed to be conducted at Clarence Jore's. I have never been there, however, and so I accepted Ole Jore's invitation to spend the night with him instead of trying to find Clarence's. I studied over my sermon, and discussed a queer pamphlet on religion, which someone had sent Ole.

Sunday July 2

Wea. Clear and pleasant

I did not get up so very early. After a lesiurely breakfast I packed up my things, hitched up to the wagon and drove to Clarence Jore's. I took Lester along to show me the road. Although it was after 10:00 when I got to Clarence's, nevertheless, nobody had showed up, and I could not begin services till almost 12:00. There was a nice crowd present.

It is usual for the family, which happens to lend its house for services, to furnish all those present with a good dinner and supper.[123] I lunched on some excellent potato salad, cold ham, and several different kinds of cake. Had my first taste of wild strawberries. Toward 2:00 o'clock I announced my intention of leaving, so two of Keough's punchers ran out and hitched up for me. I picked my way through Clarence's coulee without much difficulty, swung past the east wall of the gloomy Table Butte, and cut across prairie till Larson's. From there I drove directly to the schoolhouse, first having a long talk with "Bobby" Jannssen. At school I met Mr. & Mrs. Renkin Schnepps Fadden, and Mr. & Mrs. Levi Schoonover. I preached in English and German, and then drove down to Harm's where I expected to spend the night. Mrs. Harms was sick again. Helped Mr. Harms[124] to cook supper.

---

[123] RCJ may not have appreciated the effort it took to produce these dinners. Feeding the pastor was a major event for the hostess. According to author Carrie Young (*Nothing to Do but Stay*, Iowa Press, 1991, p. 45), "For the minister, of course, every matron threw out all of her cooking stops. By the time she had a Sunday meal on the table for him, this was as fancy as she was going to get. She had broken out her finest linen tablecloth and napkins, starched within an inch of their lives, and the table was laden from end to end with all the delicacies her garden, her pantry, and her considerable expertise could produce. It held her best preserves, mashed potatoes and gravy, two kinds of meat (*always* two kinds of meat), vegetables, homemade bread, not to mention a pie cooling in the kitchen. But when the time actually came when she would usher the minister in from the parlor and ask him to sit up to the table, she would pull out his chair, wring her hands, and say apologetically, 'Now you will have to try and make a meal out of this, Reverend!'"

[124] Relatives of this Harms family continue to live in McKenzie County.

Monday July 3

Wea. Very cloudy–rainy looking

There is going to be a big celebration of our Independence day at Sanish, in the Reservation across the river. Guenther and Minnie Harms were expecting to go, so they got up at 3:30 this morning, and left before 5:00. I got up with them, and was ready to leave at the same time. However, it took me just 1-1/2 hrs to take my leave of Mrs. Harms. She is a great talker, and I considered it my duty to answer her numberless religious questions, and offer her all the consolation in my power. Next Bobby Janssen came rushing out of his house, while I was attempting to sneak past, and held me up for nearly another hour. Then I drove six miles, past the Table and Chimney Buttes, to Ole Jore's. Here I had to talk some more; then I stopped at Berg for some new kettles and groceries, so that I did not reach our shack till noon.[125] I had figured on getting there about 9:00. – Emil was not home, and did not return till about 1:00, having fetched a load of wood from the "Breaks". He and I washed the dishes and cooked a late dinner. Then Emil hitched up to the drill and finished seeding his oats. Even he admits, that it is rather late in the season for seeding grain, but at least he managed to get through before July 4th. We are expecting to celebrate in Watford City on the 4th & 5th, and we wish to make an early start. For this reason we got everything ready tonight. I also packed up some films, and addressed the negatives to Sears Roebuck, for the purpose of having some prints made.

Tuesday July 4

Wea. Hot & windy

The 4th "dawned auspiciously", but it was very windy, and the dust bothered quite a lot. Emil & I got up before 4:00 AM, and by 4:30 we were on the road to Watford City. We took the trail that leads past "Stone Johnny", thus cutting off several miles. By 8:30 we were in Watford. It was quite chilly so early in the morning, and I wore my heavy sheep skin all the way to town. We put our horses up in a livery barn, having been so fortunate as to secure barn room.

---

[125] Clarence and Ole Jore used to haul freight from White Earth across the Missouri River to supply the Berg store. In summer they would use the ferry, and in winter they went across the ice. Their wives would sometimes take their babies and go to the top of Table Butte to watch for their arrival. (Source: Don Jore).

At about 10:30 we saw Harry Howard & family driving into town, so we went along to help them. Harry had brought a big tarpaulin and some blankets along, and we rigged up a comfortable tent just south of town. We cooked our meals there and made it our general headquarters. Later on Lloyd Buell and the Fins joined us.

During the morning and the afternoon there was little excitement in town. The band had about four pieces in their repertoire, and these they played over and over. There was a terribly stale ball game in the afternoon between Watford and Banks. After the ball game there was a very interesting bronco bucking contest. A puncher by the name of Fish was thrown badly, the others rode well. I was especially struck by the riding of Oscar Burr, a full blooded Indian. Was introduced to him in evening, and had a long talk.

Wednesday July 5

Wea. Outrageously hot. Rain in eve.   Ther. +40 +93 +82

This was an extremely hot day; there was absolutely no breeze, and the heat was almost unbearable. We men slept in the neighborhood of the camp last night. I managed to secure a blanket and my sheepskin, and had a fairly comfortable bed. After a late breakfast I hung around town, talking with Charley Carr, Joe Stevenson, Oscar Burr and other punchers.[126] Burr was dissatisfied, and we had a hard time to persuade him to enter the riding contest again, he claiming that the people would discriminate against him, because he was an Indian. I took Mrs. Howard to the ball-game, where we nearly perspired to death, and consumed untold quantities of lemonade.

North Dakota is a dry state, but beer was very plentiful in town today. The city furnished free beer to the men that applied for it in the rear of a black-smith shop; one of the marshalls acting as barkeep! Pretty rich!

Late in the afternoon there was a bareback race, and a "Saddle-and-go" race. This latter race was won by Joe Stevenson, who simply drew the cinch thru

---

[126] These three "cowpunchers" are nearly legend in McKenzie County. They have spawned numerous descendents who have been accomplished horsemen and "bronc" riders, many of whom continue to reside in McKenzie County. Charley Carr is correctly identified as Charley Kerr; he homesteaded and had a cattle and farming operation north of "Stone Johnny."

the ring, held the end of it in his hand and galloped off. Then there was another bronco busting contest. Oscar Burr's horse stampeded and cut thru between two houses. He had to throw himself from the bronc in order to avoid tearing his head off on a clothesline. The judges were forced to award him first prize. Emil & I drove over to my shack in the evening.

Figure 47: *Oscar Burr prepares to mount a bronco, July 4, 1916.*

Figure 48: *Joe Stevenson showing his prize-winning skills, July 4, 1916.*

Figure 49: *Ed Green riding on July Fourth.*

Figure 50: *Charles Carr (actually Kerr), a legend in McKenzie County.*

Figure 51: *Unidentified rider being helped off his horse in the 1916 event. Note cars being used as barriers.*

Figure 52: *A 1915 photo of unidentified riders, possibly showing George Taylor (left) and Ed Green.*

Figure 53: *Neal Stevenson thrills the crowd.*

Figure 54: *Oscar Burr*

Thursday July 6

Wea. Warm   Ther. +43 +96 +92

It was even hotter today than yesterday. After the terrible cold of last winter, this extremely high temperature comes as a distinct surprise to me.

It rained very hard last night. While closing the windows I got drenched to the skin. This morning the high wind had dried things off considerably, however, so that we did not encounter any mud.

Mr. Reynolds, who is still living at my shack, cooked a late breakfast for us, and then we drove to Schafer. Howards were already there. Emil went into Stand's land office and signed a sworn statement to the effect that Mrs. Howard had fulfilled all the conditions necessary to proving up on her homestead.[127] Then we drove off to our shack, stopping over at Croffs for our mail. To my intense surprise there was no mail for me.

Our shack was in good order. The dogs and cats, chickens, horses & cows were still alive and happy. It was just terribly hot and sultry, and I am looking for rain. At 12:00 o'clock the thermometer inside the shack still registered 90⁰.

Emil lit a smudge to smoke out the mosquitoes, and bunked outside till midnight. I undressed down to my BVD's and read. Got my new suit from M. Born & Co. of Chicago yesterday, and am well pleased with it.

Friday July 7

Wea. Sultry & hot   Ther. +42 +87 +39

Summer seems to have made a permanent entrance in McKenzie Co. It has been surprisingly warm for the past week, and indications are, that the hot wave will last for some time to come.

---

[127] The witnesses stated that Delia Green Howard had fulfilled the residence and cultivation requirements to receive title to her land. Normally, this was a five-year period. Records indicate that 20 percent of McKenzie County homesteads were granted to single women. Source: C.E. Lindgren, *Land in Her Own Name: Women as Homesteaders in North Dakota* (University of Oklahoma Press 1996, p. 52).

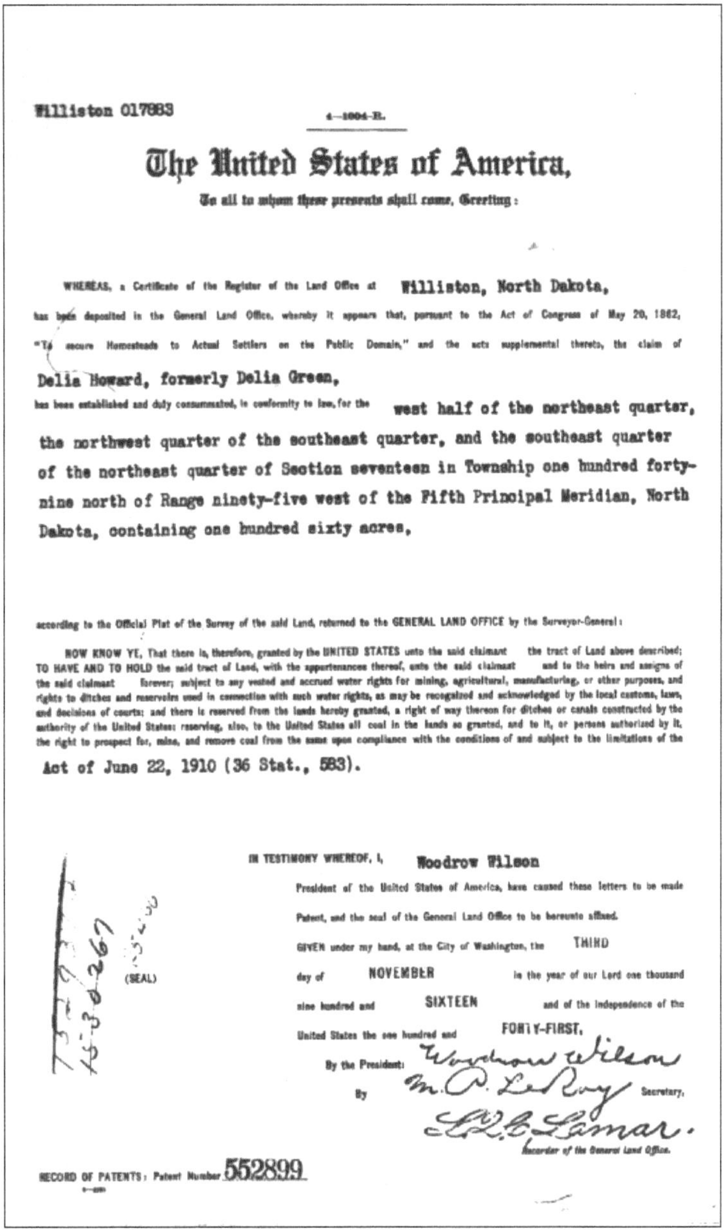

Williston 017883

4—1004-R.

The United States of America,

To all to whom these presents shall come, Greeting:

WHEREAS, a Certificate of the Register of the Land Office at Williston, North Dakota, has been deposited in the General Land Office, whereby it appears that, pursuant to the Act of Congress of May 20, 1862, "To secure Homesteads to Actual Settlers on the Public Domain," and the acts supplemental thereto, the claim of Delia Howard, formerly Delia Green, has been established and duly consummated, in conformity to law, for the west half of the northeast quarter, the northwest quarter of the southeast quarter, and the southeast quarter of the northeast quarter of Section seventeen in Township one hundred forty-nine north of Range ninety-five west of the Fifth Principal Meridian, North Dakota, containing one hundred sixty acres,

according to the Official Plat of the Survey of the said Land, returned to the GENERAL LAND OFFICE by the Surveyor-General:

NOW KNOW YE, That there is, therefore, granted by the UNITED STATES unto the said claimant the tract of Land above described; TO HAVE AND TO HOLD the said tract of Land, with the appurtenances thereof, unto the said claimant and to the heirs and assigns of the said claimant forever; subject to any vested and accrued water rights for mining, agricultural, manufacturing, or other purposes, and rights to ditches and reservoirs used in connection with such water rights, as may be recognized and acknowledged by the local customs, laws, and decisions of courts; and there is reserved from the lands hereby granted, a right of way thereon for ditches or canals constructed by the authority of the United States; reserving, also, to the United States all coal in the lands so granted, and to it, or persons authorized by it, the right to prospect for, mine, and remove coal from the same upon compliance with the conditions of and subject to the limitations of the Act of June 22, 1910 (36 Stat., 583).

IN TESTIMONY WHEREOF, I, Woodrow Wilson President of the United States of America, have caused these letters to be made Patent, and the seal of the General Land Office to be hereunto affixed.

(SEAL)

GIVEN under my hand, at the City of Washington, the THIRD day of NOVEMBER in the year of our Lord one thousand nine hundred and SIXTEEN and of the Independence of the United States the one hundred and FORTY-FIRST.

By the President: Woodrow Wilson

By M. P. LeRoy Secretary,

L. Q. C. Lamar.
Recorder of the General Land Office.

RECORD OF PATENTS: Patent Number 552899

Figure 55: *Delia Howard's grant of homestead*.

We dropped asleep so late last night, that we slept rather long this morning. I cooked dinner and then induced Emil to take several pictures of myself et familie, said family consisting of the puppies & cats.

Since I expect to drive to Schafer and Watford tomorrow, I did not ride to Croffs for the mail. The mail comes three times a week, on Mondays, Wednesdays & Fridays. It is hauled by stage from Sanish,[128] ferried across the big Mo. River, taken to Berg, and from there to Catlin.

I wrote some letters in the evening but otherwise I did not prepare for tomorrow's trip. I can get to Watford in about 4 hours, provided that it is not too hot. I expect to spend the night at my shack 2 miles south of Schafer.

Saturday July 8

Wea. Very warm

I took a bath this morning and had so many other things to tend to that it was nearly 2:00 o'clock before I got ready to leave. Emil had caught Whitie and Rex for me.

The trip along the mail road was uninteresting, as usual. But just east of the Schafer Butte I met Jack Williams. He had a huge load of groceries for his ranch, and also 2 barrels of beer for the Keough boys. We stopped to rest our teams and with the aid of my wrench and a chunk of petrified wood we opened one of the barrels and soused several bottles. The beer was warm, but sipped fine.

After completing my business in Watford, I drove over to my shack. Mr. Reynolds is still living there, and I used his stove to cook myself a good supper.

---

[128] The town of Sanish met its demise with the flooding of the Missouri River by the Garrison Dam. It was located west of present day New Town, N.D.

Figure 56:
*Laundry time
at Emil's
shack.*

View of Yin's private laundry plant.

Figure 57: *RCJ and Misery with her pups.*

Sunday July 9th

Wea. Very hot

Mr. Reynolds had to make a trip into the "Breaks", and left early this morning. I wrote a letter to Deke, and then went down to the Schafer community Hall for services. Met young Cy Ericson there; Miss Warley also attended. Took dinner at the Cherryview Hotel, and then went up to Ericson's office in the courthouse where he showed me his unique collection of pictures, mostly scenes of Hamline U.

Went to the Scand. Luth. Ch. of Watford in the afternoon. Had a good crowd there. Mr. Dietrich, the prop. of the Watford pool hall, attended for the first time. Gave Mrs. McMaster her certificate of baptism.

Mr. Reynolds had informed me last night that the Ladies' Aid Society of Schafer had sold my shack to lawyer C. C. Converse. This made it necessary to consider the removal of our goods, and we decided upon the deserted shack near the well.[129] So I made up my mind to stay tomorrow, and help Mr. Reynolds move.

Figure 58: *McKenzie County Courthouse at Schafer. The jail is the stone structure at right.*

Monday July 10th

Wea. Very hot

We got up very early, and after a hearty breakfast I carried a roll of roofing and some tools down to the shack, and proceeded to repair it as well as possible. We first had to prop up the center of the roof by fastening a 2 x 4 across the shack under the eaves, and then running a little prop under the roof to the 2 x 4. Then we cleaned out the dirt and refuse of several years, with shovels and a broom. The door of the shack is entirely gone, and one of the windows is also missing.

At noon Mr. Reynolds and I decided not to remove our belongings, until Converse has served us a formal notice. Since I do not expect to return before August, I do not feel right about the fate of my goods.

---

[129] This shack, located down the steep hill from Frey's house, was apparently built by a homesteader named Coar.

I left for Catlin towards evening, and arrived at the cabin just before dark.

Tuesday July 11th

Wea. Extremely hot   Ther. +42 +114 +51

At noon today the therm. showed 114° in the sun, and 96° in the shack. This is plenty warm to suit me, and I would not mind a cooling breeze.

Had the misfortune to lose my fountain pen somewhere yesterday. I have grown so attached and accustomed to it, that I feel the loss of the pen very keenly. In addition, I am not in the position to stand a loss of $4.50 without feeling it badly. Am having quite a time with this old stub-pointed steel pen.

Emil rounded up a one-horse cultivator somewhere, and we went out to scratch the potato field. I led "Nance" up and down the rows, while Emil guided the cultivator. The rows were very crooked and only a few inches apart in places. According to the N. D. style, Emil left the cultivator at the end of the last row, without cleaning the shovels, and even leaving them in the ground.

Ole Skaar visited us in the eve., and told Emil to work off his poll-tax[130] on the road tomorrow.

Wednesday, July 12th

Wea. Warm

Emil had intended to take a load of grain to Watford City this morning, and in order to get to town before the heat of the day he wanted to leave at about 2:00 A.M. He has an ingenious system of being able to get up at the proper time, by eating an enormous amount of sweets before he goes to bed. Then he will toss and groan around all night without being able to sleep, and thus be glad to get out of bed early. He had just finished his midnight lunch when Ole Skaar came, and it was too late then to undo his work, so he proceeded to spoil my sleep for me too. Shortly after one o'clock A.M. he ran across a mouth-organ, and from that moment sleeping was out of the question for me.

---

[130] A poll tax is a tax of a uniform, fixed amount per individual (as opposed to a percentage of income).

At intervals, when my remarks became too personal, he would sing a few bars of "My Brudda Sylvest", a song that would drive a Jersey cow wild.

At 3:00 A.M. I finally got up. Emil went outside and chopped a lot of wood by lantern light, until it got light enough so that he could see. I cooked breakfast and then Emil left for Skaars, while I wrote letters till noon. Then I rounded up "Mabel" and hitched her to Emil's buggy. Drove to Croffs, where I mailed the notices to the people that we would have services Sunday. From there I drove to Howards, to give Mrs. H– instructions in the Catechism. Took through "Confession". Harry is feeling bad. Heat prostration.

Thursday July 13

Wea. Very warm during day

Having finished working off his poll tax yesterday, Emil got ready last night and left for Watford City this morning. He and I got up at 2:00 A.M., and while he fed and harnessed the team, I cooked up breakfast.

After Emil had left, my first impulse was to crawl back to bed. I had such a nice fire. However, the dishes were nearly all soiled so that I made up my mind to attend to them. By the time I was finished, it was broad daylight, and I no longer felt sleepy, so I stayed up.

During the day I did some reading, and also looked for a suitable sermon text for Sunday. I finally decided upon Luke 12, 16-21 (The parable of the rich man) and began to dope out a disposition. Suddenly "Misery" began to bark and upon looking out of the window, I saw the Howard family approaching. Luckily I had the cabin clean and in order, so that I did not have to utter any apologies when Mrs. Howard entered.

It seems that Harry H. was still feeling ill, and Mrs. Howard wanted me to catch Rex & Whitie and drive to Watford City to see a physician. I did not show any distaste at the prospect of such a long trip, but caught the horses and left the place shortly after 6:00 P.M. We took the north trail, and met Emil just east of Schafer at 8:00. Got to town after dark.

Friday July 14

Wea. Hot, severe storm in eve.

(Partial eclipse of moon tonight about 8:20)

Immediately upon our arrival in Watford City, Harry set out to hunt up the doctor, while I put up my team in the best livery barn and secured a room for us two in the imposing Watford Hotel. Bummed around town a bit, and then returned to the hotel. Hit the hay at 11:30.

The morning of the 14th broke clear and hot. Since Harry had another appointment with Dr. Johnson[131] this morning, we decided to remain in town until evening, when the temperature would cool off a bit. I met Ed Green, Chester Alton and Bill Lillibridge during the afternoon. They had just returned from a ride to Canada, in search of a homestead, having been gone about three weeks. I talked with them for a while, telling them all the news and then attended the sale of Mennenga & Chase, but did not buy anything.

At 6:15 P.M Harry and I left town. A storm was threatening in the west, but we struck out, confident that the rain would not overtake us. Near Parrishes,[132] about halfway to Catlin, a few drops of rain struck us, however and from there on I kept my sturdy broncs at a sharp trot, uphill and downhill without a stop. We managed to stay ahead of the storm until we had passed Croffs, when some preliminary puffs of wind struck us, and soon it was raining in torrents. We wrapped up in our sheep skins, missed the trail several times, but finally landed at Howards' at 11:00.

Saturday July 15

Wea. Hot

It rained so hard after we arrived at Howards, that I gladly accepted Mrs. Howard's invitation to spend the night there. I unhitched the horses in the glaring light of the lightning flashes, and managed to grope my way into the

---

[131] Dr. P.O.C. Johnson started his medical practice in Watford City on July 28, 1915 and practiced medicine in McKenzie County for the next 46 years. He was an important member of the community, treated thousands of persons who were ill, and delivered over 3,000 babies. His grandson operates a family-owned bank in Watford City.

[132] A descendent of the Parish family continues to reside in this same vicinity today.

dug-out barn, where the water had already accumulated in big pools thru the leaky roof. I found some hay for the horses and then returned to the house.

After eating a dainty midnight luncheon I talked for a while with Mrs. Howard, and then crawled between the sheets of a snow-white little bed, and slept wonderfully. How I appreciate the atmosphere of cleanliness which reigns in a "woman's house". No bacheloring for me, if I can help it.

My unfinished, yes unbegun sermon worried me a great deal, and so I crawled out of bed at 5:00 A.M, fed and harnessed my team and did the chores for Mrs. Howard, while she cooked breakfast. I got to the cabin at 8:00, and surprised Emil in bed, of course. Geo. Taylor was occupying my bed. He had been caught in the storm, and had spent the night with Emil.

Soon after Geo. left, I wrote out my sermon, with the aid of a sermon of Rev. Buchheimer's which I happened to discover. I was interrupted a great deal by visitors and the terrible heat, so that I succeeded in bucking only the first part of my sermon, and had to leave the remainder for tomorrow morning. Emil was to Lillibridges today for Howard's.

Sunday July 16

Wea. Heavy showers

I got up at 5:00 A. M., dressed and walked up and down outside, leaving Emil sleeping peacefully. I succeeded in learning the remainder of my sermon, but the second part, especially the beginning of it, were very hard to memorize.

While I was studying it began to rain. Since the whole sky was overcast and the rain was running down in a steady drizzle, I fondly imagined that it would prove to be an all day rain, so I went to the shack and crawled back to bed. When I awoke it was 10:00 and the sun was shining brightly. So I jumped up and woke Emil, and we had to hustle to get a square meal, and to wash and dress and get out to Veeder's schoolhouse by 2:00 P.M.

I'd like to pass over my preaching, not that I got stuck, but I came close to it 4 times, and my efforts to bridge over the gaps in my memory resulted in some bad "Mulligan". However, nobody seemed to notice, and I was not requested to stop.

Just after services it rained again, Emil and I got soaked, but the shower hardly lasted for an hour. Later the sun came out, and the remainder of the day was nice.

I wrote a long letter to mother in the evening and started to write one to Art Behn, but was too lazy to finish it.

Monday July 17th

Wea. Rain in the evening

Another series of showers are visiting us at present. It rained late tonight, and there was a heavy fog or light drizzle during the greater part of the day.

We slept very long this morning. After cooking dinner Emil and I each roped a horse. I rode Mabel to Croff's, while Emil took Howard's black mare home and stayed there all afternoon.

There were no letters for me at Croff's although I am eagerly waiting for news from some of the "gang". "Daddy" Roettger has owed me a letter for several months. Billy Dietze is also due to write for many weeks, and Ban Johnson and Bill Medo also ought to write. I have no idea of what they are doing this summer, except that Ban is vicaring in Montana. I wonder how he is enjoying himself. Vicaring is not such a big joke when you have to make and buck a sermon in an afternoon.

Just about every dish in the house is soiled, and I am hoping that I can induce Emil to help me in washing them. We are washing them now as needed.

There was a severe storm in the evening. A big porcelain bowl, out of which we had fed the pups, skidded across the grass till it hit a rock, where it busted.

Tuesday July 18th

Wea. Very light rainfall, otherwise pleasant

Harry Howard pulled us out of bed at 8:00 A.M. as he has done often before. He had gone to Croff's already this morning and was quite indignant at our laziness, as he styled it. I explained to him that we were merely taking our beauty nap.

Emil and I made up our mind to catch the pinto to-day, and we succeeded, but not until we had run down two other ponies. After vainly trying to catch her, we finally opened the pasture gate and galloped around until we got all the horses chased into the barn. The pinto followed and Emil quickly threw a rope around her head and tied her up. She was mighty sore about it.

I had arranged to give Mrs. Howard instructions to-day, so I galloped after Harry and caught him near "Winie" Wherle's, where I climbed into his buggy and drove the rest of the way. I lectured on the first part of the Sacrament of the Altar, and expect to finish up in a few more lessons.[133] Mrs. Emmerson was there.

In order to amuse the little Howard girls, I gave a fancy bucking exhibition before I rode home. On the way home, the pinto bucked me off in Howard's coulee, and I had to walk all the way home. I caught her near the shack, because her bridle reins had caught over a post as she was running along the pasture fence. The fall did not hurt me in the least this time.

Wednesday July 19th

Wea. Warm

"Dutch Henry" (family name unknown) of the "Lazy S" ranch came over late last night and invited me to witness some bronco breaking, and to conduct services for the boys. Emil could not come along, because he is range-riding for the <C>bunch.[134]

"Dutch" and I left early this morning and arrived at the "Lazy S" shortly after dinner. "No War", the chink cook, prepared an excellent dinner for us, and grinned his blandest and most pleasant grin when I praised his cooking. He informed me that he would have to poison "Chuckie" Carr some day, because Chuckie had soaked one of No War's flannel shirts in croton oil, which caused an almost unendurable itching to the poor chinaman.

---

[133] RCJ was instructing her on Luther's *Small Catechism*, in preparation for her becoming an adult member of the church. This would occur on September 6, 1916.

[134] It was common among homesteaders who were struggling to get their claims proved up and keep from starving to work part-time for one of the big ranch outfits for extra cash when they could and when the big outfits were in need of extra help.

I had paid only one flying visit to the "Lazy S" before, so I rode around the corrals and shelters with "Dutch", waiting for the punchers to drive in the broncos. Really they were not intending to "break" these animals, they merely wanted to cut hay with them. Since none of these animals had never even seen a harness, I expect some of the interesting sights tomorrow. The boys came up with about 40 head of horses at dusk, whooping and yelling at No War to hurry up with supper.

Thursday July 20th

Wea. Cloudy, but pleasant

The fun began early in the morning. Several cowboys would rope two broncs, and put hackamoors on them, after which they were tied to a stout post, and allowed to jerk around for a few minutes. They were then pronounced halter broke. After this they were chased into a tight fitting chute, where one puncher dropped a heavy bar in front and behind them so they could not move. Then an extra heavy harness was thrown on and buckled very tightly. After this some punchers crowded and pushed and led the two broncs to one of the mowers. There they were held by some snubbers, while several men tied their heads and breechings together with rawhide ropes. In this way broncs could not jump apart and tear away from the machine. Then the lines were placed in the hands of a hardy puncher, the mower was set in gear, the snubbers released the broncs, and away they went at a terrible pace. Of course, it was out of the question for the driver to guide them in the beginning, and the most curious streaks were cut across the prairie. But the broncs would cool down after some time and cut round and round a definite piece.

Friday July 21st

Wea. Slight drizzle in morning

I had services last night in the Lazy S bunkhouse. Some of the "-W" and "-Y_ boys had come over, and after the meeting we had a splendid time swapping yarns and roasting "Chuckie" who had swallowed some of the kerosene which "No War" had put into coffee to get even for the "croton" oil episode. "Chuckie" took the jibes good-naturedly.

The mowing went on to-day, and will for sometime. As fast as a team played out, another one was substituted. The grass-fed broncs can gallop for incredible distances, but they can't stand heavy work very long. They dissipate their energy too much when first hitched up, and also because they lack the "bottom" of oats- fed horses.

I remained on the Lazy S till noon, when I managed to talk No War into giving me an early meal, so I could get home before dark. On the way back I stopped at Croff's for the mail. Had a dandy letter from Bill Medo, who is home in California now. Also my check for June from the Mission board, and a postal from Paul.[135] The kid wants to come to North Dakota, provided he can find work. I am afraid I will have to talk him out of it, although I certainly would like to have him out here. There is very little demand for farm laborers in this part of N.D. The ranches have plenty of men.

Saturday July 22nd

Wea. Warm and sunny

It was not really warm to-day; it was actually hot, so hot in fact that I did not leave for Table Butte till late in the afternoon.

I stopped at the Berg P.O for the Table Butte mail, and talked with Ole Jore for a while at the latter's house. Ole had just returned from a two-weeks vacation to relatives in Canada, having made the trip in his brother John's car (Ford, of course). He reported an interesting journey.

From Ole Jore's I drove to Eltins, where I had announced services. Although Eltins are very friendly and obliging, yet my reception so was queer, that I hardly knew what to do. Mr. Eltin glanced up from his paper when I drove on the place, but he did not acknowledge my greeting, nor did he help unhitch my team. He finally showed up while I was watering the horses and showed me where to put them in the barn.

Eltin's have the tiniest house I ever saw; it is about as large as an ordinary pantry. Their bed folds up against the wall, mattress and all, and is kept in place by a rope and hid by a curtain. I used a small steel cot and slept so close

---

[135] RCJ's younger brother Paul Jahn.

to my hostess that I could have placed my hand on her easily. There was no curtain twixt me and them. Such a thing would cause no end of gossip at home, but arouses no attention here.

Sunday July 23rd

Wea. Sultry

It looked a great deal like rain last night. There was a heavy thunderhead in the east and lightning was flashing continuously when I went to sleep. However, not a drop of rain fell.

The people made their appearance so very late, that I could not begin my services till after 12:00, while I had announced the meeting for 10:00 A.M. Nobody is ever in a hurry in McKenzie Co.

Buck's are having some visitors now. I was introduced to them before services. They were Mrs. Carrie Breed and Mrs. Leona Eisert, both from Minneapolis, and very charming ladies. I preached on Rom. 1, 16. The crowd was so large, and the house so small that a great many people had to stay outside. This made preaching rather difficult.

Dinner was served in the usual way. Everybody secured a plate, cup and cutlery and helped himself to whatever he pleased. I followed my usual custom of eating an enormous quantity of cake.

Immediately after eating I hooked up and drove to the Res. Corner Schoolhouse. Bobby Janssen asked me to stay and I could not refuse, although I would rather have gone to Draegerts. Mrs. Levi Schoonever (nee Hilda Draegert), had her baby, little Winnifred Louise, baptized. Mr. Schoonever gave me a five-dollar bill. I gratefully tucked it into my pocket, but he asked me for four dollars change, which dampened my enthusiasm considerably.

Monday July 24th

Wea. Drizzle in morning

Mrs. Harms is still very ill. Guenther came rushing over at about 1:30 A.M. this morning and pulled me out of bed to see his mother. While I was talking with her, the Janssen boys hitched up my team, and since everybody was afraid to drive the broncs, especially at night, I took the reins myself and drove to Charleston[136] for a doctor. It was very dark, but I managed to get there and back in a hurry. The doctor attended to Mrs. Harms, and she was pronounced out of danger.

It was now 7:00 A.M. I returned to Janssen's where I ate a good breakfast, and then struck out for home. I had hardly started when a cold drizzle, coupled with a chilly east wind set in. Although we are in the middle of summer, I put on my sheepskin, without which I never travel, and kept it on till I got to my cabin, although the rain ceased before I got to Lillibridge's.

I stopped in Berg for a few minutes and purchased some groceries, including a goodly supply of dill pickles. – Found Emil in fine spirits, he having had company almost continuously since I left. – Ed Green came over towards evening, turned his broncho in Emil's pasture, and decided to accompany him to Watford City to-morrow.

Tuesday July 25th

Wea. Pleasant

Ed Green slept till I had breakfast smoking hot on the table. Emil had rounded up two of his heaviest horses, for he had figured on hauling the remainder of his wheat to Watford City. Wheat is commanding a good price right now ($1.10) because black rust is ruining almost the entire crop for South Dakota, Nebraska and Kansas. I hope it won't strike us.

Ed left his saddle here for me, because it is more comfortable than mine. I am intending to ride down thru the Bad Lands with Geo. Taylor of the <C> who is going to look for strays. I put Ed's saddle on "Rex", lengthened the stirrups to suit my height, and rode to Howard's, where I gave Mrs. Howard her second – last lesson (on the benefits and power of the Lord's Supper). She treated me to an enormous hunk of June-berry pie, and a slice of delicious cake. Before I went home I rode out after Harry's bronc, and by lucky accident I managed to lasso him at the second attempt. Of course I acted as tho I could do this stunt with ease at any time.

---

[136] Charlson is the correct spelling.

❧1916❧

I took some bread along with me, because I was too lazy to bake myself and dumped the sack containing the "staff of life" into the open cabin door. Then I rode over to Geo. Taylor's, ate supper with him, and took him back to my shack, where we both spent the night.

CHAPTER 15

LOPING TO KILLDEER

Wednesday July 26th

Wea. Rain in morning

I had just crawled out of bed and was lacing my shoes, when the dog's bark announced a visitor. A glance at the clock showed that it was past 9:00 A.M. Geo. And I had slept so late because it was raining early in the morning and looked gloomy all day. We did not care to venture on a long ride into a country where there is no house for many miles.

The visitor proved to be Harry Howard. He jumped out of his buggy and came into the shack sobbing and crying like a baby. For explanation he pushed a letter into my hand, which announced that Mrs. Howard's mother was dying. Harry [was] very hysterical and could not control himself in the least. I loosened my pinto's picket rope, jumped into Harry's buggy and hiked over to his place as fast as I could tear along. After breaking the news to Mrs. Howard, I gave her a check for forty bucks, because she had no funds, and then I rode to Dave Wherle's asking him to take Mrs. Howard to Watford City immediately in his car. He can make the 35-mile trip easily in 2 hours. I hope that Mrs. Howard caught the train to Williston, so that she can get home by to-morrow. I cooked dinner for the girls, and then asked Mrs. Buell to stay with them during Mrs. H's absence.

Thursday July 27th

Wea. Very foggy

When I returned to the cabin, ay about 4:00 P.M., I found that Emil and Ed Green had just returned from town and were cooking dinner. We talked till late in the evening, Geo. Taylor having also come over.

My pinto has been laming a little since winter. It does not bother her in running, but it is very noticeable when she walks. Ed thinks she has sweeny,[137] so we blistered her left shoulder last night with a special salve.

Emil drove Jack and Nancy over to Howard's on the hayrack. Harry has not recovered from his sunstroke as yet, and the shock of yesterday had quite upset him, so that he is absolutely unable to work. For this reason Emil is helping him. I mounted the pinto in spite of her sore shoulder and rode down to Croff's haystack on Clark's flat, where I helped Emil to load the hay–bucker on the rack. In the afternoon I chased our stock to Clark's spring for water, and did a lot of reading. I really ought to be working on my sermon for Sunday, but am too lazy at present. Emil came home about 8:00. It was so foggy that he nearly got lost.

Friday July 28th

Wea. Cloudy, but no rain

Emil left early this morning for Howard's. I contemplated the accumulating dishes for some time, but did not have the nerve to wash them. Instead I piled them up in the tub and began writing a letter to Ruth instead. At about 11:00 A.M. Mr. Howard came driving up with the girls. He had been to the store, but had received no further news regarding his mother-in-law.

Harry said he wanted a private talk with me, and invited me to come over in the afternoon. Since I had to go to Croff's, I promised to wait for the Schafer mail to see whether he was getting any news that way.

After completing the letter to Ruth I wrote cards to the neighboring people, inviting them to services, and caught Whitie and went to the store. I could not ride the pinto on account of her shoulder. At Croff's was no news for Harry, but I had a letter from Rev. Hilgendorf promising me free transportation to St. Louis. This relieves me of a great deal of anxiety. Mr. Howard asked me for catechetical instruction and ultimate membership in our church. This is evidence of the efficacy of my mission work and cheered me considerably.

---

[137] Sweeney is muscular atrophy in horses, often onset by a nerve problem.

194

Figure 59: *Delia Howard's three daughters, Nettie, Eva and Lucille Green.*

Eva and Lucille Green,
dipping water.

Figure 60: *Eva and Lucille Green getting water from their well.*

Saturday July 29th

Wea. Cloudy, several very heavy showers

Emil left early this morning, as usual. I washed up the dishes, and then worked out a sermon on Luke 11,23: "He who is not with me is against me" etc. The sermon got much longer than I had expected, and the memorizing offers great difficulties.

At 11:30 I knocked off work and cooked a hearty dinner. After feeding the pups and sweeping the shack, I took the picket- rope off the pinto and chased the cattle and horses to Clark's Spring again. The nose-flies, a pest peculiar to the North West, were extra bothersome to-day, and I had great difficulty to control the pinto.

After watering the cayooses I put the "pincher" in the barn, so that the nose-flies would not bother her, and then I began bucking my sermon. Managed to memorize the 1st part fairly well, but will have to leave "second and third" to till to-morrow. Emil came charging in during the very worst showers, as was to be expected, and he warmed up and changed clothing while I cooked my supper.

Sunday July 30th

Wea. Warm pleasant

Had a very narrow escape indeed to-day. I only knew a bare half of my sermon this morning, and got up very early to buck the remainder. Was interrupted by Ed Green, however, who came riding over. After breakfast I got dressed up, and then we hitched the pinto and Ed's saddle-pony to the buggy and drove to Green's house where Ed dressed up, and then we went straight to Veeder's schoolhouse. While we were waiting for the people I did some more oxing. There was a very large crowd present, and luckily I got thru without the slightest hitch. Had a baptism after services. (Selmer Tilford Thofson). Geo. Taylor came over in time for supper, and Harold Lillibridge also drifted in. We did some practicing with Harold's new rifle, and then Ed and Harold rode off, while Geo. stayed till dark. I borrowed his saddle for Tuesday.

Monday July 31st

Wea. Warm; mostly clear

Emil "proved up" on his homestead to-day. He and Geo. Taylor went down to Schafer early this morning, expecting to meet Amb. Odermann, the other witness in town. They begged me, almost tearfully, to wash the dishes during their absence, and I promised them that I would think about it, but that is as far as I got. The dishes were still there when they returned at about 4:00 P.M. In the mean-time I wrote my monthly report to Rev. Hilgendorf, and dropped letters to Paul and Ban Johnson. Then I rode over to George's place and put his heavy saddle on my little pinto. Rode her to Croff's for the mail. Had two letters, one from Joe Kanth and one from Rev. Eidbo of Arnegard. The latter had just returned from Norway.

Joe Kanth wrote that he expected to make his appearance during the week of the 3rd-10th of September. This gives me nearly six more weeks in McKenzie Co. I should worry. Put the saddle on Rex in the evening and used him to chase the stock to the spring.

Tuesday August 1st

Wea. Hot

Emil went to Howard's early in the morning, after chasing Rex in the barn for me. While I waited for Ed Green to show up, I packed my camera carefully in some old clothing, put it in a sack and strapped it to the saddle. I also packed up 50 shells for my rifle. There was still a fire in the stove, and some hot water, and since the dishes were all soiled I washed till Ed came. Then I [left] everything stand as it was. Saddled up, and in a few minutes we were riding towards Croff's.

I mailed a letter to Joe Kanth and a postal to Rev. Eidbo. Then we climbed into the saddle and headed straight south for Denis Moran's ranch on the Little Missouri. I had never been in this part of the "Breaks" before, and that's why I was so anxious to have Ed as a guide because he is well acquainted in this country.

Figure 61: *Ed Green fording the Little Missouri River near Moran's ranch.*

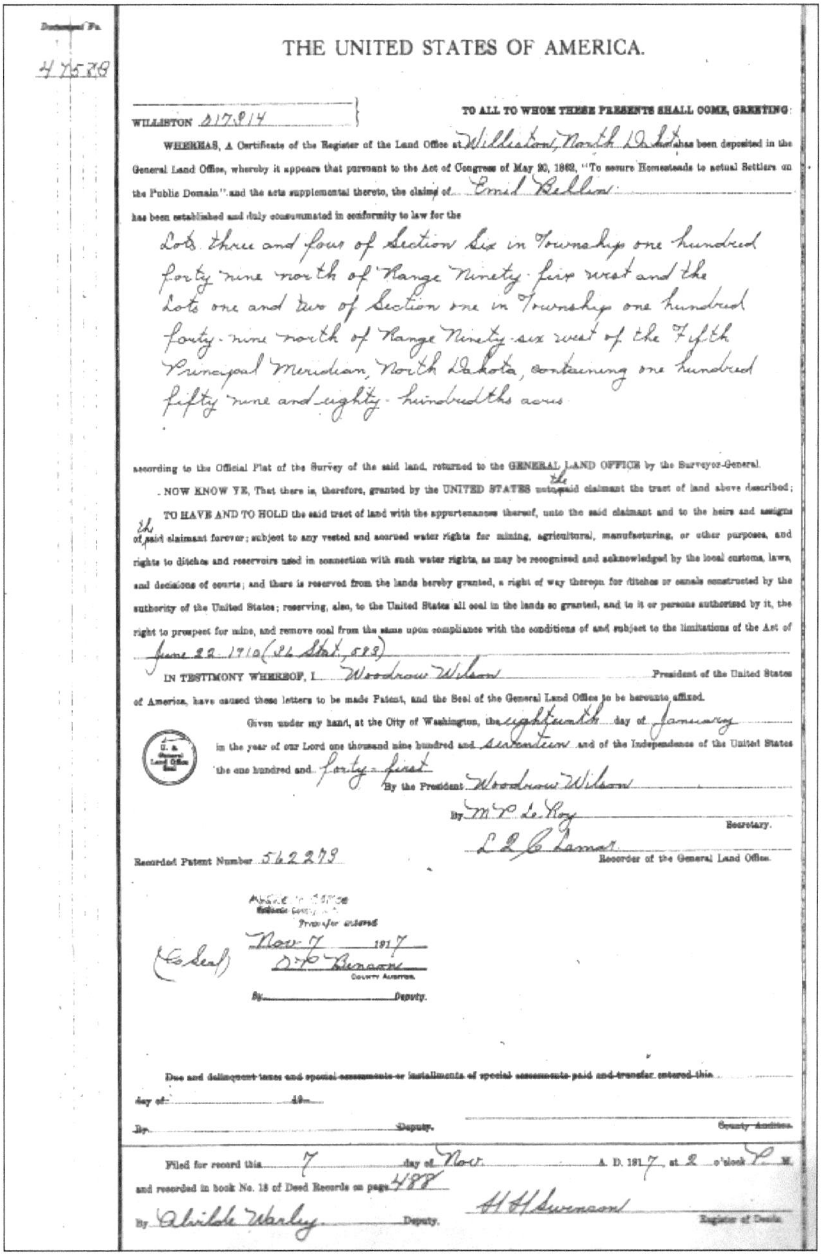

Document No.
47578

THE UNITED STATES OF AMERICA.

WILLISTON 017814

TO ALL TO WHOM THESE PRESENTS SHALL COME, GREETING:

WHEREAS, A Certificate of the Register of the Land Office at Williston, North Dakota has been deposited in the General Land Office, whereby it appears that pursuant to the Act of Congress of May 20, 1862, "To secure Homesteads to actual Settlers on the Public Domain" and the acts supplemental thereto, the claim of Emil Bellin has been established and duly consummated in conformity to law for the

Lots three and four of Section Six in Township one hundred forty nine north of Range Ninety-five west and the Lots one and two of Section one in Township one hundred forty-nine north of Range Ninety-six west of the Fifth Principal Meridian, North Dakota, containing one hundred fifty nine and eighty-hundredths acres

according to the Official Plat of the Survey of the said land, returned to the GENERAL LAND OFFICE by the Surveyor-General.

NOW KNOW YE, That there is, therefore, granted by the UNITED STATES unto the said claimant the tract of land above described; TO HAVE AND TO HOLD the said tract of land with the appurtenances thereof, unto the said claimant and to the heirs and assigns of the said claimant forever; subject to any vested and accrued water rights for mining, agricultural, manufacturing, or other purposes, and rights to ditches and reservoirs used in connection with such water rights, as may be recognized and acknowledged by the local customs, laws, and decisions of courts; and there is reserved from the lands hereby granted, a right of way thereon for ditches or canals constructed by the authority of the United States; reserving, also, to the United States all coal in the lands so granted, and to it or persons authorized by it, the right to prospect for, mine, and remove coal from the same upon compliance with the conditions of and subject to the limitations of the Act of June 22, 1910 (36 Stat., 583)

IN TESTIMONY WHEREOF, I, Woodrow Wilson President of the United States of America, have caused these letters to be made Patent, and the Seal of the General Land Office to be hereunto affixed.

Given under my hand, at the City of Washington, the eighteenth day of January in the year of our Lord one thousand nine hundred and seventeen and of the Independence of the United States the one hundred and forty-first.

(U. S. General Land Office Seal)

By the President: Woodrow Wilson

By M. P. LeRoy Secretary.

L. Q. C. Lamar Recorder of the General Land Office.

Recorded Patent Number 562279

Transfer entered
Nov 7 1917
(Co. Seal)
County Auditor.
By ______ Deputy.

Due and delinquent taxes and special assessments or installments of special assessments paid and transfer entered this ______ day of ______ 19__

By ______ Deputy. ______ County Auditor.

Filed for record this 7 day of Nov. A. D. 1917, at 2 o'clock P. M. and recorded in book No. 18 of Deed Records on page 488

By Alvilde Warley Deputy. H. H. Swenson Register of Deeds.

Figure 62: *Emil's homestead grant that was formally issued in 1917.*

We stopped for a drink at a pretty little spring. The water was wonderfully clear and cold. Our horses also had their fill, and then we traveled on. Often, the trail was so dim that we missed it completely but Ed invariably led and I followed him up hills that seemed so steep that I despaired of ever reaching their summit. We went down "cut banks" where our horses had to squat and plow a furrow to the bottom. During this entire trip we did not encounter a living thing, nor did we see a dwelling till we came to the river. After talking to Denis we crossed the river to the XT ranch, came back for some films to my camera, and re-crossed to the XT, where we spent the night. Was introduced to Pete Peterson, the owner and Mrs. Ed Green II. I knew all the cowpunchers.

Wednesday August 2nd

Wea. Rain early in the morning

The Little Missouri was much lower than I had ever seen it before. At the NT ranch the ford scarcely reached to our horses knees. Last night about half a dozen of us tried to take a swim, but the water was so shallow that we had to give up in disgust.

There are some French Army Officers in Killdeer buying horses for the European war, and Pete rounded up several broncos, which he drove off this morning with the aid of some of his men. Some of the broncs were tailed, that is the head of one bronc was tied to the tail of the other, so that they can't break away or stampede, for the leading bronc is tied to a saddle.

I took several pictures and rode over to the cuts and embankments, which the Great Northern has graded up along the river, figuring on putting in an extension Railway. Most of the ground has already washed away, and in my estimation it would require an enormous amount of work to restore and preserve the line.[138]

Ed and I left after an excellent lunch which Mrs. Green served us. We crossed the River at Moran's and swung due East, intending to cut our way thru the breaks up to the "Figure 4" and then returning to the cabin via Buells

---

[138] RCJ's prediction was correct. This line met with failure due to construction engineering problems primarily related to the soil type and nature and, after World War I, the lack of money to spend on venture capital to complete this line.

and Howards. We met three armed men, who were gunning for a lone bandit that had wronged "Crazy" Crandall's wife near Berg, and then escaped into the "Breaks" where he expected to hide. We left the "4" to our left, passed their third and fourth range houses, stopped at Buells for a drink and then rode to Howard's where we remained for supper. Then Ed and I rode home, having traveled over 100 miles since yesterday. I sure slept well.

Thursday August 3rd

Emil came home shortly after we arrived and brought Geo. Jacobson, Harry Howard's man,[139] with him. Emil wants to put up his own hay before harvest and has the service of Howard's man in exchange for his own work.

Upon me falls the terrible ordeal of being chief cook and dish-washer. During the time Emil and George tend to their four horses, I have to cook an elaborate Breakfast, consisting of pancakes, fried potatoes, eggs, meat, coffee, and some cereal breakfast food. Then I wash dishes, clean up the cabin, chop up some wood and tend to the place in general. To-day I fixed up the well curbing, for instance. By this time it is noon, and dinner must be served on

Figure 63: *RCJ with young Phil Green at the XT Ranch.*

The saddle·rack of the "XT" Ranch
"yiu's" saddle up ——— ost (with rifle)

Figure 64: *RCJ's saddle and rifle at the XT Ranch.*

time. For dinner I usually serve boiled potatoes with gravy, some vegetables such as peas, corn, beans, cabbage etc., meat, lemon and coffee with fresh biscuits. During the afternoon I have a few spare hours for letter writing, preparation and a study of sermon, hunting, riding to Croff's or Howards, etc. Then comes supper, more dishwashing, about an hour's reading and then sleep. We usually get up at 4:00 A.M., so I don't sleep late.

Friday August 4th

Wea. Cloudy   Ther. Chilly nights

Got up at 4:00 A.M., after performing my official duties as cook and house-wife. I sat down and wrote a great many letters, including letters to Helen, Dora, Searsen's and Westdahl of the McKenzie Co. journal etc. Then, after dinner I chased down my team with the pinto, hitched it to the buggy and drove to Croff's, in the vain hope of finding some vegetables and beans for

Figure 65: *An XT Ranch corral near the Little Missouri River.*

sale there. Croff is "out" of most everything, except vinegar and baking powder. In disgust I took my mail, purchased some canned fruit and drove back home. I had taken Bobby Morrison's mail along, also some chocolates for his little kiddies, and Bobby kept me talking for almost an hour. That got me home quite late.

George Jacobson has been mowing steady yesterday and to-day. Emil has been getting a load of oats from Billy's place, getting repairs for his rake and binder and thus getting ready for harvest and his part of haying. This will consist of driving the bucker and stacking. This evening Emil and Geo. drove to Lillibridges while I saddled the pinto, loaded my small rifle and rode over to the Cleveland "flat" looking for prairie dogs. I managed to get two of the smart devils, but after that I waited in vain for a head to appear, and finally beat it home.

Figure 66: *Emil Bellin, "bucking bay."*

Figure 67: *George Jacobsen cutting hay for Emil Bellin.*

Saturday August 5th

Wea. Steady rain all day

My intention was to drive to Schafer & Watford to-day, for the purpose of conducting divine services. Harry Howard had expressed a desire to accompany me, and we had arranged that I was to drive over and get him, for we expected to be gone for several days, and Harry did not want to keep a horse over here that long.

We got up very early. I cooked breakfast and began to pack up my things, when it suddenly began to rain. A look at the gloomy sky gave the promise that it was not just a passing shower, but an all day affair. So I abandoned my preparations and began rolling cigarette after cigarette, and playing the phonograph. George came in from the field just dripping wet. I gave him some dry clothing and put him near the fire, for it was very chilly outside. During a lull in the rain Harry suddenly came walking in, accompanied by "Pepper". Harry had walked down the trail to meet me and spent the first shower in the deserted house near Clark's spring. It rained till 4:00 P.M., so it was out of the question to drive in to day. I signified my willingness to go early tomor-

Lucille Green and "Pepper"

Figure 68: *Lucille Green playing with Pepper.*

row morning, however, so Harry stayed over night with us while Geo. went home.

Sunday August 6th

Wea. Very cloudy and threatening, but very little rain.

Harry and I left early this morning, and our horses traveled well, in spite of the fact that the road was very "heavy". We took the north trail and made the "Stone Johnny short cut".[140] A great deal of the grain towards Schafer is ripe, and some of it was cut and shocked, although the shocks looked rather green-ish. The soil near Schafer and Watford is quite sandy, and for this reason grain remains shorter and ripens quicker.

I suspended services in Schafer of course, for I could not get there in time. We got to Watford at noon, and at once drove down to Baumann's livery – barn, where I put up the team. I made arrangements with Mr. Baumann to take care of Mr. Kanth's books. Mr. B. has a great deal of room and also lives close to the station, while I can't get to town oftener than once in three wks.

Services had been announced for the Scan. Lutheran Church Bldg., but the door to the edifice was locked and we could not locate the key. I obtained permission to use the hall above the Watford Supply Co. I preached in Eng-lish and German on Luke 11, 23 and Phil 4, 4-7 respectively. Managed not to get 'stuck'. Bought some magazines at Lundin's drug store, went to up to my room in the hotel and read all eve.

---

[140] "Stone Johnny" is a rock shelter located approximately 14 miles west of Watford City on the south side of Highway 23. A sheepherder built it for shelter on top of a pointed hill; from that vantage point he could watch his sheep graze the grassy hills and coulees nearby. This was in the days before open range, but property lines were still recognized. Mr. Stone Johnny ended up on the worst end of a fight when he was caught grazing his sheep on the lands of a neighboring rancher, this editor's (Johnson) Great Uncle, Vanny George. Sheep never gained the acceptance in McKenzie County as they had in the southern part of western North Dakota.

Monday August 7th

Wea. Hot

Harry and I got up at nearly the same time (6:00), ate breakfast down stairs, and then proceeded to "bum" around town, waiting for business houses to open. I went to the photographers, where I got my developed film, and bought a set of views of the Medora round up. Medora is the North Dakota town where Teddy Roosevelt had his ranch head quarters, until a bad winter killed off his stock. – I got a haircut in the Dietrich pool hall, bought several cases of canned goods at S.R. Woods, and made other purchases. We met Geo. Taylor and Ed Green in town at noon. After dinner we hiked out for Schafer, where I got my Hom. Mag and the "Metropolitan". We went home via the south trails because we wanted our mail at Croff. -(The name of the post office has been changed from Catlin to Croff) I had a letter from Ma, and a statement from the bank. After deducting my checks, I have a balance of 81¢ to my credit. Quite a showing for a year's work.

From Croff we drove to the shack, where I unloaded my purchases, and then I drove Harry's home. Ate supper at Howard's and got back before dark.

Figure 69: *One of RCJ's photos of the Medora Round-Up.*

Tuesday August 8th

Wea. Cloudy; a few scattering drops of rain.

Lucille and Eva rode along with me last night. Before I could prevent her, Lucille had grabbed the whip and swung it over the horses. "Whitie" is only a half tamed bronco, and in spite of the fact that he had pulled a heavy load on muddy roads for over forty miles, he gave a violent plunge and squealed and bucked for over a minute. When he and Rex, who had also got started, were thru with their performance, there was very, very little left of Yin's whiffle-tree. I took the hitching hooks and spliced a homely but serviceable draw, and got home safely.

Emil and I had our usual argument about the advisability of getting up. He finally dumped me out of my cot, and I cooked a gloomy breakfast.

Just as I was peeling the "spuds" for dinner I saw Harry and the girls driving over the hill. Luckily I had the floor swept clean, and the cabin looking tidy. Lucille helped me with the potatoes, and then the girls played the phonograph, and amused themselves with watching my crude, but effective manner of cooking. There being six grown men, and two girls for dinner, I had quite a job, but managed to rig out a palatable meal.

Figure 70: *Medora Round-Up. Note the large crowd.*

Harry wanted Emil to come over and start cutting grain, so Emil hitched on to his binder and made a round, but it was still so green, that he quit after that, and came home late last-night. George had ridden the pinto to Jim Catlin's. Considers her a speedy horse.

Wednesday August 9th

Wea. Very sultry in morn; but clear during rest of day.

According to the new homestead law, "nesters" are permitted to take up an additional quarter section of land, provided they have "proved up" their original homestead, and that the new quarter is located within 20 miles of their home place. Emil did not want to miss his chance of "getting something for nothing". So he decided to let his haying go and look up some land in the "breaks" in Dunn Co., which he either intends to pasture himself, or sell to some renter.[141]

So he and I saddled up our own ponies and rode them thru the "breaks" to Denis Moran's ranch, where we spent the night. Emil's saddle horse had not been used for many days, and was very frisky. He cooled it down before we got to the "N.T."

I had my rifle along, of course, and was lucky enough to shoot a young coyote. The animal was so small that I did not skin it, but I took the "scalp" in order to collect the bounty of $2.50.

Thursday August 10th

In company with Alex & Chet Alton, Ed Green and Leon Eggert we forded the Little Missouri, and stuck out for Killdeer, where the filings had to be made. The River was very shallow, the water scarcely going to the horses' knees. Emil got badly soaked however, for his horse refused to go on after it got to the middle of the river. In spite of all his pleadings the cow-punchers refused to rope his pony and thus drag it out. We all sat in a circle on our

---

[141] According to Emil's son Arno, Emil never did take all the steps necessary to "prove up" this land. For a time he put some livestock on it. Arno recalls that Emil almost drowned while crossing the Little Missouri River en route to this Dunn County property. Emil couldn't swim, and after falling off his horse in the river, he saved himself by grabbing onto the animal's tail.

ponies and offered him sage advice, while poor Emil finally was forced to get off and lead his horse over. Since he threatened to maul all of us, we galloped away from him and led him a merry chase, until he had cooled down.

The trip of 32 miles to Killdeer passed without event. We got to the gap in the Killdeer mountains at noon, and loped into town at 1:00. After dinner the boys transacted their business, and it got so terribly late that we were forced to spend the night in town.

Figure 71: *Loping to Killdeer with the NT punchers.*

Friday August 11th

Killdeer is the terminal of the Soo line, and we had lots of fun at the station last night. Leon Eggert acted as a taxi "barker" and kept yelling: "Right this way, taxis for the best hotel!" Several fat drummers and some horse buyers responded. Leon took 50¢ from each, and then showed them his "taxi", which consisted of a half-wild bronco saddle horse. Needless to say, the poor fellows preferred to walk.

Before we left Killdeer we tied Chet Alton down in his bed with his own lariat, and then we "beat it". He did not show up till Emil and I were ready to leave the <C> ranch for our shack, so he did not get a chance to get even with us.

I killed a "7 pt" rattler in the Bad Lands and added the rattles to my collection of snake tails. We got home pretty early, and so Emil helped me replace a shoe on Whitie. He had torn it loose while sliding down a bad cut bank.

Figure 72: *Alex Alton and Leon Eggert at a <C> Range Shack.*

Saturday August 12th

Emil and George resumed their haying to-day and finished up by evening. I cooked breakfast and dinner, scrubbed the shack, and baked a batch of bread for the boys, because I expected to be gone for several days to the Indian Reservation, and the Table Butte post.

It was a hot day, and since the moon was due to shine (full moon to-morrow) I did not get ready to leave till about 4:00. I had gotten about three miles from the shack when Whitie displayed his bronco nature by shying at something and bolting off. Before I could stop him and Rex they had smashed my whiffle-trees all to pieces. Luckily the buggy is light and the neck-yolk held. I unhitched, rode Whitie home, got some new single trees, bolts, wrenches etc. in a sack and fixed the buggy up. But it was so late when I finished, that I decided to postpone my trip till to-morrow.

Sunday August 13th

Wea. Slight rain in P.M.   Texts: Luke 11,23

I got up very early, for it is a long way to "Tipperary", in this case to Frisby Buck's, and I am due there at 10:00 A.M. I stopped at the Berg P.O. for a few seconds to mail a letter to Ma and one to Bill Medo, then I pushed straight on. I got to Buck's just a trifle after ten, and by twelve I was thru with services, we having begun after 11:00. Mrs. Buck served us a very good lunch, consisting of salmon sandwiches, potato salad, cold baked beans, bread, coffee and cake. After loading up to my gunwales, I watered my horses and drove to the Fort Berthold Reservation Corner. There was an ominous looking cloud west of the Table Butte, and the storm overtook me before I could find any shelter. (There are no houses for 12 miles in the Blue Buttes) I was wearing my sheepskin overcoat, for it had been very chilly all day, and this is what saved me from a very bad drenching. I left my horses tied to Bobby Jansen's farm wagon. Bobby has just finished painting his house (pale green). After preaching in English and German, I was forced to return to Janssen's and spend the night with them again. Mrs. Draegert, who had invited me last time, did not come to church, and I had forgotten the way out to her place.

Log Barn, roofed with scorio.
Frisby Buck's cabin near Table Butte.

Figure 73: *Frisby Buck's log barn, with scorio roof.*

Monday August 14th

Wea. Warm

Bob and I had sat up till 1:30. Bob because he wished to talk, and I, because I knew from dire experience that millions of half starved bedbugs were impatiently awaiting me, and I was very anxious to postpone the interview.[142]

I left at 8:00 A.M. A recent hail has destroyed many of the crops completely, and the black rust is taking the rest. I feel very sorry for the poor people, but it can't be helped.

John Jore – Frisby Buck's claim.

Figure 74: *John Jore, brother of Clarence and Ole, at Frisby Buck's place.*

---

[142] Once established, bed bugs were a serious problem for the homesteaders. Some settlers had to resort to burning their mattresses to kill the bugs and try to save the springs for re-stuffing. An itinerant Lutheran pastor described his experience with the bugs in Nebraska in the 1890s, after a night in a sod house: "That night turned out to be most unpleasant. As soon as I got to bed, the bold, ever-present vermin covered me. Finally, I got out of bed and made a place for myself on what might be called a sofa in the room. Sure enough, the bedbugs found me there, too. In desperation I went outside and slept on the ground, rolled up in a blanket. It was a cool, September night, and when I awoke the next morning, every bone in my body ached." Source: *Old West Journals of the Rev. J.D. Schroeder* (Wanda S. Oelrich, Ed. 1989), as quoted in *The Man from Worms,* by William F. Arent (PRA Inc. 1994), pg. 78.

I stopped at the Berg Store for some groceries, and also took a picture of it. After I got home I had to cook dinner, for Emil and George had figured that I would be back in time. While Emil and George were stacking hay in the hay corral, I saddled the pinto and rode to Croffs for the mail, after which I had several pictures taken of myself and the "pincher".

Business district of Berg, N. Dak.

Figure 75: *Berg store and Post Office. Note the braces against the walls.*

Tuesday August 15th

I baked bread again this morning, and since I did not want to waste the fire, I put on a boiler full of water and washed out our blankets. I gave all of them a double boiling with lots of soap, ammonia and kerosene added, thus succeeding in loosening the dirt. Then I simply wrung them out and hung them on the fence to dry. – I baked my bread mostly in pound coffee tins, as usual, for thus I get the best and hardiest loaves.

Emil and George went over to Howard's early this morning to begin harvesting. I subsequently learned that Mrs. Howard returned unexpectedly at supper-time, having taken a car as far as possible and walked the remainder of the way. Her mother is much better, and they are entertaining hopes that she may recover completely. A piece of sticky flypaper blew on Emil's face and arm.

Figure 76: *RCJ and the pinto in front of Emil's barn.*

Wednesday August 16th

Wea. Very hot, no clouds

Harry came over at 7:00, just as I was finished frying my pancakes for breakfast. He took a cup of coffee, and then I rounded up "Bell" with my pinto and tied her to the back of his wagon. He asked me to accompany him since it was so very hot, and he was afraid of a relapse of his recent heat stroke. So I tied my Pinto to the wagon, mounted to the seat, and rode in the wagon with him to Lillibridges.

We bred Bell to L's stallion before dinner and then we drove to Croff's for the mail. In passing Billy's place I noticed that the wheat field was perfectly black with black rust; the grain looks so bad that Emil will probably not cut it at all. Croff will not cut over 200 acres on account of the rust. In the eastern part of this state conditions are even worse.[143]

---

[143] "Rust" is a disease that attacks wheat. Modern varieties are "rust resistant" and the problem is not as pervasive as it once was. As noted by Jahn, rust can wipe out an entire wheat crop.

From Croffs I rode the pinto home, leading Bell and carrying one of the pups, who had followed me, on the arm.

Figure 77: *Another photo of RCJ and the pinto.*

Thursday August 17th

Wea. Hot

I got up early this morning, and after tidying up the shack I prepared myself for Harry Howard's catechetical lesson. Then I rode over with the pinto. Emil had come to the shack, to see how far his grain was ripened, and I crawled in his buggy, leading the pinto, thus saving me from riding most of the way. After finishing my business with Harry, I accepted his invitation to remain for supper, and also promised to leave my pinto, so that Geo. Jacobson could ride her over to-morrow. When I went home I rode one of Harry's work horses, "Nell", and led "Beauty". Emil drove the binder over with "Mac" and the bronco, which Harry bought from the NT ranch early this summer.

Friday August 18th

Wea. Cool, Cloudy

Emil began cutting early this morning. Geo. is to shock grain for him, but did not show up till late in the evening. He had borrowed my pinto some time ago, but he led her, and walked most of the way over, being afraid to ride the sassy creature bare- backed. I set up a number of shocks for Emil and took a picture of his binder outfit. He took a view of me shocking. During the rest of the day I did the cooking and housework and also selected Rom. 4, 4-5 as the text for Sunday's English sermon. Did not begin writing the sermon till Saturday morning however. (I am writing this diary on the 21st). I have acquired the mean habit of pushing my sermon work off till the last minute.

I washed out three suits of underwear, some towels, dish towels etc. My "B.V.D.'s" did not get as snow white as the laundry renders them, in fact, they remained quite gray; but I am positive they are clean, for I boiled them up twice and nearly wore out the wash board.

Saturday August 19th

Wea. Cool & cloudy

We got up very early, and Emil began cutting immediately, in spite of the heavy dew. George Jacobson had a stiff day's work ahead of him, for he was supposed to shock up all the grain that a seven –foot binder cut yes-terday and to-day. The heavy wind bothered both Geo. and Emil. Geo. had trouble from keeping his shocks from blowing down as fast as he could set them up, and Emil could not catch a great deal of grain while cutting with the wind. Emil also was bothered by the rust, both red and black, with which the grain is infested this year. The poor kid has had a dull eye-ache for days, and I am glad that he will get a rest from cutting after to-night.

I did not get the dough for my bread mixed early enough, so I baked a batch of soda biscuits for dinner. They turned out well this time. – Geo. went home early to do the chores. Harry went to town.

Figure 78: *RCJ shocking grain at Emil Bellin's claim.*

Sunday August 20th

Wea. Cloudy

I got up at seven. Without rousing Emil I put on a sweater and jacket to ward off the chill wind and went outside with my English manuscript to finish studying for my sermon. I had planned the logical sequence of the thoughts and parts so carefully that I managed to study it without much difficulty.

After a late breakfast, which also took the place of dinner, we shaved, and dressed, and drove over to Veeder's schoolhouse, where we were the first to arrive. A good crowd (58) arrived, and I again managed to slip through without getting "stuck". I had a narrow escape in my English sermon, however, only my fertile imagination enabling me to talk without resorting to my manuscript.[144]

By the way, this is the last time I am conducting services at Veeder's school house. According to his latest letter, Mr. Kanth expects to arrive in Watford City Sept. 5th, and I expect him to make his introductory sermon here. I can hardly wait till I shall be permitted to leave here, and yet I shall miss the free and wild life of McKenzie Co. greatly.

---

[144] RCJ had a profound effect on bringing many of the people living near Emil into the fold of the Missouri Synod. Many of the families were of German descent and several were of Scandinavian origin as well. The many baptisms he performed and the funerals he officiated made an impact. However, his own self-criticism—he berated himself for failing to properly perform the ministry duties while in McKenzie County due to youthful neglect—may have been his greatest asset. The hardworking homesteaders and cow punchers saw a man of the cloth, who played hard, worked hard, endured their lifestyle and understood them because he walked in their shoes. With weather and tragedy often forcing them to take one day at a time, subsequent generations recognized that life on the prairie does not always fall into a convenient schedule. The influence RCJ had on the congregation at the Veeder School (used as a church) is evident in that even this editor (Johnson) was baptized in Missouri Synod, being a descendant of the Kummer family.

Figure 79: *Emil Bellin cutting wheat.*

Emil Bellin — putting up prairie
hay in his hay corral.

Figure 80: *Nice picture of Emil Bellin pitching prairie hay.*

CHAPTER 16

MOVING THE HOWARD HOUSE

Monday August 21st

Wea. Chilly & Breezy   Ther. +37, +69, +?

Harry Howard recently purchased the Dave Wehrle place, and he intends to move his house on Wehrle's farm, because W.- has a good well and nice barn on his place, also the better of the two farms.[145] So Harry came past our shack early this morning to get Lillibridge's wagon, and also to instruct Emil about getting some straw into Leon Veeder's coulee, so they could cross it with the house. Emil left immediately after breakfast with four horses.

I wrote three letters, and wrapped up a 12-exposure roll of film to be mailed to R. L. Redding, the photographer.[146] This makes 36 negatives that I am to get next Saturday

I rode to Croff's after dinner, to get the mail, but found that Harry Howard had taken it along. I expect to ride to Howard's to-morrow and get it. – After watering the horses I cooked supper, and then devoted myself to writing, chiefly in this diary.

---

[145] Dave Wherley owned the farm adjacent to and immediately north of the Howards' place.

[146] R. L. Redding is noted on a number of the photographs in this publication. He maintained an office in Watford City and took many photographs of early McKenzie County scenes and people. Many of his views were printed on postcards and offered for sale at stores throughout the county. RCJ bought a number of these, and they are part of his collection. Redding also developed RCJ's negatives and printed them on photographic paper. All of the surviving originals of RCJ's pictures are the same size as the negatives.

Tuesday August 22st

Wea. Warm, but chilly in eve.

Since there was nobody to disturb me this morning, I slept peacefully till about 7:00. I did not eat breakfast till about 10:00, however, since I had no very great appetite this early in the morning. At noon I chased the stock to Clark's spring, and then I rode the pinto over to Howard's. Preparations for moving the house are nearly completed. I helped put the 36-foot skids under the house, and chained them to wagon trucks. The house will "walk" to its new location to-morrow morning.

Harry had fetched my mail over, and a nice stack of letters I had. Rev. Nachtsheim sent my R.R. pass from Watford City to Sioux City and promised further transportation to St. Louis. Helen has sent a sweet letter, repeating her urgent invitation. Art Behn and Paul also wrote. Alexander, of the "Royal" Typewriter Co. wrote, offering to exchange my old machine for a new one.

Getting the house in position

Figure 81: *Howard's house – getting the skids under the house.*

I ate supper with Howard's and then rode directly home. Wrote to Alexander and Rev. Nachtsheim in eve. It was rather chilly, and the north lights were wonderfully brilliant. The north was lit up with a steady white glow, and great wavering streamers of light would blaze up to the zenith. I went to bed late.

Geo. Jacobson - E, H Bellin   Harry Howard - Dave Wehrle
Mrs. Howard - Bill Lillibridge

Figure 82: *Lunch break. Helpers are George Jacobsen, Emil Bellin, Harry Howard, Dave Wherley, Delia Howard and Bill Lillibridge. They are not individually identifiable except for Mrs. Howard. This is the only photo of Mr. and Mrs. Howard in the RCJ collection. Lucille and Eva Green are present, as is a woman inside the house.*

Wednesday August 23th

Wea. Hot, cool night as usual

The furious barking of "Misery" and her two pups roused me out of bed, and I had just dressed when Ed Green and George Taylor came driving up. Their spring ran dry, so they borrowed Emil's water keg and got some water from our well. I cleaned up the shack, cooked my breakfast, and then grabbed a bucket and went after my friend, the cow, with a sinking heart. She had not been milked in several days, so she gave me a large quantity of milk.

Shortly after dinner I rode to Croff's for the mail. I had only one letter (from Davis). Emil got notice on his recent filing in Killdeer. – From Croffs I rode to Howard's. I rode the pinto barebacked and made some record time. Harry had pulled the house down as far as Dave Wehrle's old cellar, so I was too late to see the actual moving. I helped transport the shack on the cellar etc., however, and secured several excellent pictures.

Since Harry had no level, he sent me to Ole Olson to borrow one. Foolishly I put Bill Lillibridge's saddle on the pinto and the rear cinch unsnapped for me on the way home. The strap slammed against the pincher's rear legs, of course and she "buck galloped" me all the way home. I had to "grab leather" at last, and was played out.

Harry R. Howard's house being moved.

Figure 83: *Nearing the end of Howard's house move, August 23, 1916. Note the cellar at right.*

Ready to say "Giddap"

Figure 84: *Nice photo of a house mover and his horses.*

Thursday August 24th

Wea. Sultry: rain in eve.

I got up rather early, chiefly because some crazy flies bothered me beyond endurance with their persistent buzzing. While I was busily engaged frying my usual breakfast-pancakes, young Fin, working for Bill Lillibridge, came riding up and enquired the road to Howard's. Since I was going up myself after breakfast, he sat down in the shack and waited till I got thru. It seems that his father is dying in far off Iowa, and Fin wanted the money from Lillibridge to take him home.[147]

---

[147] Tragedy would strike Bill Lillibridge the next year. On Dec. 8, 1917, his son, Lloyd, age 9, would perish in a blizzard while trying to ride home from a neighbor's house. News accounts relate that he had left the Petersons' house when the storm was just beginning. The temperature was 30 below.

Before leaving I packed a basket of cucumbers in a sack and strapped it to the saddle. Mrs. Howard had bad luck in her own garden, and I know she will appreciate some of my surplus vegetables greatly. Fin and I galloped our horses nearly all the way, in an effort to get away from "Misery" and the two pups. But our efforts were not crowned with success, for the exhausted pups arrived about half and hour after us. I put the pinto in the hay corral, and made myself generally useful about the house, carrying water, disposing of refuse, etc. I also helped put the new foundation under the house.

Since I had been using Bill Lillibridges saddle, I had to ride the pinto home bare back. She is feeling far too good to suit me, for when I once turned around to see how well the puppies were following me home, I accidentally placed my left hand on her hip, and she nearly succeeded in bucking me off. I spent the afternoon with cleaning up.

Friday August 25th

I spent this day in utter solitude, neither seeing nor hearing another human being. After having bachelored for over ten months one would naturally suppose that I was used to being alone, but I must say that I am greatly oppressed whenever circumstances force me to be alone.

I killed a big rattler in the weeds near the well. I told Emil some time ago that I thought I had heard a rattle near the shack, but he merely laughed at me. I am willing to admit that I am much afraid of snakes, and I shot to-day's rattler with my .44 instead of using a club.

The pinto is walking a little lame with her left front leg. I think she is sweenied, although her shoulder does not show it yet.

CHAPTER 17

LAST FULL MEASURE
OF DEVOTION

Saturday August 26th

Wea. Warm during P.M. – killing frost at night.

I wanted to make a very early start for Watford City, where I am due to preach to-morrow, but so many little things turned up, that I did not get away till nearly 11:00, although I was up at five. Ed Green was here this morning, got a package of "Peerless" and talked till I left. Ed is shocking for Geo. Taylor.

Instead of running down to the old tumbledown shack where I am keeping my trunk etc. I drove straight to Watford, where I landed in the early afternoon. I put my suitcases and bag of books in the Watford Hotel, and then drove down to Mr. Baumann's livery barn, where I put up the team.

After doing some business with the bank, I went to the photographers and got the pictures that he had developed and printed for me. Out of the 36 views 33 were good. I got some really pretty pictures.
The Watford Hotel has been in the active possession of Jim Catlin for a week. Catlins greeted me with enthusiasm, and gave me a dandy room.

Sunday August 27th

Wea. Cool

Bright and early this morning I went to the barn, where I tended to the horses. Then I went back up-town and ate breakfast, got my books ready and drove down to Schafer for services. I felt very blue when the hours dragged by and nobody showed up, although I had the notice in the paper. There is a big celebration at Grassy Butte and dancing etc. is more interesting to the people than hearing the word of God.

After eating dinner in the Cherryview Hotel I hitched up and drove to Watford again. Here I had a little better luck, but the crowd was dishearteningly small. Since this was "menschlich geredet", the last time I will ever preach here, I felt a little discouraged, although I was well aware of the great laxity of the people of Schafer and Watford.

Late in the evening I made the acquaintance of Rev E.E. Eidbo, the Norwegian Lutheran minister of Arnegard. We went to the vestry of his Scan. church and smoked and talked.

Monday August 28th

Wea. Warm

"Whitie" showed his bronco nature again this morning and nearly got the best of me. He jumped on to me, because I had made a quick, jerky movement and pinned me against the wall. One of his front feet struck me a gashing blow on the left leg, ripping my overalls and tearing a gash in my leg. He also injured my left hand severely before his bit cling rope tore, thus releasing him. I found most of his harness tack and, and after quieting him, I managed to get him harnessed and hitched.

From Watford I cut across prairie, past Starlings, till I got to the deserted claim-shack where I stored my things. Drove on to Mrs. Alex's without stopping, and got my wash. Mrs. Alex kept me to dinner and showed me how to bake "Johnny Cake". After dinner I put my horses in the old barn and examined my goods. They had been exposed to two heavy rains and many things were hopelessly damaged. I loaded up all the books and took them along, expecting to ship them with the other books from Catlin.

Took the south trail home. Got my mail (a letter from Rev. Frey) at Croff's and hit the cabin at 7:00.

Figure 85: *Action at Grassy Butte on September 4, 1916. It was "Frontier Day".*

Tuesday August 29th

Emil is cutting his oats for hay, and he pulled me out of bed at 7:00. I was so sleepy that I spilled a lot of pancake dough on the floor while cooking breakfast.

Shortly before dinner I went out with a bucket and the camera. Took two pictures of Emil and had one taken of myself. Then I dug up several hills of potatoes and cooked dinner.

Emil finished cutting at about 3:00 P.M. By that time I had watered the stock, and so I rode over to Howard's with the pictures that I had taken of the little girls. Little I knew the surprises in store for me. For while I was sitting around, dressed in a blue shirt and overalls, with an ugly bull-dog pipe in my face, there suddenly came a big drove of women intending to surprise Mrs. Howard. I excused my rotten appearance as well as I could, and ate heartily of the excellent lunch which the ladies served. Helped Geo. Jacobson get a load of hay, and promised to come back tomorrow to instruct Harry. The double baptism is set for Monday, Sep. 4th.

Emil H. Rellin – Cutting oats on his claim.

Figure 86: *Emil cutting oats.*

Wed. Aug. 30

Wea. Warm and clear

I slept til about 8:00, and had barely dressed, when Emil came dashing up with Howard's bay mare, expecting to dump me. He told me to be sure to reach Howard's by noon because they were going to have chicken for dinner.

I had not sent in my report to the Mission Board for August as yet, and was just engaged in writing it, when I was interrupted by a knock on the door. The intruder turned out to be a man by the name of C. E. Langberg, a traveling propagandist of the Seventh Day Adventists. He was under the impression that I was Emil, and I did not remove that idea. I argued with him for over an hour; finally he got sore and left. It was after eleven o'clock, and I had close to ten miles to ride (via Croffs to Howard's), so I dropped my unfinished report, jumped on the trusty old pinto, and let her go as fast as she pleased. When I got to Howard's she was dripping wet, but I was in time for the chicken. Talked religion with Harry, was home for supper.

Figure 87: *RCJ posing on Emil's cutter.*

This means you!

Thursday August 31

Wea. Gloomy, heavy wind; small showers

Got up at 8:00. I had begun a story in a magazine last night, and I sat down this morning immediately after getting up, and read til the end of the magazine. By that time it was noon, and I was very hungry. I cooked an elaborate meal and enjoyed it immensely. I kept the fire going, and set a boiler full of water on the stove, for I had to wash out a lot of towels. After completing this disagreeable job, I finished the report to the Mission Board, wrote a long letter to Rev. Frey, and took the mail to Croffs, for I had a film that I wanted to send to Watford City for development. The pinto felt extremely good, stopping every half mile for a hearty bucking. Wrote letters to Helen and Art Behn in eve, also invited people to services for the 10th.

Emil Ballin – Cutting oats for hay

Figure 88: *Another view of Emil and his oat crop. Barn is in the background.*

Friday Sept. 1

Slept exceptionally long this morning but got up in time to cook dinner. I had promised Mrs. Howard to come for dinner so I left early for Croffs to get the mail.

"Pauly" Gruetzner packed about half a dozen catalogs in my grain sack, and the weight nearly pulled me off the pinto, because I was riding barebacked and the beast kept galloping with me.

As I was riding through Isham Ike's pasture, I met Mrs. Howard and Mrs. Emmerson in a buckboard, bent for the store. With great relief I deposited the mail in the buggy and rode on to Howard's for some bread. Since there was nobody home, I just simply helped myself to bread and rode straight home.

Saturday, September 2

Wea. Hot and windy, frost in low lands

Emil went to Howards this morning to build a wagon box for Harry. I was supposed to go to Table Butte to day but I felt so queer and tired, that I finally pushed it off til tomorrow.

I rode "Rex" over to Tolle Johnson's to have a new shoe put on his right hind leg. Then I took the top off my buggy, for the wind was whipping the curtains to pieces. Emil came home towards evening; he hadn't eaten any supper, so we cooked up a late supper which we ate at about 4:00. I should have written letters in the evening, but felt too grouchy.

Sunday, September 3

Wea. very windy, rain in evening

I got up very early this morning, for I had a long trip before me. Still, so many things turned up, that it was past eight o'clock before I got started. I had announced services at Ole Simmonson's at Table Butte, but I had not the remotest idea where that gentleman lived. Since I was so late, I was afraid I would not find anybody to direct me. Luckily I found Ole Jore still at home, and Lester Jore took me down to Simmonsons. About half an hour after

I got there, I began services and got through nicely. Ate a hearty meal and took my final leave of the people, promising however to bring Joe Kanth around next Thursday. Then I drove over to the Reservation Corner school-house, where I preached in German only, because it was late and I expected to drive partly to Watford City in the evening to get Mr. Kanth. First I called upon Mrs. Harms, however. She is feeling a little better, but I hardly hope for recovery. Harms, Larsons and Draegerts declared their willingness to board Mr. Kanth, should he be willing to stay with them.

After eating a hearty lunch at Harms, I struck out for Watford. It was 7:00 PM and getting quite dark and cloudy. It also began to sprinkle, so I finally turned in at Ole Jore's and passed the night there. Mrs. Jore fixed me up a good lunch. I talked with Ole for a while before going to bed. He is sickly again.

Monday, September 4

Wea. very stormy.

I am a very sound sleeper and rarely wake up by myself, so I overslept greatly this morning, it being after 7:00 before I arose. I helped Mrs. Jore with breakfast by making and frying sour-dough pancakes. Left for Watford City at about 8:00 and drove the team as hard as possible, averaging about ten miles per hour. I got to Schafer at noon and went straight to Core's deserted shack[148] where I planned to pass the night with Rev Kanth. I had bought a chunk of bacon, weighing 1 1/4 lb. for 60 cents, also bread, vegetables, etc. After feeding and resting my team and cooking a bite to eat, I drove in to Watford City.

I put the team in Dutchie's livery barn, and walked to the station, confidently expecting the train to be late, as usual. This time, however it was on time. The agent informed me that it had come and gone. In great anxiety I went up town to see whether Rev. Kanth had arrived and almost ran into him. We sure were glad to see each other, especially Joe, who naturally was in a blue funk. Besides, all stores were closed, it being Labor Day, so we could not get in anywhere. So Joe and I loaded his suit cases in the buggy and rode the six miles to Core's shack, where we cooked supper and spent the night.

---

[148] The rest of Rev. Frey's house had been moved by this time.

Tuesday September 5

Wea. hot, slight wind

Early this morning I packed my trunk and dispatched it to Watford City with W. N. Raymond who was going in with a big wagon. I had an enormous raft of stuff in the trunk, and had to stomp the stuff down with my feet.

Joe and I cooked breakfast, washed up the dishes and drove to Schafer, preparatory to going to Bellin's place. In Schafer we stopped for some groceries and a talk with Diehm, the post-master. Then we started out on a nice twenty mile hike to Croffs. Joe got a little restless after a while and asked me whether we were nearly there. I told him we only had 14 miles left, and he got plumb disgusted. Still the trip was quite interesting to him, for the fantastic scorio buttes etc. were something brand new. We stopped at Croffs for the mail and some additional groceries, after which we cut across prairie to Emil's place. Emil and Harry Howard were busily engaged in shocking oats on the patch west of the barn. We talked a while after introductions, and then went down to the cabin. True to his threat, Emil and Harry had piled up all the dishes, so that Joe and I got a good taste of housework right away. We lunched on some beans and olives and ate so much more for supper. After supper Emil and I washed the dishes and played the gramophone. Before dark I rounded up the stock with the pinto, and gave Rev. Kanth a fancy riding exhibition.

Wednesday September 6

Wea. light showers

In spite of all my protest and arguments Emil pulled me out of bed at 4:30, so that I would have breakfast ready after he did the morning chores. Harry Howard came riding over on Nell early in the morning and helped Emil put up Oats - hay all fore noon. The baptism of Mr. and Mrs. Harry Howard was set for this afternoon, so Mr. Kanth and I dressed up, packed up our books, and got ready shortly after dinner, in spite of the threatening rain clouds. Mrs. Howard came out to greet us and took our books in. I put the team in the barn and went into the home with Joe. After Harry and Emil showed up we played the phonograph, while I discussed the final details of the ceremony with Mrs. Howard. Then we set up a bowl of water on the sewing machine. Rev. Kanth sat down at the organ and after signing an appropriate hymn, I read the prescribed prayer and proceeded to question Mrs. Howard and baptized her. I reduced Mr. Howard's questioning, because his instructions had been greatly curtailed.[149]

After the ceremony Mrs. Howard served us a dandy lunch and gave me two pieces of lemon pie. I ate so much that I could barely move. After it quit raining Emil, Joe and I went back to the shack, played the phonograph, talked bunk- stories, and went to bed late.

Thursday September 7

Wea. Warm, slight wind

We got up early this morning, since I wanted to take Rev. Kanth to his two final mission posts - Table Butte and Res. Corner. We did not leave til 9:00, however, since I wanted to arrange it so that we could have dinner with Ole Jore. At Berg we stopped for the Table Butte mail and then "humped" the horses right along so that we made Jore's by noon. After a dandy meal we hooked up again and drove to Frisby Buck's, where we ate a good lunch, and where I bid them good-bye. Then we swung north past the Table Butte, over the rough trail, making our first Reservation Corner stop at Elvin Larsen's. We had barely greeted Mrs. Larsen, when our friend, Bobby Janssen, came driving up, yelling all the way. I introduced him to Rev. Kanth, and then we drove to Pete Harms, where we spent the night.. I turned Rex and Whitie into the pasture and spent the evening talking with Mrs. Harms, who is feeling much better.

Friday September 8

Wea. warm, hot Chinook winds

I tried a new experiment this morning after leaving Harms. I wanted to bid good-bye to Mrs. Draegert and introduce Rev. Kanth, but I had no idea where she lived. "Rex" and "Whitie" had been down there several times before I came out, so I pointed them in about the right direction and let them

---

[149] RCJ's baptismal records show that Delia Mary Howard was the daughter of Mr. and Mrs. Calvin Church. She was born Aug. 15, 1880 in Lowell, Michigan. Harry Rois Howard was the son of Mr. and Mrs. John Howard. He was born Jan. 26, 1880 near Grinnell, Iowa. Reverend Kanth's real name was Martin; his name may be spelled Kauth.

have their heads. Joe and I settled back for a good smoke while the horses trotted along the Reservation fence and then swung off on several dim trails and finally landed us at Mrs. Draegert's combination log and sod house. We talked awhile and then drove to Bob Janssen's, where I took leave; also stopped at Elvin Larsen's and swung down to the foot of the Chimney Butte, where we again ate dinner with Ole Jore's. Ole kept us til after three o'clock, so that we had to go pretty sharp to get to Emil's by supper. I stopped for some groceries at Berg and talked with Tolle Johnson before going to Emil's. While Emil was cooking supper, I rode the pinto to Croff's for the mail, making the six miles, including a good stop, in 40 minutes.

Saturday September 9

Wea. cloudy and drizzly

My stay in McKenzie Co. is now rapidly drawing to a close. I am figuring on leaving from Watford City Monday noon, getting as far as Williston on that day. My R.R. Pass expires next Friday, so I won't have much time to spare, for I am traveling to Sioux City exclusively via the Great Northern, and my route thus is very circuitous.

Emil and I had a grand house cleaning to-day. It was so foggy and wet outside that he could not haul hay. While Emil cleaned off the top of the cupboard and the shelves along the north and west wall of the cabin, I hunted my books, the fur coat, and some old clothing together and packed my box. Emil is willing to take me to Watford Monday and also haul my box in, while he will take Rev. Kanth's trunk and books on the return trip. Emil washed some clothing and began scrubbing the floor, while I got my dear little "pinty" and took a last ride to Howard's for bread. The pinto had been oats-fed for several days, and was feeling wonderfully well, galloping almost all the way. I took supper with Mrs. Howard and rode home with a heavy heart, for I had grown quite attached to her.[150]

---

[150] The Howards were still in McKenzie County in 1920, but they later moved to Washington.

1916

Sunday September 10

Wea. rainy; very violent wind

Rev. E. C. Schutt of Wildrose, ND was supposed to install Rev. Kanth in Veeder's school house to-day. Since he failed to show up, Rev. Kanth proceeded to buck his "antriterpredigt" in order to play safe.– It rained and stormed just terrible all day, but in spite of this we got ready for services immediately after dinner. We bundled into sheep skins, covered with some heavy blankets and chased the horses with might and main.

At the school house nobody showed up of course, except Howards, and they came for several other reasons, namely to return "Nancy" and "Jack" to Emil in exchange for "Roky" and "Mac," also to bid me good bye. After waiting for a long time at the school house, we finally decided to go home. Howards drove immediately behind us. Emil and Harry made the exchange of horses, while Mrs. Howard and the girls came into the shack to warm up. I took leave of them with a heavy heart, knowing that I would probably never see them again.

I spent the evening by cooking my last supper, and in packing my suitcases. Took a bath with a basin and rag. Played casino with Emil. Bed at 11:00.

Monday September 11

Wea. Pleasant, cool

I am filling out the page in the waiting room of the Great Northern R.R. in Williston, ND. I have just returned from a tour of inspection thru town, and found it so horribly stale that I decided to return to the station for a snooze.

Emil and I got up shortly after 3:00 AM. I cooked breakfast, perhaps the last meal I shall cook for years. Rev. Kanth also got up with us. While breakfast was cooking, I packed up my last belongings, also slipped my old overalls over my gray traveling suit, as it was pretty chilly outside.

We left the old shack shortly after 4:00 - It was so chilly that we all wore heavy sheep skin overcoats and mittens. I also had my cap pulled over my tender ears. We had hitched Emil's heavy farm team ("Nancy" and "Jack") to a lumber wagon, for we had to haul my box and trunk into town and take Rev. Kanth's goods out.

After a short stay in Schafer, we went to Watford City. I shipped a box of books to Unc. Herman also checked my trunk as far as Williston. Emil could not wait for the train, since he had to make the return trip before dark. So I bid him and Rev. Kanth a sorrowful farewell at about 1:00. After that I got a hair cut and shave, bought some more bucking pictures and a new fountain pen at Lundin's D.S. and finally went to the station, where the train actually pulled in on time. I left Watford City in the company of Mrs. E. Emmerson at about 2:00. It took us over 8 hours to make the 70 miles to Williston. Some accommodations.

Tuesday September 12

Wea. sunny, pleasant- rain in Minnesota

I am writing this paragraph in the Great Northern flyer, as we are speeding across the monotonous flat North Dakota prairie between Church's Ferry and Devil's Lake. I am traveling in a tourist sleeper, and enjoyed a wonderful sleep last night, although the train arrived so late in Williston that I could not get my berth til 4:30 AM.

Osakis, Minn: We arrived from N. Dakota into Minnesota at about 3:20 PM. Since then we have passed thru a very beautiful lake region. There is a very big sheet of water here at Osakis. The ground was so very level in the Eastern part of N.D. that its monotony made me sleepy, and I dozed off for a few hours. Grain looked pretty bum because of the hail and black rust.

Wilmar, Minn: 2:30 AM. - I have just landed in the "Merchant's Hotel" after making the run down from the Twin Cities. The reason I did not say in Minneapolis was because I was afraid of spending too much money there, and because I wanted to sleep till about noon, and since my train will not leave Wilmar til 2:00 PM tomorrow, I am going to have a good sleep.

In Minneapolis I ate a big smothered steak, took leave of Mrs. Emmerson and the Hills, whose acquaintance I had formed on the train, and after three beers, I beat it for my train. Slept almost all the way to Wilmar. I suppose I will have to spend tomorrow night in South Dakota.

Wednesday September 13

Wea. warm and sultry - lightning late in eve.

Garretson, So. Dak, 7: 20 P.M. - Our train is very late, but I should worry, having to wait in Sioux City till at least 7:30 tomorrow morning. I left Wilmar, Minnesota at 2:45 PM after eating a hearty dinner. Wilmar is a very pretty town with a beautiful lake adjoining it. I slept til nearly 10:00 in the morning, having gone to bed very late.

All afternoon I have been passing thru Minnesota. What I appreciated especially was the great number of trees and lakes, and the large and pretty farm buildings. Compared to the rough, unpainted shacks of far-away North Dakota, there is an enormous difference. The crops looked alright, as far as I could judge from the swiftly moving train.

I arrived in Sioux City at about 11 and took a cab to the Mitchell Hotel at 4th and Jackson. After registering and disposing of my grips I went uptown in the fond hope of putting a "few under my belt" before retiring to my virtuous slumbers. But all my efforts were in vain, for nowhere was there a drink establishment in sight. While eating my lonely supper, I remarked to the waiter: "Sioux City is dry, isn't it?" "Well," he drawled, "some say it is!"

My fountain pen was dry, so I could not do any writing. The hotel clerk was willing to lend me some of the vermillion paint he called ink, but after examining the stuff, I declined with thanks. There being nothing to do, and the town having a very stale aspect to me, I finally hit the hay, having first given orders to be aroused at 6:00.

Thursday September 14

I got up at 6:00, dressed rapidly and went directly to the station, where I disposed of my "grips," and tried to make arrangements about getting my trunk at the Union Station. The Sioux City Union Depot is a rotten hole, at least in comparison with the other large stations I know, and I know quite a lot of them. Everything was 'dead', the baggage room was locked, and so I finally returned to the Northwestern Station in great disgust.

There I ate a solitary breakfast of hot cakes, coffee, and pears. Then I hired the baggage master to tend to my trunk and steamed to Lyons, Nebr on the 7:40 Northwestern. I could hardly keep from whooping with joy when we crossed the "Big Muddy" which took me once more to the state of my birth. I arrived in Lyons on time, and at once phoned up Mr. Burmeister to come in with the car and get me. While I was waiting for him to show, I wrote a card to Howards, and made myself at home in Stile's store, where I entertained a group of awe-struck clerks with hair-raising stories of the North West. 'Unc' came in soon and my welcome at Burmeister's certainly was enthusiastic enough. I helped Kiddie wash the car in the afternoon, although we washed our faces as much as the car. In the evening, "Unc" and I killed a porker. Then we talked a while and finally Helen and I got a chance to have a few spoons, and she sure was nice to me.

to solve my problems myself

Watford at this time marked the terminus of the Great Northern Railway, which had run a little spur-line into this part of the county, and which, by the way, was the only railway in McKenzie Co., although there were rumors of proposed routes by the "Soo" line and the Northern Pacific R.R.

Watford then was only seventeen months old; a typical western "mushroom" city. It contained about 600 inhabitants, had several hotels, livery barns, 3 blacksmithys, several restaurants etc. When I came a catholic church and a new school-house were just being built; the Norwegian Church, served by Rev. Eielbo, was practically finished. Until the new public school was finished I conducted my services in a ramshackle, tumble down tin school, scarcely big enough to turn around in. I remember that the first time I ever entered this school, the water bucket was filled with a cake of solid ice (Nov. 14th 1915)

Schafer, four miles east of Watford, had lost heavily since the railway had been built. It was still the county seat, although Watford and Arnegard were continually striving for this honor. A lot of the business houses moved over to Watford, because Watford naturally had a bigger trade because of the railway. Schafer, for instance, had no bank, no drug-store, no restaurant, no smithy, although it had two hotels, two garages and several nice general merchandize stores. Divine services were held by the presbyterians (Rev. Cowgill) and myself in the "Community" or Schafer Hall, a rather big building, but badly heated and not completed inside. This building also served as a dance-hall etc.

At Schafer there was a regular, organized congregation, but the people were

PART III: RCJ'S RECOLLECTION

Figure 89: *Watford City under construction, July 1914.*

RCJ's Recollection, Written a Few Years Later

It was on the seventh of October 1915 that I first made up my mind to vicariate. My intention had always been to study straight through, if possible. But this call had a strange appeal for me, and then, too, my financial circumstances were very bad. I could not find work in St. Louis, and I did not wish to impose upon the generosity of my friend and benefactor, Mr. Deke. It was mainly on his written advice that I decided to go.

Naturally, my intention raised a storm of protest among my roommates and at home. The severe climate of North Dakota was painted to me in its most appalling and repellent aspect. But the main reason, which also filled me with doubt, was the hard work connected with this place. My call specified eight congregations scattered over McKenzie Co. and one place in Montana, 41 miles away. In addition, I was supposed to teach 3 classes of children desiring to be confirmed. My mind was, however, firmly set on going, and so Prof. Fuerbringer sent my ticket on the 13th of Oct. I attended lectures until the 15th and went to some especially interesting ones during the following week. The remainder of my time I spent in type writing sermon outlines, etc. Since most of my work was to be in the English language, I wrote two complete English sermons and one extra German one. And then I settled down to a policy of "watchful waiting." To me it seemed as though my railway tickets were delayed unaccountably. I filled two big boxes with books and stowed them in the basement of the Seminary. It was rather hard for me to part from them, but I could not pay the transportation charges on them.[151]

---

[151] Concordia Seminary is located in Clayton, Missouri, an inner-ring suburb on the western border of St. Louis. The institution trains clergy for the Lutheran Church - Missouri Synod (LC-MS). Concordia Seminary is the oldest seminary of the LC-MS but not its first; that distinction goes to Concordia Theological Seminary in Fort Wayne, Indiana, formerly in Springfield, Illinois. The St. Louis institution is also the largest Lutheran seminary in the United States. Concordia Seminary was at one time considered the "theoretical" (i.e., academic) seminary of the LC-MS, while Concordia Theological Seminary in Fort Wayne was considered the "practical" seminary, although those distinctions are no longer widely agreed-upon.

At last my suspense was ended. Rev. Nachtshein, the railway agent for the N. Dakota District, happened to have some business in St. Louis, so he brought my railway passes along. This was on the 27th of October. On the following day I took leave of my friends, the majority of whom I probably would not see again in this life, and left St. Louis for Chicago on the Wabash, at 9:17 p.m.[152]

I spent the day in Chicago by looking over the big city. It was my first visit there. Then I took a Pullman[153] on the "Soo" line[154] for St. Paul, Minn., leaving Chicago at 6:30 p.m. and arriving in St Paul at 8:00 a.m. From here I took a little side-trip to Jordan, Minn., where Rev. Ad. E. Frey was then stationed. He had been in charge of the mission-field in McKenzie Co., and was able to give me some first hand information. He was very nice to me and gave me a lot of his time. I found that the work I had undertaken was even harder than I had expected, but I still looked at it cheerfully.

By Sunday night I was back in St. Paul and left there at 10:45 p.m. on the Great Northern The train whisked me through Minnesota during the night, but when we struck the border of North Dakota I was wide awake.

What struck me was the peculiar aspect of the state at that time of the year. Everything was of the same dull, brownish hue. Not a speck of green to relieve the monotony, not a tree or shrub in sight. Besides I noticed that, in spite of the advanced season, nearly all the grain was still standing in shocks, that very little threshing had been done. It was noticeably colder than St. Louis had been. I found that most of the pools and creeks we passed had a thin coating of ice.

---

[152] The Wabash Railroad (AAR reporting mark WAB) was a Class I railroad that operated in the mid-central United States.

[153] A sleeping car on a railroad. The Pullman Company owned and operated most such cars in the United States through the mid-twentieth century, attaching them to passenger trains run by the various railroads.

[154] The Soo Line Railroad (AAR reporting mark SOO) is the United States arm of the Canadian Pacific Railway, serving Chicago, Illinois and the areas to the east and west. Formerly known as Minneapolis, St. Paul and Sault Ste. Marie Railway (and commonly known as the Soo Line after the phonetic pronunciation of Sault), the present name was adopted as a trade name in 1950. In 1961 the company was consolidated with several subsidiaries and reorganized under the current name.

Monday night, Nov. 1st, I arrived in Williston.[155] Here I had to spend the night, and I was so tired that I retired immediately after supper, at about seven o'clock. A rather disagreeable thing happened to me the following morning. I had forgotten how far west I had traveled, and since, according to my time-table my train left at 6:00 in the morning, I arose before five in order to get ready. I got to the station at 5:50, and there I discovered that the train left at 6:00 mountain time, or at 7:00 according to my time. So I had to wait there a full hour.

The train from Williston to Snowden Mont. was a wretchedly slow affair. But it was heaven compared to the train from Snowden[156] to Watford,[157] N. Dak. This latter train consisted of a series of freight cars, with an antediluvian passenger coach in its rear. I subsequently learned that this train ran only every two days; that on other days they had freight trains only.

As I approached my destination I began to feel wretchedly blue. Everything was so strange and a peculiar sense of loneliness stole over me that was very apprehensive. Judge my joy, therefore, when I saw that good old "Daddy" Roettger was at the station to meet me. "Daddy" had been in charge of this place since Rev. Frey left it in the middle of Sept., and he had been due to take charge of a school in Gardena, N. Dak. on Nov. 1st. Loyal as he always was, he had waited for me, however, and he helped me load up my trunk and took me over to Schafer, the county seat of McKenzie Co., although it was not situated on any railroad. The home which I was to occupy during my stay here, was not in Schafer at that time, although the people intended to move it soon. It was two miles in the country in the bleakest and loneliest spot imaginable, so it seemed to me.

I think a description of my home would be appropriate here. The house was located on a big hill, or table land, with comparatively level ground on the

---

[155] Williston, North Dakota is located in Williams County, just north of McKenzie County across the Missouri River.

[156] Snowden is a place name in Montana just across from the North Dakota border. The railroad had built a bridge across the Missouri River at this place, and it is still in use today. Until recently it was used for rail and single land automobile traffic. It is located west of Fort Union National Park.

[157] "Watford" was the official name of the town at one time. However, early in its existence the name was changed to Watford City to avoid confusion with Wolford, North Dakota.

Figure 90: *Frey's house, where RCJ found himself too lonely to stay.*

West and North side. On the southern and eastern side there was a steep
slope to a big valley. At the foot of the hill, about two blocks away, there was
a deserted house, which some settler had abandoned years ago. Near this
house there was an open well about 50 ft. deep, with a staunch frame- work
supporting a pulley. The water was raised by means of a bucket. Here I obtained my drinking water. Near the well I found an old tin wash-tub, where I
watered my horses.

On the north side of my house, about 20 yards away, was the barn for my
horses. It consisted simply of four walls and a "North Dakota" roof. The roof
is constructed this way: A ridge pole runs the length of the building, from the
center of each short side, and is raised about a foot above the walls. The roof
consists of a series of boards, nailed with one end on a long wall, bent over the
ridge pole, and nailed on the outer wall. Probatum est; simple but efficient.
The barn had room for one team and a little compartment containing a barrel
for oats and some boxes. In one corner there was a pile of slack wire, while
on the opposite wall, built in the barn, was the toilet. In front of the manger
was a flap door communicating with the outside, thru which one would feed

---

[158] North Dakota was "open range" at this time.

"Ayin's barn, view taken during a typical Mckenzie's storm.

Figure 91: *The barn at Frey's house.*

hay. Beginning with the month of November, it is customary here to let the stock roam around at will.[158] Naturally, my little supply of hay was continually being attacked by stray cows. I had a fence around the hay, of course, a so-called hay corral, but the cows seemed to treat it with supreme disdain, walking through the wires whenever they pleased.

It was impossible for me to be continually outside and chasing the cattle away, so I finally became desperate and carried all the hay in the barn, stowing it away as well as possible. There was no room for my buggy in this barn; it had to stand outside and naturally suffered severely in the fierce winds. My house consisted of two rooms. They were not plastered, but covered with wall-board; one of them, which I used as a living room, was also tastefully papered. Each room contained two windows, and from the inside it looked nice and cozy.

Before my house was moved to Schafer it also had a kitchen built against the south side of the house. I was forced to spend all my time in it, because it contained the heating stove, and I could not heat the other rooms in addition to the kitchen. For a few nights I slept in an adjoining room, but it was so cold in there that I was forced to move my cot into the kitchen.

The kitchen windows were small, about 2 ft square, while the house proper had regulation sized windows. When I came, the room intended as a bed-room was filled with wheat, and I consequently could not use it.[159] Its fur-niture consisted of a few pictures (old calendars) and a corner, which was curtained off and had spaces for hanging clothes, with a convenient shelf on top. For this room the house contained a folding steel cot with extension rods and no head or foot board, no mattress, and no springs. I had brought all my bed clothes along and improvised a mattress by spreading several layers of "Christian Heralds" on the steel frame of the cot, to keep the cold from un-derneath away. On this I spread a folded horse blanket and one quilt. I could not spare anymore covers for a sleeping pad, because it was too cold. Later on Mrs. Frank Alex,[160] my wash-woman, made me a big bag out of some straw ticking. This I filled with hay and straw and used as a mattress.

I made my own table or desk, with 2 X 4 planks for legs. In one corner of the living room there was a bookcase, and on one wall there was a clock shelf. A few pictures, and roller shades for the windows, completed the furniture.

The heater in the kitchen was my property. The rest of the furniture, ex-cepting the wash-stand, belonged to Mr. Hofman,[161] who had bought the barn and the kitchen part of the house. The "ash-stand" I made by setting a box up-right, nailing some white oil-cloth on top, and a calico curtain clear around it. The kitchen had a built-in cupboard for dishes and groceries, and a space for hanging clothes, similar to the arrangement in the bed-room. It also contained a nice, tho home-made, table but these articles were not mine.

---

[159] It was not uncommon to use an empty room to store grain at this time. Building materials were at a premium and grain storage buildings rare.

[160] Frank Allex was the son of Martin Allex I. The Allex family has been in McKenzie County since 1910. Frank's brother Lucas moved to Schafer in 1911 and opened a harness-making shop. Source: Watford City Diamond Jubilee Book.

[161] There are several Hofman families located in this area today. The correct spelling is actually Hoffmann. RCJ is referring to Andrew Hoffmann. The foundation where this house sat can still be found and the land is owned by a descendent of Andrew Hoffmann named Ronald Broderson.

In addition to the above mentioned articles of furniture my house contained a few dishes, some mason-jars, a wash-basin and a few kettles and a frying pan. For a water bucket I used the pail from the well.

Underneath the kitchen was a cellar, about six feet deep. In one corner I found a pile of coal, and a sack with a few rotten potatoes.

The entire property, together with eighty acres of land, formerly belonged to Rev. Frey, who took up a homestead there. He sold his farm, the barn, and the lean-to kitchen to his neighbor, Mr. Hofman, who lived about 2 miles away. The Ladies Aid Society of my Schafer congregation bought the house. They had to move it away later on of course, because the land did not belong to them.

Contrary to most of the other neighboring houses, my home had a shingled roof and a brick chimney. It also had one coat of white paint.

My team belonged to a young man near Catlin, Emil Bellin. He was generous enough to allow me to use the horses and buggy or later, his sleigh, free of charge, thus saving the mission board much money. The horses were young and very spirited, capable of trotting mile after mile without a stop, up hill or down hill. On some of my 40 mile trips I did not even water them. They were typical western broncos, horses that will run till they drop dead. One of my horses, "Babe," was a perfect pinto, the finest saddle horse I ever rode. My buggy was provided with side springs, which continually gave one the sensation of tipping over. It was in pretty bad condition, because of the mean roads and trails.

This leads me over to an account of the nature of my work. My chief preaching stations were located at Watford, Schafer, Catlin, Table Butte and Reservation Corner.

When I came to McKenzie Co., I was the only Lutheran minister of the Missouri Synod in the entire territory. There was a Norwegian-Lutheran minister at Arnegard, Rev. E. Eidbo, and one at Rawson, Rev. Hockenstedt, but these men concerned themselves not at all about my work, since they belonged to a different synod. So I was practically my own master. It is customary that vicars are under the direct supervision of some older minister, to whom they can turn for advice and aid, and who can take the heavier burdens off their shoulders, but I was all alone in a strange country, with absolutely no experience in mission work. When doubts assailed me, when I was perplexed about what course to take, I had to solve my problems myself.

Watford at this time marked the terminus of the Great Northern Railway, which had run a little spur-line into this part of the country, and which, by the way, was the only railway in McKenzie Co., although there were rumors of proposed routes by the "Soo" line and the Northern Pacific R.R.[162]

Watford then was only seventeen months old; a typical western "mushroom" city. It contained about 600 inhabitants, had several hotels, livery barns, 3 blacksmiths, several restaurants etc. When I came a Catholic church and a new school-house were just being built. The Norwegian Church, served by Rev. Eidbo, was practically finished. Until the new public school was finished I conducted my services in a ramshackle, tumble down tin school, scarcely big enough to turn around in. I remember that the first time I ever entered this school, the water bucket was filled with a cake of solid ice. (Nov. 14th, 1915) Schafer, four miles east of Watford, had lost heavily since the railway had been built. It was still the country seat, although Watford and Arnegard were continually striving for this honor. A lot of the business houses moved over to Watford, because Watford naturally had a bigger trade because of

---

[162] The railroad system into McKenzie County boasts a rich history in itself. McKenzie County has earned the nickname "Island Empire" as it is nearly impossible to enter without crossing a river—the Big Missouri to the north and east, the Yellowstone to the west, and the Little Missouri to the south. The settling of McKenzie County was much delayed due to the difficulty of moving people, freight, supplies and agricultural commodities in and out of the county. Watford was the result of a "winter camp" and "supply camp" from which the railroad was built in McKenzie County. To enter from the west, the railroad had to build a bridge spanning the Yellowstone and then dig a tunnel through a large hill; this greatly delayed the building of the rail line. To move things along more quickly, a spur line was build from the Missouri River north of Watford to Watford. This line was known as the "Wild Cow Spur"; railroad-building supplies were ferried across the Missouri River and then hauled by train to Watford where the line proceeded west to meet the line being built eastward. Rumors of proposed routes began to materialize a few years later when construction began from Watford to the southeast, where it terminated at the Little Missouri River. Even though the plans were grandiose, engineering difficulties with the soil at the Little Missouri and the lack of money after World War I ended this dream of a railroad transforming the county and connecting it to a railway leading to Bismarck and Fargo. It is interesting to note that the rail company had no plans to connect Schafer to the rail line, which meant a certain death to the town, the county seat at the time.

Figure 92: *Another photo of Watford City under construction in July 1914.*

Public School Building Watford City, N.D.

Figure 93: *Public school building in Watford City.*

the railway. Schafer, for instance, had no bank, no drug store, no restaurant, no smithy, although it had two hotels, two garages and several nice general merchandise stores. Divine services were held by the Presbyterians (Rev. Cowgill) and myself in the "Community," or Schafer Hall, a rather big building but badly heated and not completed inside. This building also served as a dance- hall etc. At Schafer there was a regular organized congregation, but the people were divided up between Watford and Schafer, so that I always had a meager attendance at both places. At my first services in Schafer there were only five women present.

Schafer had about 150 inhabitants. It is located in a deep valley and cannot be seen very far. "Table Butte" was no town or post office. It was merely a convenient way of labeling a preaching station, and derived its name from the huge butte by that name.[163] At the foot of this butte there lived a splen-

---

[163] This is part of a series of buttes in the eastern part of McKenzie County. The reference to "labeling a preaching station" after this butte coincides with the fact that the Hidatsa Indians of this vicinity have long considered the "Thunder Butte" sacred to their culture. They have conducted religious and tribal ceremonies from the top of it for many years, continuing today.

did Norwegian man who was clean and well bred. Since there was no school nearby, I was forced to conduct all my services in private residences, and I was always glad when Mr. Ole Jore[164] invited the crowd. His wife was totally deaf, but she was a perfect lip-reader.[165] On the whole, the other people were also nice. I always had a good attendance there, when the weather was favorable. Table Butte was to be reached only by following a very round about trail, so that I usually had to cover about forty miles from my house, in order to reach it. I always spent Saturday night there, usually at Jore's; I conducted services Sundays at 11 a.m.

PUBLIC SCHOOL BLDG.   SCHAFER N.D.

Figure 94: *Public school building in Schafer.*

---

[164] Descendants of Mr. and Mrs. Ole Jore still reside in McKenzie County.

[165] Her name was Jessie Buck Jore.

After dinner I had to drive over to "Reservation Corner," a school-house situated at the corner of the Fort Berthold Indian and Military reservation,[166] about 6 miles from Table Butte. Here I conducted services at 3:00 p.m. in the German and English language. Some of the people were fairly well to do, having modern houses and good machinery. Others, through shiftlessness, were in poorer straits.

Here I usually spent my nights at Draegerts, living about seven miles from the school. They were nice, clean people. Mrs. Draegert had recently become a widow, her husband having died in Spring.

Draegert's occupied a spacious log-house. My bed was built in one corner and separated from the rest of the house by a calico curtain. Mrs. Draegert, while a great talker, was a sweet, motherly woman, and a good cook.

Figure 95: *Richard C. Jahn as a seminary student.*

---

[166] Home to the Three Affiliated Tribes: Mandan, Hidatsa and Arikara Indians.

APPENDIX I

1917 DIARY EXCERPTS
(AT THE SEMINARY)

Wednesday January 10

Colonel W. F. Cody (Buffalo Bill) passed away in the home of his sister in Denver today. Col. Cody has been seriously ill since January 5th and was reported dying January 8th. With him one of the most picturesque characters has gone away.

Thursday January 18

One of the most influential newspapers in the world is the "Shafer Record" It is the main connecting link between me and good old McKenzie Co. Today the "Record" contained the news of a fearful blizzard, the worst blizzard in years that is sweeping McKenzie Co. I know from experience what that means, and I and thanking my lucky stars that I could hug the radiator instead of having to buck the "White Hell," as the "old timers" call a bad storm.

Friday February 2

I wrote a long letter to Mrs. Howard this afternoon, she has had a terrible time lately. (I got an 8 page letter recently.) She and the little kiddies were very sick with LaGrippe and a slight attack of Diptheria. Emil fainted away in her kitchen, so they had to take care of him in addition. According to her letter, Harry was still able to be up and around. I hope he staid well.

Tuesday February 13

I type wrote a letter to "Joe" Kanth this afternoon. Also wrote Dora (during Hans Bente's lecture).

Wednesday February 21

"Joe" Kanth sent me a notice that Mrs. P. Harms, of Charlson, ND. had died. She was very sick and weak when I knew her, and death was certainly a relief for her.

Friday March 16

I got a letter from Mrs. Howard…as she wrote they had all recovered from their illness, and were feeling well. Her mother has died, as was to be expected.

Thursday March 29

…wrote a letter to Mrs. Howard…

Wednesday April 18

I got three letters today…Rev. Frey discussed business matters and his little baby girl…

Saturday April 21

I typed another hunk of dogmatics during the day. Also wrote a long letter to Rev. Frey. Rev. Frey had asked me about the stove and things which he had left at Core's shack and which Mr. Reynolds sold on him.

Monday April 23

After supper I wrote a letter to Schnutzie Pallmer, and enclosed a picture of myself at my "laundry plant" in No Dak.

Wonder of wonders! Emil Bellin actually wrote a letter. It arrived today! It contains very little news, but it was written with pen and ink! (He excused himself for not using a pencil.)

Tuesday May 1

Had a letter from Joe Kanth this morning. North Dakota is having its influence upon him too. The lazy life got on his nerves. He has not been able to get to Watford City since January, similar to my own experience last year. According to all newspaper accounts, and all my letters from the northwest, the past winter must have been by far worse than the season 1915/16, and believe me!, that winter was bad enough.

Tuesday July 3

Wrote to Rev. Frey.

Sunday July 8

The papers (Saturday Topeka Journal) announced a daring feat by a fleet of about 22 German aeroplanes flying over London and doing great damage. No German casualties were recorded.

Dora and I looked over my collection of pictures.

Tuesday July 24

I finally got a letter from Ban Johnson again. Ban wrote his letter in Bear Springs, Mont. where he is temporarily engaged in teaching school. Including a dog, two tomcats and a canary bird, the population of Bear Springs is approximately 6, wrote Ban. He claims it would take an expert to tell one of his pupils from an ape. – Poor Ban! And yet I know he will grow so attached to his surroundings that he will ever continue to long back to the West. The "Call of the Prairie" gripped everybody.

Tuesday August 21

(At Burmeisters in Lyons, Nebraska)

I got up just as the folks were beginning to eat breakfast. After the meal I walked around the farm on a tour of inspection, and then I hunted around till I found my old working top. But while my old shoes were still in serviceable condition, my overalls (both from No. Dak.) were in excellent shape, but my shirts were all hopeless, so I had to wear a dress shirt. I think I must have presented a ridiculous sight.

Tuesday October 23

This was one of the rare days on which I had no mail at all. I got my "Schafer record", however, and noticed that Jacob May has died. He was an old friend from the Catlin vicinity.

Tuesday November 6

A year ago today I attended lectures for the first time after having vicared. According to my diary, the class-room seemed perfectly natural to me. To think, it is over two years ago since I went to North Dakota! Time certainly does fly!

Thursday December 6

In glancing back over my diary the thought often strikes me: what will a stranger think, if he or she should ever read this diary? I have given myself just as I am, with all my faults standing out in glaring relief, laying due emphases on laziness, etc. But there are redeeming features to me too. I sat down immediately after dinner today, and only left my machine for a few moments at a time until about 12:30 am. I did not even go into the dining room for supper.

APPENDIX II

BIOGRAPHY OF RICHARD C. JAHN

Figure 96: *Pastor Richard C. Jahn (top left) delivering a prayer to open a session of the Arkansas Legislature in 1957.*

❧Appendix❦

Richard C. Jahn was born in 1895 in Watertown, Nebraska, a town near Amherst that no longer exists. His father Konrad, German-born and well educated, gave up a career in business to immigrate to America and become a Lutheran minister. His mother Frieda, who "emigrated" with her family from Minnesota to Nebraska to homestead, was born in a sod hut. Richard spent his childhood in rural Nebraska, something that must have helped him later to adapt to the rugged life he faced in North Dakota.

At age 13, Richard's parents sent him to Missouri to follow in his father's footsteps and become a Lutheran minister. He spent the next 10 years there, first at St. Paul's College in Concordia, Missouri then Concordia Seminary at St. Louis. While at the seminary, he accepted the call to become a "supply" minister to congregations in McKenzie County, North Dakota in 1915. Roughly one year later he returned to finish his studies. In 1918 he graduated and became an ordained minister. He also married Martha Pallmer, a girl he met in St. Louis. "Billie," as she was fondly known, remained a cheerful "helpmeet" by his side for the next 57 years.

Then, for more than four decades, Richard served various congregations. His first was in Hecla, South Dakota, followed by a short stay in Oakes, North Dakota. He left there to go to Columbia Bottoms, a St Louis suburb. Major stints then took place at First Lutheran Church in Chattanooga, Tennessee (1925 to 1950) and First Lutheran Church in Little Rock, Arkansas (1950 to 1963). He held many leadership positions within the Missouri Synod and continued to preach and teach almost until his death.

He and Billie returned to Chattanooga following his retirement in 1963 to be near their son Richard, his wife, Anne, and their three children, Rick, David and Janna. Their daughter Mildred, "Millie," visited often from her home in Hawaii with her husband John and two children, Carol and Bruce.

Richard was a lifelong scholar and theologian. According to his brother, Erich, "It must be said he was never happier than when he was in his study surrounded by his books." The volumes numbered over 5,000, some of them quite old and rare. Richard died in 1977 at the age of 82, just two years after Billie, who was 79. But his legacy lives on not only through the meticulous diaries he kept throughout his life but also through the rich German Lutheran heritage of faith, intellect and humor he and Billie left to their children and grandchildren.

APPENDIX III

BIOGRAPHY OF EMIL BELLIN

Emil Henry August Bellin was born in Wisconsin on August 21, 1890. His parents had 13 children in a span of 21 years; Emil was the youngest. Unfortunately, the names of Emil's parents have not been found.

As a young man, Emil had worked at a truck farm in Wisconsin. At meal times he would be sent to various taverns to get a half gallon of beer for 5 cents. Emil always said that he was "raised on beer."

Emil was closest in age to his brother Billy Bellin. Billy came out to McKenzie County, North Dakota in about 1910. He homesteaded just south of Johnson's Corner. Emil followed him out from Wisconsin in 1912. Unfortunately, Billy got pneumonia in 1914 and died. Emil had chosen a homestead that was about four miles from Billy's. Another person had previously homesteaded on the site, but gave it up. After Billy died, Emil farmed on his land and used Billy's shack for grain storage, as related in the diary.

During World War I Emil was able to get a farm deferment. However, late in the war, he was told that he had to report for active duty. He had arranged for others to take care of his animals and was preparing to report when he suddenly got word that the war was over. He did not have to serve.

Emil never learned to swim. He did come to own a tract of land in Dunn County, as related in the diary. Once when he was fording the Little Missouri to get to it, he fell off his horse and almost drowned. He managed to grab his horse's tail and by that means saved himself.

On November 20, 1920 Emil married Leta Kummer. She had been born near Sauk Centre, Minnesota or Oshkosh, Wisconsin in 1900. Her parents, Lawrence and Minnie Kummer, moved the family to Catlin, N.D. in 1911 and homesteaded there. The Kummers had a large family, consisting of nine girls and three boys. When she and Emil married, the service was performed at her home. Two of her other sisters got married there at the same time. Emil remarked that it was cheaper that way.

To prepare his place for his bride, Emil moved Billy's shack - pictured in the diary - and attached it to the rear of his cabin. This served as the marital bedroom for Leta and him until 1955! On their wedding night, several of Emil's friends took a large school bell and put it in the attic of the log cabin while he was away. They attached a rope to it and carefully worked it out of the east side of the cabin and over into the east coulee. The culprits laid in wait in the coulee until the lights went out in the cabin. At that time they yanked the rope many times, ringing the bell. The couple survived this raucous wedding night. Emil never bothered to take the bell out of the attic, and it remained there until the cabin was torn down in 1955. Over all these years the main entrance to the property came across the west coulee, but Emil did not really try to improve it or build a bridge over it. Later owners improved the driveway by using culverts and fill.

Emil and Leta had one child, a son Arno, who was born in 1925. Arno's "room" was in the main cabin where Richard and Emil stayed in 1916. He spent his entire youth there. The cabin never had running water or electricity. Another boy, cousin Arnold Peterson, lived with them soon after Arno was born. His mother was Leta's sister Tille; unfortunately she had lost her husband Martin when Arnold was only three. One of Arno's toys was the phonograph used by Richard and Emil. He devised all sorts of creative uses for it, even long after the big speaker part had fallen off.

Arnold Peterson's mother had a steel-wheeled tractor. She allowed Emil to use it as long as he would put in a crop for her. For a time, Emil was farming his place, Billy's homestead, and the Peterson land at the same time.

Emil worked many hard jobs. He was farming in the early 1930s when he was hired to work on a Works Progress Administration dam project near his place. He worked on his farm, then put in many hours with his team working on the dam. Unfortunately, it was not designed properly and failed, but the remains are still there; one can still see the stream flowing through the break in the wall.

On another occasion, Emil was working on a county road bridge project. Large timbers were used instead of pipes. He tripped over some timbers in the weeds and fell onto another one and broke his kneecap. The doctor wired it together. However, Emil had to use crutches for a long time. He would walk out to his fields on those crutches, laboring hard and painfully to move his knee. Arno watched him sweat profusely when he tried to do chores on those crutches. After the bone had healed, the doctor wanted to take out the wires. Emil said that they didn't bother him, so he left them in the rest of his life.

The well mentioned in the diary was abandoned soon after 1916. Arno recalls that it was never in use during his lifetime. The family obtained their water from the coulee or, whenever possible, from clean wells of their neighbors. The only electricity to be installed at the cabin was wind-powered. In the 1930s, Emil made a windmill. To it he attached a car generator. Wires from the generator ran into the cabin to charge a car battery there. The battery powered a car headlight installed in the main room. This way the family could come in and turn on the headlight until they could get their lanterns lit. Arno recalled that the headlight didn't burn very long, but it was a very welcome addition on dark nights.

In 1950 Arno became engaged to get married. He and his wife, Dorothy Schoenlein, planned to build a house about 100 feet from Emil's cabin. They did get married, but they had to live in a tiny granary near the cabin for several months while the house was being built. His wife was not fond of it. Her father built a small window in the granary to allow some light to come in. When the house was completed, it had no running water, but in 1951 electric lines were run to it.

Dorothy's father, W.A."Tony" Schoenlein, was himself an interesting character. In the early 1900s he had been a trail hand on several cattle drives that started in Texas and ended in North Dakota. There were no fences along the way, and the cattle were driven over the vast plains without man-made obstacles. Many hands would typically quit during the journey, so that by the time they got to North Dakota, only a few loyal cowboys would be left with the huge herd. They had learned, however, that the herd would typically follow one particular cow, so they kept close track of it.

Emil and Leta lived in the log cabin until 1955. The logs were torn down at that time. A house formerly belonging to H. L. Clark was moved and placed on the cabin's foundation. Emil and Leta lived in the Clark house until about 1960. At that time Arno moved to Watford City with his wife, and so Emil and Leta moved into their house next to the cabin site. Alex Alton's wife, the former Mildred Tiegs, bought the Clark house. She had been living in a log house. The Clark house was moved out to her place, and it is still there. Mildred's log home was moved and can be seen today at the Heritage Center in Watford City.

Arno recalls that in the1960s he and his family (he had three children) took Emil and Leta on a car trip to Wisconsin, among other places. They went to Emil's birthplace—Arno doesn't recall the name of the town—and they stopped at Emil's old house. They did not know who lived there and didn't go in. After arriving in North Dakota in 1912, Emil took few trips, and he never saw the ocean.

Appendix

All his life Emil liked to play cards and stay up late at night. He often slept well into the mornings, just as related in the diary. Emil never danced. He believed that it showed disrespect for the woman. Interestingly, he never had a camera, and the only known photographs of him are the ones taken by Richard in 1916. Arno recalls seeing copies of these photos in the cabin when he was a boy, but they have long since been lost. There is a photo of Emil and family in the Watford City Golden Jubilee book (1964, page 92), but Arno says it is not the Bellin family.

In 1971 Emil was 80 years old and suffered from arthritis. He had a heart attack at his farm and was taken to the hospital in Watford City. He passed away the next day, July 13, 1971. Leta moved to Watford City immediately thereafter. She died on May 2, 1994 at the age of 94. Pastor Jay Reinke, a Lutheran Church – Missouri Synod pastor from Williston, preached her funeral sermon. Emil and Leta are buried together in Schafer cemetery. Dorothy passed away in 1996. (The above information was related to Editor Jahn in personal conversations with Arno Bellin and Jay Reinke in March, 2006). Arno resided in Watford City until shortly before his death in 2012. Arnold Peterson still resides in Watford City.

Figure 97: *Richard and the Pinto at ease on the vast prairie.*

Figure 98: *Richard C. Jahn later in life.*

APPENDIX IV

REVEREND FREY'S BRIEFING

The following probably occurred on Saturday October 30, 1915 and the next day. En route to McKenzie Co., RCJ stayed overnight in Jordan, Minn. He met Reverend Adolphus Frey, who briefed him about the parishioners of McKenzie County. The notes were written by RCJ in his 1915 diary.

Schafer
- Andrew Hoffmann, Catholic, 1 mi. from the claim. Stay there. Meals-.25; bed-.25. likes to "rope" a person. Nice clean place.
- Ask Mrs. Christiansen to play piano at Schafer. Mrs. Harms at Reservation Corner
- B.J.'s (Bobby Janssen) kids in order of age: Carl, Alvin, Paul, Willie, Margaret
- F.J. Otto, 5 mi. east of Schafer, family man, best man at Schafer
- Mr. and Mrs. Nickel, very good
- Mr. and Mrs. Balsizer, very good, best woman
- L. Bergen (2 boys for confirm. class)
- J. Ellickson,1 boy to be confirmed, 2 instructed
- Mrs. Dean, Post mistress, Ladies aid
- Bernanthe, very dirty, don't eat there; well-meaning

Schafer and Watford
- Schuck, Edward. (McMaster, his daughter), German = Russian
- J. Marten, nice; hardware store; brother to Mrs. Balsizer, always in the hole, lives in Watford
- W.R. Dietrich, pool hall man, treasurer of congregation, best man at Watford;
Presbyterian wife, confirmed as Lutheran
- H.P. Lundin, druggist, secretary of congregation, indifferent
- William Sahr, 1 mi. from Watford, voting member, strange man, in with Presbyterians, blow-bag, well-educated
- Services at Norwegian church with Rev. Eidbo of Arnegard, try to stay with him.

- Lud Krueger, butcher, good wife, lodge man and drinks, lax, wants German church family

Catlin
- E. Bellin—Mr. and Mrs. Howard to be instructed
- Lawrence Kummer, collector, family large
- Herb Veeder, family, fine fellow, comical; son-in-laws: Theo. Thofson, Olaf Sorensen, Paul Oderman
- J.W. Tiegs, wife not confirmed, he's not either
- Ambrosious Oderman, he is catholic, she is Lutheran
- William Kummer, Lawrence's brother, never comes to church, 2 children to be confirmed
- Mrs. Wells, engl., comes at times
- Mr. and Mrs Omar Hart, engl.
- Mr. and Mrs. H.R. Howard
- Frank Tank—family: good wife
- (Palmer) Greete, Olsen (Dodge) ask Tank about them and Kieson
- Paper: Schafer Record

Table Butte—5 mi. NE of Berg
- Ole Jore, Frisby Buck, Clarence Jore
- Newt. Simonson, af. Eltin,
- Buck's son-in-law, Mr. Wiedermann
- services at 11 a.m. in houses
- Charlson Journal

Reservation Corner, school house, $35.00 per an.
- (German and English)   class on Monday
- Peter Harms; Mrs. Draegert, A. Reuken
- R. Janssen, Mrs. Bee (Mrs. Wiedermann's daughters)
- Daughter of E. Larsen, Levi Schoonover, Draeg.; son-in-law---Amos Dickinson
- Otis Larsen, McKenzie Co. Journal at Charlson
- Services at 3 or 3:30

From Schafer:
- Reservation Corner, 30 mi. east (and north of Table Butte); German and English

- Catlin (Veeder's School House) East.—English and German
- Table Butte-25 mi. north east of Schafer- English only
- Watford (try for German work)
- Mrs. Howard at Catlin (stay with Emil Bellin) wishes to be confirmed

Rolf's schoolhouse 3.5 mi. SW of Arnegard
- They are supposed to go to Hackenstedt
- Ad. Aucklam; Ernest and Jul. Rick--bachelor
- Walt. and wife; Henry Olsen; ask Aucklam about William Harry Bauman post- master in Rawson
- Oscar Gessner near Arnegard; very lax
- Gust. Schultz. 1 mi. S of Arnegard, good. John Dumdre; Mrs. J. Burr; he is nothing; she is good

Fairview, Mont.
- Arnst Weemann and wife; Mrs. Harm, Mrs. Sying and fam., Mrs. Kinderson and children.
- at Catlin: stay with Emil Bellin (bachelor)
- at Table Butte, Miss Norma Jorgenson c/o Peter Harms
- Rev. Cowgill
- Mr. Randall, helper of hotel
- Drof. Dodge and Fairview

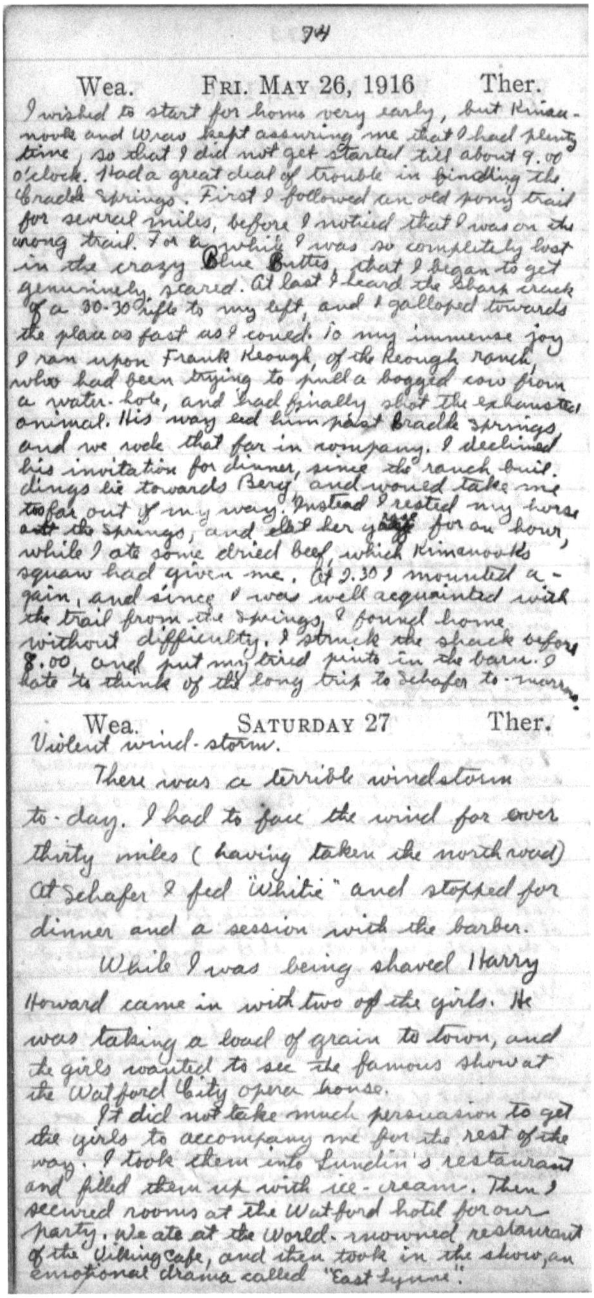

94

Wea.   Fri. May 26, 1916   Ther.

I wished to start for home very early, but Kinnan-nook and Wrou kept assuring me that I had plenty time, so that I did not get started till about 9.00 o'clock. Had a great deal of trouble in finding the Cradle Springs. First I followed an old pony trail for several miles, before I noticed that I was on the wrong trail. For a while I was so completely lost in the crazy Blue Buttes, that I began to get genuinely scared. At last I heard the sharp crack of a 30-30 rifle to my left, and I galloped towards the place as fast as I could. To my immense joy I ran upon Frank Keough, of the Keough ranch, who had been trying to pull a bogged cow from a water-hole, and had finally shot the exhausted animal. His way led him past Cradle Springs and we rode that far in company. I declined his invitation for dinner, since the ranch buildings lie towards Berg, and would take me too far out of my way. Instead I rested my horse at the springs, and let her graze for an hour, while I ate some dried beef, which Kinnanook's squaw had given me. At 2.30 I mounted again, and since I was well acquainted with the trail from the springs, I found home without difficulty. I struck the shack before 8.00, and put my tired pinto in the barn. I hate to think of the long trip to Schafer to-morrow.

Wea.   Saturday 27   Ther.
Violent wind-storm.

There was a terrible windstorm to-day. I had to face the wind for over thirty miles (having taken the north road) At Schafer I fed "Whitie" and stopped for dinner and a session with the barber.

While I was being shaved Harry Howard came in with two of the girls. He was taking a load of grain to town, and the girls wanted to see the famous show at the Watford City opera house.

It did not take much persuasion to get the girls to accompany me for the rest of the way. I took them into Lunchin's restaurant and filled them up with ice-cream. Then I secured rooms at the Watford hotel for our party. We ate at the World-renowned restaurant of the Villing cafe, and then took in the show, an emotional drama called "East Lynne".

Figure 98: *Actual size of diary page.*

INDEX

COMMON NAMES AND PLACES SUCH AS BELLIN AND SCHAFER ARE OMITTED. APPENDIX I IS INCLUDED.

❧Index❧

❧Index❧

❧Index❧

❧Index❧

❧Index❦

❧Index❧

❧Index❧